Patti Miller was raised on a farm in central western NSW. Her many books include *Writing Your Life* (Allen & Unwin, 1994, 2001), *The Last One Who Remembers* (Allen & Unwin, 1997), *Child* (Allen & Unwin, 1998), *Whatever the Gods Do* (Random House, 2003), *The Memoir Book* (Allen & Unwin, 2007) and *The Mind of a Thief* (UQP, 2012), winner of the NSW Premier's History Award. She has taught writing for over twenty years, including at the innovative Faber Academy in Sydney.

Ransacking PARIS

A YEAR WITH MONTAIGNE AND FRIENDS

PATTI
MILLER

UQP

First published in 2015 by University of Queensland Press
PO Box 6042, St Lucia, Queensland 4067 Australia
Reprinted 2015

www.uqp.com.au
www.lifestories.com.au

Cataloguing-in-Publication entry is available from the
National Library of Australia
http://catalogue.nla.gov.au/

ISBN (pbk) 978 0 7022 5339 3
ISBN (ePdf) 978 0 7022 5461 1
ISBN (ePUB) 978 0 7022 5462 8
ISBN (kindle) 978 0 7022 5463 5

Typeset in 12/16.5 pt Bembo by Post Pre-press Group, Brisbane
Printed in Australia by McPherson's Printing Group

University of Queensland Press uses papers that are natural, renewable and recyclable products made from wood grown in sustainable forests. The logging and manufacturing processes conform to the environmental regulations of the country of origin.

For Charlie

CONTENTS

Les abeilles pillotent deçà delà les fleurs, mais elles en font après le miel, qui est tout leur; ce n'est plus thym ni marjolaine.

Bees ransack flowers here and flowers there, but then they make a honey which is entirely theirs; it is no longer thyme nor marjoram honey.

Michel de Montaigne

ONE

ARRIVING

This great world of ours is the looking-glass in which we must gaze to come to know ourselves from the right slant.

Michel de Montaigne

The studio in the rue des Trois Frères on the slopes of Montmartre looked out onto a shadowy courtyard, just a couple of strides across. On the other side of the courtyard was a small theatre, Théâtre du Tremplin, which my dictionary revealed meant 'springboard' or 'stepping stone' theatre. In the foyer there was a poster for the next production – *La Grenouille mode d'emploi*, Frogs, How to Use – with a photograph of two frogs, one right side up, one upside down. One of the actors, young, dark-haired, hung out the back window overlooking the studio, smoking and talking to someone behind him.

The sky wasn't visible from where I was sitting – the studio was on the ground floor and the courtyard was too narrow – but there was enough light to see a scraggly locust tree in a pot under the actor's window. I'd noticed it as we dragged our suitcases in; it looked as if it needed more space and light with its spindly branches and some of its oval leaves yellowing. I stood up and stretched, arms over my head, feeling the kinks of twenty-four hours in flight straighten out. My joints clicked after being locked into place for too long. I sat down again and looked around the studio.

Our bags were half unpacked on the lounge. Dresses and jeans were thrown over chairs, and books – Montaigne, de Sévigné and Rousseau – were stacked on the floor. Stendhal and de Beauvoir and Annie Ernaux too, all writers looking out at 'this great world' as Montaigne called it, trying to set down what they saw. They had come with me to Paris and I was hoping they might keep me company throughout the year. I had placed them in chronological order, but they made an unsettled, uneasy tower, threatening to slip into a heap at any moment.

'*Ça va?*' Anthony asked. How are you? He was sitting on a kitchen chair near the French windows, holding his cigarette outside with one hand and a glass of wine with the other. His dark hair was greying but his eyes and smile were youthful, fully engaged and observant. He shifted his stocky body on the chair and leaned back to catch my distracted gaze. Beside him on a stool were the leftovers of a baguette and corner shop camembert we'd eaten as our jetlagged dinner. It looked like a tableau ready for a romantic painter: bread and cheese and wine in front of a window in midsummer twilight, the long soft embers of an evening that didn't want to end.

A kaleidoscope turned in my head, disjointed scenes, confusing and exciting at once; the green iron and glass fan of the Guimard-designed Metro entrance at Abbesses Metro, a busker's voice echoing Joni Mitchell's 'Free Man in Paris' up the long spiral staircase from the platform, light glittering on the gold-tipped obelisk at place de la Concorde where a guillotine once stood, a gypsy woman in layered skirts in front of the Tuileries gate offering me a fake gold ring. We had walked around the gardens trying to stay awake. Children sailed boats in the pond, chestnut trees clipped into cube shapes grew in neat rows, the heavy-headed blossoms of asters and anemones and cosmos leaned in the summer heat, bees staggered from flower to flower. 'Where the bee sucks, there suck I; in a cowslip's bell I lie,' Ariel sang in my spaced-out brain. After lunch, Anthony and I sat in a café in the Tuileries, drinking Stella Artois, legs stretched out, shoes dusty from the white crushed gravel paths. Even then, our arrival at Charles de Gaulle airport that morning seemed a century ago.

My diary sat on the kitchen bench alongside the laptop, and pages of the manuscript I'd begun back in Australia were still lying in the suitcase. The manuscript was the story of a friend who had died from a brain haemorrhage and of her baby son who has become part of my life ever since. In Paris, away from ordinary life, I thought I might be able to piece together their stories, Dina's and the child Theo's, and mine. Our paths had crossed and become tangled and then she had died. A young mother dying and leaving a child bereft is an old story, a story from the beginning of stories, but it was the first time it had arrived in my life.

It was still the evening of the day we arrived and time had acquired a stretching quality, as if the day had lasted several lifetimes, as if time, in fact, didn't pass but circled forever. Perhaps it was days since Anthony asked me how I was. His cigarette smoke went straight up in the still twilight.

I looked around my new home. The one-metre-square kitchen was delineated from the rest of the studio by a bench; the remaining space contained a lounge, a desk and another chair, and the bedroom was a futon on a mezzanine up a steep ladder and so close to the ceiling we would have to be careful sitting up in bed. The only separate space was the bathroom with a toilet and shower, both of them, we soon found out, as temperamental as cheap camping equipment. The only picture on the wall was a poster advertising an exhibition of Aboriginal art at a gallery in an outer suburb of Paris.

'*Ça va*,' I answered. All going well. I loved every little thing about our studio. It was just as I had imagined it all these years. Even the small cement courtyard and the dodgy loo and the bed platform I couldn't stand up on were perfect. I could hardly believe that it had somehow happened. We were together, our two boys had grown up and we were young again. Maybe you could set time back to start again. To gain a dream long after it seemed possible made the world glow as if the light that comes after the sun has set had spilled gold on everything.

*

Thinking about that year it seems as if it were outside time, or a dream. It's not an unusual dream; it's so common that if I say it aloud I have to use an ironic tone or an American accent: *who doesn't wanna be a writer in Paris?* Part of me shifts uneasily – not another writer in a garret living in illusion in Paris – but another part feels tender. It must mean something, a dream that can propel you to the other side of the world. Couldn't it be the heart wanting something it needs, this longing for elsewhere? After all, we are all strangers wandering around this planet, apparently lost most of the time, looking for something or someone – or some place. And then, when we arrive there, we await revelation, or we impatiently turn things over, demanding answers.

Montaigne wrote, 'Bees ransack flowers here and flowers there, but then they make a honey which is entirely theirs; it is no longer thyme nor marjoram honey.' I ransacked all year; I'm not sure if I was the hard-working bee or the beekeeper who simply bided her time until the honey was ready, but it doesn't matter as both bee and beekeeper are thieves. I feel a bit twitchy admitting that, a propensity to theft, and it's not something I can defend except to say that I've always been that way.

In childhood I had a great uncle who kept bees. In memory he's an unshaven, wrinkled bloke in shabby clothes who turned up at my grandmother's house in town once a year with a battered drum of honey. I thought he lived in a hut in the hills behind the town although I'm not sure about that now. When we drove home after visiting Gran, through the hills along Bushrangers Creek Road to our farm, sometimes we would see his bee-boxes up under the gum trees, so that may have led me to imagine he lived there as well. Thinking back on it he was probably shy, perhaps a recluse, and the honey was his offering to his sister, his connection with the world. When we were visiting, I sneaked into the washhouse where Gran left the drum and put my finger in to steal a scoop of eucalypt honey.

*

I glanced at the poster for the '*Exposition d'Art Aborigène d'Australie*'. It was reassuring and unsettling: a dot painting in ochre and brown and black painted in the Western Desert, thousands of kilometres from where I lived on the other side of the island continent. It described country, the sacred sites of the desert places, where the rainbow serpent had slept and where waterholes could be found. I was born on Wiradjuri country in eastern Australia and walked on it every day of my childhood; I had no painting of it, but the shape of every fold of land, every rocky outcrop, was printed, is still printed, in my memory. I can see the anthill by the dry creek, the slope of the fallow paddock behind the house-yard, the muddy hoof prints of sheep and cattle around the shrinking dam. If that landscape was erased from me I am certain I would no longer exist. Why had I left it behind? What else did I think I would find here? It was something to do with an imaginary life, that much was obvious, one that had begun when I was still a child and that bore small resemblance to my actual life.

*

At the end of January during the long 1960s drought of bare brown earth, blue skies and bony animals, the new French teacher, Mrs Berman, walked into my classroom at St Mary's high school in a country town 300 kilometres west of Sydney. It was a parish convent school, run by Irish nuns who taught the sons and daughters of the poor – cocky farmers and struggling shopkeepers – and a few Aboriginal kids from the Mission. We were a ragtag lot, some of us dressed in hand-me-downs, but not wild. Religion had a strong hold, keeping us mostly obedient and believing the rest of the world was on the road to hell.

'*Bonjour mes enfants*,' Mrs Berman said. She smiled as we sat in puzzled silence, none of us daring even a '*bonjour*'. There were only six in the French class; the rest had sensibly enrolled in Commerce. I gazed at her critically; she wasn't French. She was just a nice, plump Australian woman about the same age as our mothers; she dressed in the same quiet skirts and neat cardigans, had the same short tidy cap of hair and spoke with the same Australian accent.

I was thirteen years old and young for my age. I still read Enid Blyton schoolgirl stories and had met Mam'zelle, excitable Mam'zelle, her dark hair in a bun with wisps that kept escaping. She stamped her foot with un-English temper and had a great sense of humour and was afraid of mice and beetles. The girls played merry pranks on her and she scolded 'ze girls like ziz'. That's how a French teacher was supposed to be.

'*Comment allez-vous?*' asked Mrs Berman and then she smiled and began handing out a French textbook with a red cover. 'You can find the question in here – and the answer,' she said. I was hooked already.

Although she was calm and correct and Anglo-Saxon, nothing like Mam'zelle, Mrs Berman did love French and, most impressively, had been to Paris. We learned the conjugations of *avoir* and *être* and *aller* in the first few weeks and a new vocabulary list every week until, by the end of the year, we could all ask *Comment allez-vous* and answer *Je vais très bien merci* or *J'ai mal à la tête* with only the usual amount of stumbling.

I complained with the others about the never-ending lists of 'vocab', but I loved being able to say *le chien* and *le chat* and *mon frère* and *ma soeur* at home on the farm. It was like having a secret language, one that set me apart. Having some small distinction was at times necessary amongst eight brothers and sisters, but it also hinted at the possibility of another kind of world, the faint beginning of awareness that there was a connection between language and perception. Other words for things created the idea that there was another way of seeing, of thinking, of knowing, that things didn't have to be what everyone agreed they were. Not that anyone in my family was impressed.

'*Bonjour Maman*,' I said.

'Oh for heaven's sake,' my mother said and handed me a tea-towel.

Mrs Berman brought in madeleines and éclairs, which she made at home and let us eat in class, and told us about the cafés in France where everyone sat outside at round tables and drank wine with their meals. We sketched maps of the 'hexagon of France' with the Dordogne, the Rhône and the Seine rivers marked, the Alps and the Pyrénées cross-hatched, and Provence, Languedoc and all the other provinces outlined; we learned that Napoleon crowned himself emperor in an ermine-lined purple cloak decorated with gold bees, and that Marie Curie was a woman scientist who won the Nobel prize. It was a pure, old-fashioned version of France.

Mrs Berman also told us about the novels of Balzac and Zola and we read Guy de Maupassant's stories and the short essays by the exquisitely truthful Michel de Montaigne, for whom I was not yet ready. I started to dream that one day I would go to Paris, but apart from Mrs Berman, I didn't know anyone who had made such a miraculous journey. There didn't seem to be any way for a girl from a scrabbling farming family to get to Paris.

When I sat on the broken veranda at home, I could see patchy grass, the pepper tree, a sagging chicken-wire fence. Outside the fence was the dry creek, windmill, dams and paddocks, and to the west, the farm sheds and, in the distance, Baron Rock, the monolith behind my childhood. To the east was the lane out to the road which went past the tin church we prayed in on Sunday mornings and then past the one-teacher school where I spent seven years, then twenty kilometres through the bush-covered hills to town where there were shops, a wheat silo, a high school and another, bigger, brick church. I had been to Sydney once that I could remember. That was the size of the world, except in books.

The only other French writer I remember reading in high school was Camus. *The Plague* was set for English; I'm impressed now that the nuns were willing to set existentialism loose on bush teenagers in the 1960s. I sat on the back veranda on my great aunt's old rocking chair, which we eventually rocked to pieces, and ploughed my way through the tumult in Algeria, a country I'd barely heard of. It's hard to recall now the effect of existentialism and the absurd on a fourteen-year-old girl, but I do recall a feeling both of pride in reading something which I knew to be 'literature' and a worrying sense that the world was much stranger and more frightening than I had been told.

Perhaps it was then that the paddocks and sheds finally lost solidity, or at least, became unconvincing. Ever since I could read, the three-dimensional world inside books had taken up more and more space, become more detailed, had come to be the world I wanted to live in. In my mind there were apartments with balconies, stairways and attics, narrow streets and shops and parks with iron railings, and beyond the cities, stone villages and meadows and running streams and oak forests, all made of words, and all the spaces, the air in the streets and rooms and over the meadows, that too was made of words.

I left the farm and moved to Sydney and then to New Zealand and back. Within a few months of meeting him when I was only twenty years old, I was pregnant to Anthony and gave birth to a boy with reddish gold hair. He was one of those babies who smiled at strangers and strangers smiled back. I waited until he was walking and talking and then I enrolled at university to study literature and writing.

The French thread was picked up by a mismatching collection of writers – Voltaire, Balzac and Duras, Artaud, Robbe-Grillet, Colette, Françoise Sagan, de Beauvoir (but not Sartre at that stage as we were a feminist faculty), fragments of Rousseau, and reams of French theorists, Barthes and Foucault and Irigaray. Like de Beauvoir, 'literature took the place in my life that had once been occupied by religion, it absorbed me entirely and transfigured my life'.

At home in a shambolic share house, I read Anaïs Nin, Henry Miller, Hemingway, James Joyce, Scott Fitzgerald. I tried Proust, just because I thought I should, and certain lines – 'as a rule it is with our beings reduced to a minimum that we live' – appealed, but mostly I was in too much of a hurry for his precise world. At the time the whole household was passionately devoted to the film *Les Enfants du Paradis*, seeing it several times and falling in love with both Baptiste and Garance. I wasn't the only one with romantic French symptoms.

After I finished my degree, the household broke up and I moved with Anthony and our son and two friends to a house in the Blue Mountains near Sydney. Matt started school, sturdy and independent, and my body started to long for another small body to nestle under my chin and to fit around the curve of my breasts and stomach. Another boy arrived on a cold blue day. Matt, who was seven years old by now, stroked the baby's arms and said, 'So this is the person we have been loving all this time.' The baby lay on my belly and gazed at me and in that instant I saw the sweetness of his nature.

Afterwards, I changed Patrick's nappies, was often exhausted, stole time to write, dug in our garden and dreamed about the world outside the Mountains. Anthony drove taxis in Sydney and we got by.

One day in the Mountains we met Jean-Jacques, a French-Swiss who gave us French lessons around the fire and became our friend. He spoke a fantastical half-French version of English with no care for tense or grammar, but once a week turned up with French books and red wine and sat with us reading *Le Ballon Rouge* and laughing at our accents. He gave our boys, Matt and Patrick, a copy of Antoine de Saint-Exupéry's *Le Petit Prince*, the first whole book I read in French. I still can't look at the drawing of the elephant in a python in *Le Petit Prince* without thinking of Jean-Jacques.

He busked as a shoeshine clown, Monsieur Polish, to earn a living, and when he and his girlfriend, Olive, came around to our place after busking, he always pulled a handful of coins out of his pocket to give to Matt. Jean-Jacques collected objects – kangaroo skulls he found on the roadside, a twisted branch, a carved elephant, cockatoo feathers – and made them into sculptures. He also painted disturbing pictures with thick paint and violent colours. In the evenings, he and Anthony smoked joints together on the back veranda and their talk ranged all around the world and I could see there was a matching discontent and a sweetness in them both.

In a few years, Jean-Jacques' story had become a saga of art and heroin addiction and flight, but, at least for now, it's enough that he held the French thread for me for several years. He opened the door to a playful sensibility, *ludique*, and a child-like imagination, which has ever since seemed to me to be intrinsically French. But by the time we went to live in Paris, we hadn't seen him for nearly fifteen years.

*

All those Mountain years I wanted to live in Paris, it was my dream, but everyone has unfulfilled dreams. *C'est la vie.* I began to turn to memoir, more and more interested in exploring the self in writing, 'the self as a physics and metaphysics' as Montaigne put it. Why on earth couldn't the self be a respectable subject for literature? It was a territory as complex, as vast, as any other; a moment-by-moment hallucination of sense impressions, emotions and thoughts, continuously creating the experience of a shady chestnut tree, an itchy leg, a smiling face, a sense of belonging, of love and grief and delight. Wasn't an ungraspable sense of being, in fact, the only thing that connects each one of us?

I read *La Batarde* and *Memoirs of a Dutiful Daughter* and *The Diving Bell and the Butterfly*, looking out through their authors' eyes at a world with a light and shade so much more dramatic than the light and shade in my mountain back yard that I wondered if it was their gaze or their world that differed so much.

From the back veranda I could see a rough lawn sloping down to a trampoline and a clothesline slung between two gum trees. Orchids grew untended under one of the gums and, one year, a nearby waratah planted in memory of my father burst out with seventeen extravagant red blooms. Along a wooden fence hung with two of Jean-Jacques' wooden masks, dark mauve lilacs and port wine magnolia scented the air. Beyond the clothesline were angophora gums, banksias, grevilleas, wattles, random and tangled, sloping all the way down to a creek. I couldn't see the creek from where I sat but I had seen yabbies in the pool created by a stone dam the boys had built. Matt and Patrick were almost seven years apart, but they worked together hauling and balancing the stones, which stayed in place for years, even when the roar of brown flood waters tumbled over them.

I was immersed in my days, I wrote, I enjoyed the feel of children's arms holding me close and wasn't discontent. I don't want to give the wrong impression, or rather I don't want to tempt the Fates who have given me more than my fair share of love and luck, but nothing lasts. I am at least old enough to know that. Even if it lies dormant for years, sleeping like a hibernating bear, restlessness always returns, no matter what.

And then an aneurysm in Dina's brain burst and she died and Theo's eyes were bruised forever and I knew for certain that life and dreams and getting up in the morning could stop without warning. A blood vessel can split in the head and in an instant all is lost and nothing anyone can do or say, no clichés about holding on and having courage and living the dream, will make the slightest bit of difference. Plans for building an extension on the house are left mid-air, a child is left motherless and a clever and beautiful young woman is a handful of ashes.

And even if catastrophe doesn't arrive just yet, the body still changes, the monthly flow of blood starts drying up, the skin thickens, and then one day someone asks an innocent question: what have you been up to? It's an everyday conversation, but suddenly the answer feels too heavy to say.

I waded through muddy water against the current. Marianne Faithfull sang 'The Ballad of Lucy Jordan' on the CD player while I ironed. I was already older than Lucy; she was only thirty-seven. What had once seemed over the hill was already in the past. She would never ride in Paris in a sports car. The plaintive voice released vast territories of youthful longing. I put down the iron and cried. I hadn't known that all dreams come back as forceful and demanding as babies. I had thought I had found my place here, but I was longing for elsewhere.

I knew what would assuage the restlessness; it's not that hard to recognise an old yearning when it resurfaces. I told Anthony my dream, and he, being always ready to jump sideways, dreamed with me. We began to plot and save. I made lists, researched apartments in Paris, taught extra classes, calculated endless sums and currency conversions, looked for someone to rent our small house in the Mountains. Our younger son, Patrick, left school and enrolled at university to study politics and watched with bewildered astonishment as Anthony and I shut the door behind us.

*

It was ten o'clock, still our first day in Paris and still twilight outside, but Anthony was asleep. I was too excited to sleep, unwilling to miss one moment. I had been annoyed with him for climbing the ladder and collapsing on the mattress with the daylight only just faded.

'How boring you are!'

He'd shrugged and closed his eyes and gone to sleep. He could always do that, even after a real argument. I wanted him to feel everything the way I did but he'd never had any need to dance to my tune. I was afraid of fading away. I wanted to stay awake every second, make the day last forever.

I stood up and took more clothes out of the suitcases but I couldn't think where to put them. There was no wardrobe or chest of drawers and I couldn't see any hooks for hanging

TWO

JULY

I myself am the subject of my book.

Michel de Montaigne

I still have the diary I kept that year. It's just notes, handwritten in a French exercise book, the kind with graph-paper, *papier scolaire*, which I bought on the first jetlagged day at WH Smith's bookshop over the road from the Tuileries. It was too big to carry around with me, not useful for jotting observations, but now as I try to recall what happened that year it has the heft of a convincing record.

On the front page I taped a black-and-white postcard of a girl standing on the pont d'Arcole, one of the bridges spanning from the Right Bank to the Île de la Cité, the larger of the two islands in the Seine. The girl has her back to the camera looking eastward down the river towards the Île St Louis and is wearing plain clothes – a cardigan, narrow skirt and sneakers – but her arms are uplifted in a joyful salute. Even though you can't see her face, she looks like a naive, happy girl, probably a country girl, just arrived in the city of her dreams. It's a well-known image – you see it in racks outside all the postcard shops in Paris – but I don't care that it's commonplace. It's exactly how I felt at the beginning of my sojourn.

At first I wrote excitable descriptions of streets and cafés and people in the diary, a series of postcards, clear edges against bright blue skies, but it soon enough became patchy, often just instructions like 'Ring Mum today' or 'Choir 19.00'. While it allows some checking of dates, much of that year is a sequence of memories overlaid since then with other sojourns, not a history but a kind of layered honeycomb of stored memory.

*

Despite scrambling up the ladder to bed so late the night before, the first morning I woke early, still on an Australian clock, tired but wide awake. Anthony was up already and had been down to the *boulangerie* in the rue des Abbesses. The croissants and *pain au chocolat* he had bought were still warm in their paper bag.

'We can't do this every day,' I said. 'Pastry and chocolate for breakfast.'

'This is not every day. This is today. First-morning party.'

I sat on the stool over by the window with my cup of tea and gazed with an unfocused stare out at the courtyard. I was in Paris at last but a ritual as deep as tea was not going to change. I took a bite of the *pain au chocolat*. The warm runny chocolate dribbled down my chin and I wiped it off with my fingers. Anthony leaned over and licked my chocolate fingertips, not sexily but as if he were licking the back of a spoon.

'Sorry for saying you were boring last night,' I said. The small and ordinary failings had come with me.

'Let's explore,' he said.

Out in the rue des Trois Frères it was already warm although still fresh on the shady side of the narrow street. Anthony turned right and I followed but within seconds we stopped at Bonjour l'Artiste. There was a painted jester on the door in front of a cascade of gold streamers and the windows were scattered with blinking lights and crammed with masks and magic tricks and a stuffed white rabbit. It looked like a shop out of a children's book where elves and gnomes might work, where you might find yourself transformed into a bird or a dormouse. A fall right through the looking-glass; Alice quivering in anticipation. It was closed at this early hour, 11 am.

Near the end of my childhood the muttering white rabbit and the raging Queen of Hearts still frightened me, but I wanted to be Alice nonetheless. To grow tall, or small, to fit through looking-glasses and tiny doors and rabbit holes into other worlds; how lucky she was. She could have half a cup of tea with the Mad Hatter and see a smiling cat and answer riddles and play croquet with hedgehogs and flamingoes. Heads might be cut off and babies might change into pigs too, which was worrying, but the possibilities of entering another world were too enticing to turn away.

Anthony pointed out a bird mask that reminded him of Jean-Jacques. We still had a couple of masks of his at home. He had left all his possessions with us – animal skulls, masks, photographs of malformed creatures, a hash pipe, Balinese puppets, pots and pans and sheets and a wardrobe – when he fled Australia. We kept a lot of it, put our clothes in the wardrobe, hung the puppets up in the hallway, and the disturbing papier-mâché bird-man mask sat on the mantelpiece for fifteen years.

He had sent a couple of postcards from Paris soon after he left fifteen or so years ago, and a photograph of himself sitting in a window. Last we had heard, he had a new Spanish girlfriend, Ana, and he was thinking of working with his parents in Switzerland.

Further down, the cobbled street turned a sharpish corner and then lost itself in a five-ways. One corner was occupied by a *boulangerie*, which became our local for the next few months. We crossed over into the rue Tardieu where the shops sold Eiffel towers of all sizes, Sacré-Coeur in snow-domes, Mona Lisa mugs and tea-towels. We came to an open square with a large nineteenth-century carousel, and there, high on Montmartre above us, were the symmetrical white domes and cupolas of Sacré-Coeur cut out against the blue sky. I want to say it perfectly reproduced its thousands of photographic images, but of course, it's the other way around.

I read aloud from my pocket Paris history that it was built as a penance for the excesses of the socialist Communards who seized power in Paris in the brief revolution of 1871 just after the Franco-Prussian war. The Communards had hidden several hundred cannons they had somehow dragged up to Montmartre and after fierce battles with the army had established the Commune and ruled Paris for a few months.

'Penance?' Anthony scoffed. 'You mean it was the Catholic Church reasserting its power!'

I bridled a little. My childhood days were immersed in ritual and incense and Benediction and confession and making lists of sins and coveting a lacy white communion dress. My brother and sister and I constructed an altar rail out of boxes in the laundry and made communion hosts by pressing round

Vegemite lids into bread and played at being priest and congregation. Every evening I knelt on the lino in my bedroom and prayed for the Fall of Communism, even though I was from a poor family and even though I didn't know what communism was. I might be on the side of the Paris Commune now, but my history was against me.

'Let's walk right up,' Anthony said. 'You can show me how to genuflect.'

I ignored him and set off up the hill past the young French-Africans approaching tourists with braided wrist bracelets. They smiled and held out the bracelets and deftly tied them to wrists before tourists had time to protest. I had only just arrived but I'd read my guide book; I wasn't going to be caught.

From the terrace at the top, the basilica wasn't nearly as white and had a blocky squat air. The travertine stone was like concrete close up and had lost its drama.

'One of the many things in life that look better from a distance,' said Anthony. I looked away. I hadn't wanted it to be said.

There were hundreds of tourists on the terrace gazing out over Paris. The steps below were crowded with young travellers; a boy played his guitar and sang 'Brown-eyed Girl', a couple were setting up a puppet show, more young men held out bracelets and Eiffel tower earrings.

We surveyed the city for a few minutes, not able to name anything except Notre Dame and the Eiffel Tower, but it all felt recognisable; it could not have been any other city in the world. The overarching whiteness of it gave it the appearance of an imagined town, a place that had constructed itself to be looked at. This wasn't the real-life red roofs and green-grey gums of Sydney or the washed-out honey colours of country towns, it was a fantasy city where all the buildings were the same whitish-cream and the same dimensions. It created a sense of order and calm – and unreality. Around the edges, outside the *périphérique*, the ring-road, there was a rash of skyscrapers, threatening the perfection, but they were not enough to disturb the dreamy sense of looking at a mythical city.

We walked down the side of Sacré-Coeur. There would be plenty of time to go inside another day; today we just wanted to see the lie of the land in our *quartier*, the eighteenth. For local government, Paris is divided into twenty arrondissements and Parisians name where they live, not by suburb, but by the number of their arrondissement, the sixth, the eleventh, the eighteenth. Each number carries a connotation: the sixth connotes 'bobo', bohemian-bourgeois or *intello*, the eleventh suggests young and cool, the eighteenth is the artistic world of early last century.

Around the corner was place du Tertre, with its cafés and checked tablecloths and geraniums in boxes and shops selling Toulouse-Lautrec, Dali and Picasso prints and artists sketching pencil portraits – a marketed version of its own past. 'A picture of Madame,' the artists called out in English, holding their pads and pencils and pretending to start sketching. People streamed all around us, picking up posters of Aristide Bruant, the cabaret performer in his black cape and red scarf, and key-rings with melting Dali clocks and music boxes playing 'La Vie en Rose'.

We bought takeaway coffees then went around the back of Sacré-Coeur, away from the crowds. Down the rue de la Bonne we saw a park with a children's playground, a sandpit and swings at one end. Kids were playing and parents sat around on benches in the shade. We sat down on a bench facing back up the hill where we could still see the white dome.

The mothers and a few fathers, all of them much younger than us, chatted to each other. A couple of nannies, young African girls, sat watching two white children. I could understand a word or two here and there, but not enough to even know what anyone was talking about. Politics? Buying a new apartment? An affair? They talked as parents do, watching their kids the whole time, occasionally jumping up to pick up a fallen child or retrieve a toy. I sipped my milky coffee, not liking the bitter taste.

'*Regarde, Maman*,' a small boy cried out in the warm air. Look, Mummy. I had heard the words in English hundreds of times. He needed a witness. I'd been a witness for twenty-five years, the one who watched and acknowledged each step, each new task. Watch me walk down steps. Watch me kick a soccer ball. Watch me. To witness appears self-effacing, but I didn't feel effaced or diminished by being the observer. I wonder if it's because a writer is also content to watch, is already practised at being the one who doesn't take part and isn't seen. The boy stood up, bending forward to keep his balance. The skin on his chubby arms looked silky soft.

Anthony and I looked at each other. I could feel his shoulder warm on mine. We didn't say anything. Accidentally we had made creatures together for whom we would both crawl across deserts of broken glass, but mostly it had been washing nappies and spooning avocado mash into mouths, then later, cheering on the side of chilly soccer fields and reading endless chapters of *Lord of the Rings*, and later again, ferrying them to parties and discussing homework and marijuana and girls. There was nothing to say but my heart felt tight to bursting.

I remembered the wave of loss that had surged through me a few days earlier as we crossed the Australian coast and flew out over the Timor Sea. I had known in that instant that it was Patrick's loss that I was feeling, that I was experiencing the tearing of the umbilical cord from his side. I had said to Anthony, 'I can feel Patrick missing us, right now,' and he nodded. It has only happened to me a few times in my life – I am not especially sensitive – but it has been unmistakeable when the surge of someone else's feeling has hit me. I had cried over the Timor Sea.

'*Regarde, Maman*,' the little boy said again, holding up a red match-box car he had found in the sand. Behind him, on top of a dome high in the cloudless sky, was a statue of St Michael slaying a dragon. Time and weather had turned it verdigris, a milky green that I have always loved. His mother nodded and smiled but it seemed she was thinking about something else.

The streets on the northern slope of Montmartre are steep and cobbled and crooked. Away from place du Tertre, the scruffy village that once clung to the hill pokes through in rough stone walls and patches of *maquis*, native scrub, and a *rocher de la sorcière*, witch's rock, and houses with messy gardens and bees buzzing and ants scurrying. There's a vineyard too – Montmartre used to be scattered with vineyards and orchards and windmills – and ivy crawling over walls and unpainted shutters and a white cat sitting on a windowsill, dreaming in the sunlight. Cobbles are worn smooth and old-fashioned pink roses bloom in the garden of the house where Renoir and Utrillo lived. Le

Lapin Agile cabaret, with its ragged hedge and faded cerise walls like an old country house that sees no need to smarten itself up, communes with the vines climbing up the slope across the lane. There are chestnuts and oaks in gardens, shady and damp underneath, grasses growing out of walls and plaques declaring Tristan Tzara, the Dadaist, lived here in this fine house. And there's a bishop with his severed head in his hands, ready to walk across Montmartre and put it down where he wanted to be buried – it's St Denis, his head chopped off by the Romans, looking calm and unperturbed. There's a young woman singing 'Les Temps des Cerises', the ripe cherries symbolising the fruitfulness of summer and the blood of those who died when the Commune was overthrown. And here are three boys playing soccer in front of the statue *Le Passe-Muraille*, a fictional man who could walk through walls, as he emerges from the stone wall in place Marcel Aymé. Or is *Le Passe-Muraille* caught there, forever imprisoned by his magical ability?

From the park we wandered the backstreets until we came to a paved area at the top of a flight of steps. There was a bronze bust of a woman – Dalida, it said on the plinth – and a bench under a tree and, behind her up the hill, the park where St Denis held his mitred and severed head. I didn't know then, but Dalida was born in Egypt and had longed to come to Paris – she arrived the year I was born – and soon became the most loved singer in France. A pale boy about eleven years old was playing the violin in front of her. He wasn't busking – there was no receptacle for coins – he must have just wanted to be outside in the warm afternoon doing his practice. He had his violin case and a few music books on the bench and a flimsy stand for his score. He was playing 'Flight of the Bumblebee', one of the few pieces I can recognise, slowly and carefully.

We stopped to listen, standing to one side so as not to put him off, but he was concentrating so intently that he didn't seem to see us. He stood upright, his back straight, his elbow out, his thick dark hair, a bit long, tucked behind his ears. He looked as if he had been selected by a film director who wanted to convey the fine beauty of a sensitive boy – his skin was creamy, his lashes long, the hairs still soft on his bare arms and legs – just before his life changed. The notes buzzed in the air, hectic in the summer heat, triggering memory. I was stung by a bee at the water-bubblers at primary school one day. Bees often hung around the bubblers, hoping for water, I suppose, but I didn't notice one alight on my finger until I felt the sharp sting. And then the throbbing ache afterwards and my pride in the 'blue' the teacher put on it to take the sting away. 'The bee dies when it stings,' we said to each other, satisfied that there was retribution.

Anthony and I didn't watch and listen for long, but when we left, a small smile and a nod escaped the boy. I walked up the hill, smiling. I might not be able to understand most of what I saw but Montmartre was telling me stories, welcoming me.

*

It was my first day ransacking Montmartre and the pleasure was in a kind of eating – I felt as if I were devouring the world and being nourished. Simone de Beauvoir wrote that she loved to gaze at random strangers; 'their faces, their appearance, and the sound of their voices captivated me'. It was a confession that revealed her secret soul to me, that strange desire to absorb others, suck them in through the eyes.

I'm told there's a kind of water bug that sucks the insides out of its victim, leaving only its skin, but I have no desire to take anything from the people I watch. I want something more than witnessing though. It isn't so much to invade or know their inner geography, but to gaze out through their eyes, to know what the world looks like to them. To live more than my own life.

Colette too wrote of the 'inscrutable human beings who plucked me by my sleeve, made me their witness for a moment and then let me go'. When I read that sentence in one of her stories, I felt it hit its mark like an arrow. It was not the responsible witnessing of a parent, but a random and greedy and yet almost reverential gazing at strangers that I'm also addicted to.

What *is* it like for other people to be in the world? Even as a self-absorbed teenager, that was the question: what was it like for other people – passing strangers, people seen out the bus window, families in suburban lounge-rooms – what was it like for them to be here?

It's still the same. It could be just curiosity, which is a good enough motive, and I could just ask, and I do, but it's not a question anyone can answer straight out of their mouths. What *is* it like for you to be in the world? It's elusive, disturbing, so infinitely faceted, that I think the words have to be spread out one by one on the page before they can make any sense at all.

Montaigne described the world as the 'looking-glass in which we must gaze to come to know ourselves from the right slant'. My gaze was more voracious than that. I suspect he was talking about a more detached observation of others to reconsider his picture of himself. But he too was a hungry soul, I think, and he admitted to his own ransacking.

I like Montaigne's truthfulness, but even more I like that he didn't try to convince his readers of his truth. He merely said, 'these are my humours, my opinions; I give them as things I believe, not as things to be believed'. This is not the way things are, just the way I see them. It astonishes me that he knew that in the sixteenth century. Does it still need to be defended?

Montaigne understood the contradictory nature of who he was: 'My aim is to reveal my own self, which may well be different tomorrow.' He knew he could be a thief one day and a protector the next. It meant he always allowed himself to be unsure: 'Only fools have made up their minds and are certain.' He knew others wouldn't see it that way, that he would be attacked for self-absorption and vanity, but he didn't appear to care about that. In fact, on the opening page of his *Les Essais* he boldly writes: 'Reader, I myself am the subject of my book: it is not reasonable you should employ your time on a topic so frivolous and so vain. Therefore, farewell.'

What beautiful cheek! It's all about me, so see you later!

I'd love to be able to get away with that kind of insouciance, but I don't dare. I will offer a cup of coffee and the best macaroons and a glorious view of Paris, tiled mansards and balconies and red geraniums – please sit down, please stay – as I run about trying to mix up the honey pooling in the waxy cells of memory.

I can't do it alone. Montaigne ransacked the writers of Ancient Rome and Greece in his efforts to know himself. I'll have to keep ransacking Montaigne and de Beauvoir, de

Sévigné, Rousseau, Stendhal, Ernaux; rob the bees and the beekeepers.

*

Perhaps I ought to introduce them. Here and there, one by one.

What needs to be known about Michel de Montaigne? Let's see: his dates are 1533–1592; he lived in a chateau in the Perigord in the south-west of France – a landscape which I first saw that year and which has since become almost as familiar to me as the plains of my childhood; he was woken each morning of his childhood by the sweet thrumming of the harpsichord because his father believed a child should not be rudely awoken; he had a Latin tutor from babyhood and learned to speak and read Latin as his mother tongue; he had a dear friend who died and to whom he dedicated his writing; he had a wife and daughter whom he hardly ever mentioned; he was mayor of Bordeaux for several years; he had dark observant eyes and a neat Spanish conquistador-style beard and wore soft hats to cover his prematurely balding head; he came to Paris a few times and travelled as far as Italy; he wrote a book exploring his own nature, *Les Essais*, which every French schoolchild is expected to read.

I arrange to have coffee with Montaigne. We meet in the rue des Martyrs at Café KB (Kooka Boora) because they make good coffee – they have an Australian barista – and it's clear Montaigne couldn't be bothered with a poor brew. He doesn't believe in the value of hardship, seeing such belief as a kind of masochism: 'As for whacks and afflictions, you can make me do nothing but curse them: they are meant for men whose desires are aroused by only a good whipping.'

We sit at one of the tables on the footpath because it's crowded inside and most people are using their laptops or mobile phones. Montaigne is wearing dark trousers, a white linen shirt and a loosely knotted tie – he's not handsome, but stylish in an easy-going way. He orders a double-shot long black with a Portuguese tart. He's relaxed, and even though I'm impressed by the fact that he speaks four languages, he doesn't make me feel awkward or inadequate.

'I need to handpick my companions,' he says with a smile. 'But we must direct our desires and settle on things that are nearest and easiest.'

'Like the song,' I say. 'You can't always get what you want.'

He laughs. His brown eyes are attentive and amused. He says he loves the ease of popular culture. Then he adds, as if it were related, that he loves the internet, the access to vast knowledge, the branching connections which he finds himself addicted to, but is troubled by the fact that it does not allow for silence and unfilled time.

'I can never get to the bottom of things, I look things over, ripple the skin, and sometimes pinch to the bone,' he says.

He talks in a rambling fashion for ages. I enjoy his dry ironic humour and his eclectic mind, the way he explores ideas without dogmatism. We talk about philosophy and books, natural wonders we have seen on television, even exchange, with a smile, stories of our sexual habits and desires. I know he likes talking with women and that these days he acknowledges we are as capable of loving friendship as any man. He admits that for him desire is only really satisfying when it is accompanied by love and I am moved by his sensitivity. We exchange email addresses and decide to stay in contact.

And now, as the fairytales say, it was still the day I set out to explore my new home. In my old world, ten years could go by in a flash, leaving only a buzzing of memories, but in the first weeks in a new world, days are long, perhaps five times as long as usual.

By the time we were back in the rue des Trois Frères we had circled Montmartre, like pilgrims circling a mountain in Tibet. We came in the other end of the street, past the corner shop from the film *Le Fabuleux Destin d'Amélie Poulain*, as several newspaper articles taped to its window explained, and then, in a small square, we discovered the Bateau Lavoir. It was the studio where Picasso and Matisse and many other painters and writers and sculptors worked. It was painted a shiny dark green and the name was lettered in gold above the window. I knew it wasn't exactly the same studio – it had burned down thirty or so years ago with only the facade remaining – but it felt near enough to the real thing.

Much later I found an old back-and-white photograph of the original Bateau Lavoir and the shabbiness of the building reminded me more of the house I grew up in on the farm than the glossy shop-front with gold lettering I saw that day. The Lavoir where Picasso passed, he said, the most beautiful years of his life, was a shambles of a building patched together with tin and buckled boards and mismatching windows. It looked as if it might fall in on itself any minute and in the wind it had swayed and creaked like the washing boats on the Seine it was named after. It was freezing in winter and boiling in summer, dark and dirty, and there was only one water tap for the whole building. Here in this scrap-yard in 1907, Picasso painted *Les Demoiselles d'Avignon*.

But history in Montmartre began a long time before Picasso.

*

Two thousand years ago the Romans built temples to Mars and Mercury on the summit of Montmartre, one of which stood until 944 AD when it was struck by lightning. Two of the columns in St-Pierre, the church hiding in the shadows of Sacré-Coeur, are from the temple of Mercury.

St Denis had his head chopped off in the rue Yvonne le Tac in 250 AD and then picked it up, washed it in a fountain and carried it ten kilometres, preaching a sermon as he went.

When Henry of Navarre, later Henry IV and a Protestant, laid siege to Paris, the Abbess of the Convent on Montmartre, a beautiful seventeen-year-old girl called Claude de Beauvilliers, became his mistress and his army stayed at the convent. Parisians called the convent *un magasin des putes*, a shop of prostitutes.

In the sixteenth century St Ignatius Loyola founded the Jesuits on Montmartre, some say at St-Pierre on the summit, others say in a small chapel at the foot.

When the Cossacks attacked Montmartre in 1814, one of the four brothers who defended Moulin de la Galette, a mill which is now a restaurant, was cut into four pieces and one piece was put on each sail of the windmill and sent spinning.

Vincent Van Gogh stayed with his brother for a year in the rue Lepic, which crosses rue des Abbesses and winds right up around Montmartre.

During the Prussian Siege of Paris in 1870–71, after which the Montmartre Commune seized power, the people had to eat rats and mice and animals from the zoo, tigers and giraffes, and even each other. A restaurant menu extract from the time reads: '*civet de chat aux champignons*', cat stew with mushrooms; '*cotelettes de chien aux petits pois*', dog chops with peas; '*salamis de rats, sauce Robert*', rats in sauce.

In the nineteenth and early twentieth centuries, Montmartre became a favourite drinking haunt because it was outside the city limits where wine was cheaper. People came to the Moulin Rouge and Le Chat Noir to see red-and-black cloaked Aristide Bruant, and can-can dancer Jane Avril, and La Goulue, who caught coins in her vagina.

All of this happened a few minutes' walk from my studio in the rue des Trois Frères. The stories of Montmartre multiply on plaques on walls, pamphlets in souvenir shops, books in libraries, in Zola's *L'Assommoir,* in the Montmartre museum and in paintings of its wooded hill-top in the Carnavalet where the history of Paris is displayed.

I didn't know any of these stories when I grew up on the farm – but I longed for them. There I was surrounded by stories of country, rocky hills and whirlwinds and caves and fossils that whispered to me all day long, but they were so quiet I had to strain to listen. I wanted stories with crimson velvet and silver trumpets in them, and steep stairways and falls from grace and artists drinking absinthe and centuries unfolding one from the other with time divided into precise dates.

Forty thousand years of Dreamtime floated like a mist, poetic and sacred, but I could not read anywhere that, in 52 BC or 944 AD or 1590 on the banks of the Macquarie River on the central plains near where I grew up, a battle had been fought, or a temple built, or an artist celebrated, or a saint sacrificed. It wasn't a failure of the Dreamtime, it was my own need for articulation, for time and space to be delineated.

That evening I bought a phone card to call my mother. She lived in a retirement home in town – the farm had been sold years before when my father was still alive – and she was becoming frail, although she resisted using her walking-frame.

I sat down with my cup of tea and punched in the endless sequence of numbers on the phone card. It took several attempts before I got it right but then I heard the phone ringing in Australia and my mother's tentative 'hello'. There was always a question in my mother's hellos, as if she wasn't going to give anything away until she knew who it was on the line.

'*Bonjour Maman,*' I said.

'Oh for heaven's sake,' she said. But I could tell she was thrilled. 'How are you?'

I was good. Everything was good. In front of me next to the photo of Baron Rock was a sketch that one of my friends, a cartoonist, had made before we left. It showed a couple sitting outside a café looking at a *Paris Match* headline announcing '*Anthony et Patti arrivent à Paris.*' 'Ah, Paris will be like ze thirties again,' one of them remarks. I had blushed at my long-out-of-date dream.

'It's the best of all possible worlds, Mum,' I said. And then I told her of my adventures, displaying my day in Paris like a pretty thing I had found for her. As if I were a child and not a woman with adult children of my own.

THREE

AUGUST

What's the use of knowing the movements of stars if we don't know our own minds and hearts?

Michel de Montaigne

The *Amélie* shop in the rue des Trois Frères had a sloping counter outside with baskets of fruit and vegetables artfully arranged and garlands of grapes and vine leaves twisted along the awning, looking as pretty as a picture-book. Inside it was an ordinary corner shop. I was buying the usual milk, apples, cheese, honey and cereal, using the shop as a mini-supermarket. I was afraid to try the *fromagerie* with its thousands of unrecognisable cheeses, or the *marchand des légumes*, greengrocer, or the *pharmacie*, or the *épicerie*, deli, or the *cave*, wine shop. If I went into those shops I would have to be able to discuss what I wanted – I had loitered outside the *fromagerie* a number of times and had observed the lengthy discussions between the shopkeeper and customer. In the corner shop, all I had to do was say hello, I thought.

'*Bonjour Madame,*' the shopkeeper said.

'*Bonjour,*' I replied.

'*Il blah de blah aujourd'hui. Blah blah du soleil blah,*' he responded sociably.

I nodded, blushing. I remembered the advice Jean-Jacques had given during our fireside lessons – when you don't understand, he said, consider what people usually say in the situation; in a shop, as you are paying, it's 'do you want a bag' or something about the weather. I did hear *soleil* so he must have been saying something about the weather, surely okay to agree to. But then who knows? Whenever anyone spoke to me since I'd arrived I'd not understood anything more than occasional words from Mrs Berman's vocabulary lists. It was as if my ears were stuffed with a strange cotton wool that blurred most words and let one or two through but not enough to respond with any safety.

Still, I had been trying my shop French every day. '*Je voudrais une baguette, s'il vous plaît.*' I'd like a bread stick, please. I believed in language immersion theory; if I just listened to French enough, its meaning would seep through my pores and into my brain like a kind of dye, the way it did with children. The way it did with Montaigne, who learned Latin from babyhood 'without art, without books, without grammar, without rules, without whips and without tears'. His father not only engaged a Latin tutor when he was a baby, he insisted on all the servants learning a few words too, so the nurse and maids all spoke to him in the language of the Ancient Romans. It became his mother tongue of course, and Gascon, a local dialect, was his second language, and French his third. He said that even after not using it much in his adult life, when anything surprising or demanding happened he burst into Latin. Asking for bread would have been no problem: *da mihi pauxillum panis?*

I didn't have enough money for a tutor and, besides, now that I was surrounded by all things French, surely I would pick it up? I did have those lists from Mrs Berman after all, stored in exactly the same order I had learned them, they must all come together into sentences one day. All I needed to do was practise.

I bought newspapers – *Libération,* and *Le Monde* – and painstakingly decoded the front page and the arts pages; I easily read all the ads on the Metro; I studied my French textbook, which I still had from Jean-Jacques' fireside lessons. And I watched television. There was a small set in the dark under the mezzanine, so I began watching a quiz show each evening. The questions were repeated a number of times and were written up on the screen as well: *Qui est l'auteur du roman Les Misérables? a) Émile Zola, b) Honoré de Balzac, c) Victor Hugo d) Guy de Maupassant.* I could read that easily – I even knew the correct answer. As long as I could see the words I was fine. I sat with my dictionary on my lap, looking up new words and attempting to memorise them.

Anthony worked for a university trying to persuade international students to study in Australia, which meant he had to travel often in Europe and Asia. After much argument, his boss had agreed that he could work from Paris, especially now that his main region was Europe. Back home he had an office at the university, but here he had to work from our tiny studio. I found it hard to write with someone in the same room – thinking is a noisy business and takes up a lot of space – and so did my manuscript. I had already written a hundred or so pages; they were spread out on the floor and I was literally piecing them together. I had claimed the old-fashioned writing desk and Anthony sat on the lounge with his laptop on a chair. He stepped carefully over my pages to get to the kitchen or bathroom.

The studio had no wifi connection but I found an internet café at place des Abbesses right next to the Metro. There weren't many on the 'tourist side' of Montmartre but I discovered later there were plenty on the north side, 'behind' the hill. It was a poorer area with a lot of French-Africans so there were telephone and internet shops in every street for people to connect with their mothers and sons and wives back in Mali or Senegal or Gambia.

Anthony soon started going out to cafés to work; Camille's in the next street was his favourite.

'You're tossing me out on the streets,' he said.

'I could go instead,' I offered, unconvincingly. It was a ritual – we both knew it would be him. I had always worked at home, and besides, he needed a smoke. All the cafés still allowed smoking then, so he sat outside Camille's and worked on his laptop and smoked and watched the passers-by.

I struggled with Dina's story. I had begun writing it in an old beach-house then daily life had taken over. It had been difficult from the start, but now that I was working on the third section, the period after she had died, I didn't know how to go forward at all. It wasn't just because it wasn't clear what stories to include, but that I felt more emotionally tender. It was ten years since she had died and I thought it shouldn't have been too demanding, but I found writing made the experience of her death more intense than perhaps it had been in life.

I kept thinking how young she was. I hadn't realised it at the time because she had been older than I was and now she was younger, thirty-seven years old forever, dark-haired, eyes sparkling, unchanged – and Theo was motherless forever. The writing pulled things out of the dark and made me feel how near death always was. I was spending too much time staring at the screen and crossing paragraphs and pages out in my notebook.

One hot morning I sat down early, determined to unfold the next part of her story. Anthony was away in Lyon in the south-east for a few days' work and I wanted to take advantage of uninterrupted time. We were practised at staying out of each other's way, but here in such a small space and with the temptations of Paris outside the door, it was easy for both of us to down tools and take off. Today with only myself to struggle with, I could stay and work it out. I opened the laptop and read what I had written the morning before. Just as I began to write a new sentence, someone upstairs picked up a hammer and started banging.

Bang! Bang! I waited. There was a pause. Then it started again and this time continued in a perfectly regular rhythm for several minutes. How long does it take to bang a nail in? My shoulders tensed and my head started thumping. Then it stopped. All done. I sighed and picked up my pen. If I scribbled a few things by hand first, the writing would flow more easily. Then it started again. I looked at my watch as if by timing it I could control it. It continued in the same unvarying rhythm, on and on. I should go up and yell at him to stop. What was the word for hammer? I looked it up: *marteau*. But who was I kidding? I was a foreigner in his country – I wasn't going to start yelling *arrêtez*, stop, with the bloody *marteau* in a bad accent.

I'm sure Montaigne and de Sévigné and Stendhal and all the rest never had to put up with hammers banging while they wrote. They would have just told the servant or workman to stop and that would have been the end of it. I flicked open Montaigne: 'I have a mind which is delicate and easy to distract: when it withdraws aside to concentrate, the least buzzing of a fly is enough to murder it.' I couldn't help laughing; there he was in his tower, annoyed by a fly buzzing in through the open window, trying to ignore it, but soon chasing it around the room with a rolled-up manuscript.

After an hour of stopping and starting and several imagined violent retributions, I faced the fact that the hammering was never going to end. I grabbed my map-book and keys and headed out.

In the streets it was hot and quiet. The *boulangerie* in the rue des Abbesses and the *fromagerie* were both closed and had handwritten signs on the door: *congé annuel.* Annual leave. I was puzzled – so the whole shop just closed for the summer? Surely they wouldn't just shut up shop and go – no-one did that. I discovered that was exactly what the French did, that summer holidays were a sacred right of the republic and many shops had blinds drawn and signs on the doors. There was a slow, dozy feeling in the streets, as if most people were away or indoors and if you did have something to do in Paris, you ought to do it slowly. There were fewer cars parked in the street too, less traffic, and fewer people walking about, except, I soon noticed, in the tourist areas, which were more crowded. The banging faded out of my brain in the bright heat.

There were a few things I could attend to. One was finding a choir. I wasn't really a singer, had only started to learn a couple of years earlier and could barely hold a tune, but I wanted to continue. I had been in a choir in the Mountains for only a year and I knew I would lose courage if I didn't keep going now. Singing was part of the story about Dina and Theo. Dina had been a singer, but I was also drawn to the deep connection in singing with others, something beyond the grasp of intellect. Even though my voice was weak, I had felt at least moments of communion when it merged with everyone else's. It's curious, the release of being at one with others, almost as if we were made for it.

On the way down to the Metro I decided to go to Shakespeare's bookshop to find a *Fusac*, a magazine for expatriates listing accommodation, jobs, things to buy – and classes. And I would pick up a *Pariscope*, the 'what's on' magazine. I could find a singing class in one of those.

Shakespeare and Company is on the Left Bank in the rue de la Bûcherie, directly across the Seine from Notre Dame. It was started in the 1950s by an American, George Whitman, who named it after Sylvia Beach's bookshop of the same name. Sylvia, also American, was famous as a supporter of writers during the mythologised golden years of expatriate writers in Paris, the years of Gertrude Stein, Ezra Pound, Ernest Hemingway, DH Lawrence, Samuel Beckett, James Joyce – and she was the first person to publish James Joyce's *Ulysses* when no publisher would take it on. I had already visited the bookshop once and liked its ramshackle dimness and uncertain towers of books.

The *Fusac* magazines were stacked outside the door of the bookshop in a rack. I didn't go in this time because I knew I'd be trapped in there for hours, pulling books off the shelves and stacks, filled with both desire and a kind of hopelessness that always nibbled at my frayed edges in bookshops. All the books I'd never read. I grabbed the magazine, went to the news-stand around the corner in the boulevard St Michel and bought a *Pariscope*, then headed up away from the bottleneck of tourist cafés around Fontaine St Michel.

I turned into the rue St Jacques, the main road south from Paris for hundreds of years, and then further up the hill came to the rue Pierre et Marie Curie. Along one side of the street was the Foundation Curie, a severe-looking building. Marie Curie, the Nobel Prize-winning physicist and chemist, had worked in this very street! She was the only woman I'd heard of who was a scientist and in high school I had toyed, for a while, with the idea of following in her footsteps. Montaigne said there was no use knowing 'the movements of stars if we don't know our own minds and hearts', but I wanted to know the movement of the stars no matter what use it was – all of it, from the structure of atoms and wave theory right out to galaxies and black holes and how one single particle came into being from non-existence and unleashed the whole universe. Fortunately for science, I realised even before I left high school that I was too inclined to make things up and that I would have been one of those scientists disgraced for fudging test results to fit my favourite theory. I liked the stories too much to let the facts get in the way.

I found a café and sat down outside. It was a quiet street, no tourists.

'*Bonjour*,' I said.

'Do you want a menu?' said the waiter in English.

I shook my head, dispirited. What was it about the way I said *bonjour* that gave me away?

'*Un café crème*,' I muttered.

He shrugged as if I'd said I wanted sugar in my wine and walked away. I was just another tourist trying to extract meaning from other people's daily lives.

I opened the *Fusac* and read through notices for yoga retreats and children's drama classes and English lessons until I saw a small announcement about a choir. It was in French and indicated that no audition was required. It also said that a '*bon niveau*', good level, was expected, but I clung to 'no audition'. If I didn't have to sing alone I'd be okay. Standing next to a strong singer I could hold a tune. The choir met in the Marais, the oldest part of Paris in the fourth arrondissement. I wrote the date and address in my diary.

I flipped open the *Pariscope* and started looking through the concerts. I had grown up with almost no music. Neither of my parents was musical although my father sometimes tunelessly sang 'Home on the Range'; we had no musical instruments and I don't recall a record-player in the house until some of my older brothers and sisters were teenagers and started listening to rock'n'roll. There was the radio, or wireless as we called it, but it was turned on for the news and the Argonauts Club, an on-air club for children, and for weather and stockyard reports, not for music.

As a child Montaigne woke to the sound of a spinet, a type of harpsichord, but he didn't like musicians playing at dinner because it disturbed good conversation. Madame de Sévigné often mentioned musical performances she had heard: 'The music was indescribable, Baptiste [the composer] has done the utmost with all the King's musicians ... I don't believe there can be any other music in heaven.' But music was just part of her intellectual life, a few lines here and there. Of the other memoirists, only Rousseau was deeply interested in music. Before he became a writer, he taught music, composed a few pieces including an opera, wrote theoretical discussions on music and came up with a new system of musical notation to make music 'easier to write down, easier to learn and much less diffuse'. He presented it to the French Academy of Sciences, but while versions of it were eventually used in various countries, it wasn't accepted at the time.

When people say that music was important in their childhood I still feel a pang of envy. There is a world of patterned sound inside them that is silent in me and I know their souls have been refined in ways that are too late for mine. I have a friend in the Blue Mountains, Peter, who once told me he heard whole symphonies, note for note, inside his head when he was gazing out over the escarpment or at work at the writers' centre he ran, or even just when he was driving along the highway. He said he didn't know what the world was like without a musical accompaniment, what it was like to gaze over the cliffs and valleys filled with eucalypts and not hear Bach. Dina too lived inside music, although for her it was the beat of rock'n'roll, raw and energetic. Her voice was throaty, the music in her body rather than her mind, the sound and beat of blood and the throb of sex. I felt as if I had been shut out of a vast room in myself; there was flat silence in me where they had a detailed landscape of chords and notes and songs.

I would not be able to fill in all the silence, but at least I might be able to hear a few notes, pattern some scenes in Paris with music. There were pages of concerts in the *Pariscope*, every day of the week, and on Sundays performances in churches which were free or only cost a few euros: string quartets, solo sopranos, piano recitals, choirs, symphony orchestras, organ recitals, cello and violin duets, all over the city. I circled the notice for Mozart's *Requiem* at the Madeleine Church and thought of Dina, long dead. There had been no requiem for her. Just a strange scratchy funeral in a modern cemetery chapel before the coffin slid behind the curtains, her pale-faced little boy looking as if the whole world had become a vast and terrifying blank. Music and singing and death were beginning to mingle in my story in a way that I hadn't planned but which seemed inevitable. Death – and love too – has always needed music it seems. Words take us to the edge of their vast territories, but music can take us right through them; it can delineate the shape of every strange mountain and lost valley in those landscapes.

I stretched out in the midday heat. As I extended my arms I felt a twinge in my shoulder; I must have been crouched in front of my laptop for too many days. I'd give the man with the *marteau* a little longer before I headed back to the studio.

After leaving Madame Curie, I zigzagged through the narrow streets of the fifth arrondissement, along the rue Tournefort where Balzac's characters in *Père Goriot* lived, and along the rue du Pot de Fer where George Orwell was down and out, and into the place de la Contrescarpe where Hemingway drank in the cafés. The streets were narrow and silent and occasionally smelled of piss but I felt a delicious sense of a world shivering into place around me, a pleasure that was soothing and exciting at the same time. The streets were not just ordinary three-dimensional roadways and apartment buildings and shops, they existed as stories, as places inscribed. Here was where Orwell heard 'the desolate cries of street-hawkers' and where Balzac's fictional Rastignac began his long ascent into society and where Hemingway held up the zinc bar in the Café des Amateurs. Even though I'd never seen any of these streets before, I was aware of a curious sense that they were more real to me than the streets of my hometown. I could read these streets as well as walk them. They had been imprinted in my brain already and as the written image slipped over the actual, each street and café became imaginary. It was pleasurable, as if I were seeing a landscape unfold itself out from an open page and become real. I nearly laughed aloud – the world had become a 3D fold-out book and I was living inside it.

The rue Mouffetard wound up from the place de la Contrescarpe. It was lined with cafés and there were more people about because it was lunchtime and the rue Mouffetard was a tourist street, noisy after the silent summer heat of the backstreets. A market was just beginning to pack up and vendors were crying out their best prices to get rid of the last of their raspberries and strawberries. There were lettuce and other vegetable leaves everywhere on the cobbled street, and the smells of salmon and prawns and cheeses, mouldy blues and Normandy camemberts, were overpowering. One man was selling honey and honeycomb and I stopped to look at the neat hexagonal shapes of the cells. How had creatures come up with such a precise way of making and storing their nourishment, stealing nectar so arduously from hundreds of flowers – it takes 150 flowers to fill each bee's nectar basket – and then storing it in matching hexagonal cells until they needed it or until it was stolen by the beekeepers? It seemed a kind of alchemy, to turn flower juices into liquid gold.

I decided to head back to the studio; the hammerer no doubt would have stopped for a long lunch by now. On the way I passed the Panthéon where Rousseau and other *Grands Hommes*, famous men, of France are buried and then I was back in the rue St Jacques walking down by the buildings of the Sorbonne, quiet now with all the students away for the summer. Even the street was empty of traffic. It was hot and still. I suddenly felt that I was the only person out in Paris, that everyone had gone somewhere they all knew about and were laughing and talking under shady chestnuts by the water. Somewhere along the Seine out in the country. Or by a beach under sunshades. No-one knew I was here in this street. In this city of millions I didn't know anyone at all, not even a casual acquaintance, certainly no-one who needed to tell me what they were doing or where they had gone. I'd thought I was absorbing daily life but this was all show and the real people had gone elsewhere. I was standing in a street where people had walked with donkeys and ridden in coaches for more than a thousand years, where scholars and poets and musicians, medieval François Villon and Rabelais and twentieth-century Serge Gainsbourg and Coluche had laughed and drunk wine, and where travellers from the south came to see the great capital, but now I was the only one here. I wasn't part of this place. I was like a ghost, unseen. My imaginary world had become real and solid – I could feel the cobbles under my feet – but I had become invisible. Had I come so far to disappear?

*

When Jean-Jacques Rousseau first saw these streets on his way into Paris from the south, he didn't like them at all: 'I saw nothing but dirty, stinking little streets, ugly black houses, a general air of squalor and poverty, beggars, carters, menders of clothes, sellers of herb-drinks and old hats.' That was nearly 300 years ago, and most of the buildings were still medieval, crooked and falling down, with no sanitation, and it was a much poorer area than it is now, but Rousseau wasn't keen on towns anyway. He was more of a hippie really – the original hopeless romantic. He was happiest when he lived with Madame de Warens in the country near Chambéry in the Alps, wandering through the woods and wildflower meadows, gardening, making honey, taking care of chooks and pigeons and cows: 'I strolled through the woods and over the hills, I wandered in the valleys, I read, I lazed, I worked on the garden, I picked the fruit, I helped in the household and happiness followed me everywhere.'

In Paris, like me, he was an outsider. He came from Switzerland and he was a Protestant – although he converted to Catholicism for a while – and it was difficult to find his way in. He recognised that 'nothing is achieved in Paris except by the help of ladies' and was regularly received at their homes, but he was often slow in conversation, and, unfortunately for him, the essence of French society for a long time had been quick and witty conversation. Madame de Sévigné, a hundred years before Rousseau, was a mistress of the art and mixed in all the highest circles, but Rousseau was afraid of quick wit and 'women who prided themselves on their brains', especially those who employed the 'trick' of asking lots of questions without giving anything away of themselves. I don't think Rousseau would have liked de Sévigné's famous account of an investiture at Versailles where two courtiers got their ribbons and swords and lace so tangled up with each other, 'they had to be torn apart by force and the stronger man won', and, even less, her brutally amused tone as she tells the story of Vatel, the chef at Chantilly who killed himself because the fish he had ordered for the king's banquet had not arrived.

But Rousseau did love France: 'My continuous reading, always confined to French authors, nurtured my affection for France and finally transformed it into so blind a passion that nothing has been able to conquer it.' It's disarming the way he just comes out and admits it. There's nothing to defend in a blind passion, it simply is.

And he liked the French: 'They are naturally obliging, kindly and benevolent, and whatever may be said, really more sincere than those of any other nation. But they are fickle and flighty. The feelings they profess for you are genuine, but those feelings go as they come.'

That may have had more to do with him than the French – he was hypersensitive and never really fitted in – but he did change France from the inside out. He literally made a revolution – many revolutions in fact – in politics, education, literature, in ordinary attitudes and way of life. For him, feelings, passion, nature and imaginary life overruled rationality and the practical world every day: 'Never mind how great the distance between my position and the nearest castle in Spain, I had no difficulty in taking up residence there.'

I had no difficulty either. I was fifteen and lying on my bed reading one of Guy de Maupassant's nineteenth-century stories, *Clair de Lune*. A severe priest, fearful of sensuality and tenderness, is won over by the beauty of a moonlit night in his village. On the farm it was a hot January afternoon, the day flattened by the tedium of Mass that morning and by the sun heating the corrugated-iron roof until the rooms underneath were ovens. The day was still, curtains unmoving, the lilac painted bedroom walls and three china half-cups hanging on nails unchanging. Even my brothers and sisters were quiet, stunned by the heat. But I could hear distant nightingales as they 'shook out their scattered notes – their light, vibrant music that sets one dreaming, without thinking, a music made for kisses, for the seduction of moonlight'. It was cool in that world and the full moon silvered a fine mist around a line of poplars.

I could easily take up residence in any imaginary village or town.

I don't suppose that people were only practical and rational before Rousseau, but he was the one who turned the life of imagination and creativity into a kind of cult. In fact, even though I didn't read him when I was young, and even though I don't think I'd like him if I met him now, it was almost certainly because of his strange stormy mind that I ended up in Paris, standing invisible in the rue St Jacques several centuries later.

I should really introduce him.

*

Rousseau was born in Geneva in 1712 and died in 1778, ten years before the English came to settle in Australia. His mother died when he was born; his father read to him all night long when he was a child, which gave him 'the strangest and most romantic notions about human life, which neither experience nor reflection has ever succeeded in curing me of'; he became passionately and often hopelessly attached to various women in his life; he liked to be spanked, a pleasure mostly unfulfilled; he believed that 'Man was born free and is everywhere in chains'; he wrote *Of the Social Contract* which revolutionaries carried in their pockets, and *Émile*, a sensitive and natural approach to bringing up children; he had five children, every one of whom he forced his mistress, Thérèse, to put in a foundling home where they probably died; he was neurotic and became paranoid ('After long being maddish, he is plainly mad,' said the philosopher Hume when he met him in England); he was the father of Romanticism; and he wrote *The Confessions*, in which he claims to examine his mind and heart with complete honesty: 'I have bared my secret soul as Thou thyself hast seen it, Eternal Being', but there's something about him that I don't believe.

It's to do with a certain dissembling in myself, I know that much. I recognise something in him that I've struggled against for years without being able to name it. I've sensed it, rather, as a type of sticky coating on my mind and spirit. Rousseau said he struggled between weakness and courage, self-indulgence and virtue, but I think it was a struggle between self-deception and the desire for truth. At least that's what I've come to see in myself, a leaning towards self-deception. I suspect it comes from a desire to be thought well of, from caring too much about what other people think. Read the signs carefully, don't let anyone catch a glimpse into the narrow chamber of the soul.

It's the opposite of my reaction to Montaigne, whom I'm happy to admit I adore. When Montaigne argued that we couldn't change our essential natures, we could only try to cover them over and hide them, I felt myself breathe out at last. It wasn't an excuse, just a truthful observation. But I owe Rousseau, because it wasn't until I started examining my reaction to him – he's a revolutionary hero and a defender of the imaginary life, I should be bowled over by him, so why was I disliking him? – that I started to see what it was. Perhaps it was Montaigne's looking-glass I needed to gaze into.

For coffee with Rousseau I selected Le Chant des Voyelles in the rue Lombard because I thought the name, The Song of Vowels, a poem by Rimbaud, would appeal to him. He orders a *tisane*, a herbal tea. His hair is slightly longer than the fashion and he wears a cream shirt and a violet velvet coat like the one he once bought in Lausanne when he started work for the Archimandrite of Jerusalem. He doesn't look much different from the way he did in the eighteenth century, a bit retro late-1960s, a cravat and waistcoat, gentle features, soft brown eyes. In London or Melbourne he'd hardly be noticed, but here in the dark chic of Paris he looks as if he is trying to draw attention to himself. True Parisians don't do that; it's gauche to so obviously signal who you think you are.

'Tell me about living in England,' I begin, thinking we could share our experiences of being in a different culture. But he darts me a suspicious look and I remember that when he was in exile there he often believed people were attacking him. I change approach.

'But I should tell you about myself first. I come from Australia. As a lover of nature, you might be interested to know there are many plant species in my country that don't exist here – banksia, eucalypt, bottlebrush.' I know he has made a study of botany.

He relaxes and tells me all about living near Annecy with Madame de Warens and how he loved to walk across the hills and observe nature. He says that living in the natural world and a natural upbringing is best for children, who are all 'born free'. I'm tempted to ask him about putting each one of his five babies on the stone at the foundling home, but it would be pointless. I'd have no patience with his justification that he was saving them from a poor upbringing in his mistress's family. Instead, I ask if he would discuss *Of the Social Contract*, which expands his theories on the relationship between the natural man and the State, and he becomes passionate. This is his Big Idea. I tell him there's a street not far away named after him, rue Jean-Jacques Rousseau, and he tries to hide how pleased he is. Although he is trying to be humble, I feel a surge of irritation – he's driven by ego just like the rest of us. It makes me feel less tolerant of even his brilliant ideas. We part with no arrangement to meet again. I suspect we don't like each other that much, our mirrors too self-reflective.

*

The day after the hammering was Patrick's nineteenth birthday. He was born on a cold August day in the Blue Mountains and every year it had been a rugged-up celebration: rosy cheeks, fires burning, mittens, wild children running through the bush, swarming in like birds to be fed and flying out again. It felt strange to wish him a happy birthday on a hot midsummer's day from the other side of the world. Strange not to see his face. I remembered the first time I had seen him lying on my belly, coated in vernix, the purity and sweetness of his being.

I woke before dawn in the rue des Trois Frères with the pang of missing both Matt and Patrick deep under my ribs, an aching pang. I lay in the dark on the mattress under the low ceiling and wondered what I was doing on the other side of the world so far from them. What if a crack opened up in the earth and they were on the other side of it and I could never get across? The planet may as well hurtle off its orbit because nothing else would matter anywhere in the world. The before-dawn thoughts settled as the greyish light came in from the courtyard; they were young men now and they were going their own way as they were meant to. And they might come my way again. Patrick had applied to study at university in Amsterdam because his course in international politics required a year's study overseas, and Matt wanted to come and visit, but he had no money.

When I woke again I felt unformed, like a runny sea-creature without a shell. I got up and wrote until lunch but in the afternoon I cried. It wasn't sadness or distress, but almost as if I had become liquid. My sons had grown and my body was losing its capacity to ever make children again. I didn't want any more babies – babies and children were relentless hard work – but a fundamental ability was leaving my body and would never come back.

That evening I went to Mozart's *Requiem* at La Madeleine, the Greek temple church with its Corinthian columns and tympanum, built by Napoleon III. Apostles and saints circled the base of the dome, and below it, at the back of the altar, a marble Mother of God was supported by two gloriously winged angels. It was a monument to Church and State power, a long way from the tin church in a paddock I'd knelt in as a child. The glorious music poured through me, the sound of earth and heaven, the soaring voices and the heartbeat of violins, and again I felt as if I'd become liquid, as if I could be poured into a mould and remade as anything at all. I breathed in and out, conscious my breath was in rhythm with the music. I had not realised before that having babies had kept me solid. For them, I was the origin of being, cells, blood, breath. If I'd come to learn the difference between real and imaginary, then right now everything else was imaginary.

Still, the weather was always real. It's what we've all had to share from the beginning: sun, rain, wind, storm. August was humid and there were storms often in the afternoon. Paris is in the basin of the Île-de-France region, and in summer the hot air is held in it like a bowl of soup. The heat rises and the air molecules become electrically charged as they rub past one another and then late-afternoon thunderstorms crash around the stone buildings. Because I'd not heard thunder echoing and re-echoing off stone buildings before, storms were much louder than I was used to. I loved watching from the safety of shelter, high up in a building like a bird in a cliff cave, but one day on a busy Friday afternoon in town, I was caught outside.

Anthony had had a meeting in another *quartier* and when he finished he'd sent me a text to join him.

'Rendezvous place Colette 4 pm near Académie Française.'

I finished writing for the day. It was inching forward into detailing how life continued after Dina's death as it does after everyone's death. The ordinary, even the banal, keeps on happening. Annie Ernaux wrote of her mother's death and was stunned to see how the ordinary phrases suddenly had power: 'the first springtime she will never see, sensing now the force of ordinary phrases, even of clichés'. Theo had often gone to sleep on my lap, had nosebleeds, played soccer with Patrick, been sad and bewildered. Each morning in the dim under the mezzanine I breathed in another time on the other side of the world – and often the rest of the day seemed a review of the morning as fragments of times, weather and places floated through me.

Map-book in hand, I caught the Metro to Concorde and walked down alongside the Tuileries and crossed over the street in front of the Louvre. I waited on the edge of place Colette, standing in the shade by the colonnade. Beyond the Louvre the south-western sky had darkened. The heat had become moist and even while I stood still my skin was damp, clinging in the way I loved when I was naked in Anthony's arms. Sexual weather.

Within a few minutes the dark sky shadowed overhead. A breeze swirled bits of rubbish, pages of a newspaper blew off a café table, and then a flash of lightning followed too quickly by a loud crack of thunder made me jump. It rolled loud and long, seeming to crash from building to building. Large drops of rain began to smack onto the cobbles and onto my arms, slow-motion explosions of water. Because of the dim light, this memory seems to be without colours, like a black-and-white photograph, more convincing in its detail as memories are often more convincing than life.

The lightning zigzagged, making my heart thump in anticipation of the ear-piercing thunder each time. I felt like a cave dweller attacked by terrifying lights and explosions, but it only lasted about twenty minutes. Anthony found me a few minutes after the storm finished and we held hands and laughed like kids.

To recover ourselves, and for me to dry off, we had a drink in L'Entr'acte, behind the Comédie Française. It was an ordinary bar restaurant where actors probably came after the show. Perhaps Molière came here for a wine between acts. Legend has it that he died on stage right behind us in the oldest theatre in Paris – like Shakespeare he was an actor as well as a playwright; it seems to have been usual in those days – but in fact he collapsed on stage then died at home not long afterwards. Like St Denis carrying his head over Montmartre, preaching as he went, a good story grew into a better one.

Montaigne remarked that as stories are handed along, 'the whole fabric is padded and reshaped so that the most far-off witness is better informed about it than the closest one'. He wasn't talking about the reshaping due to gaps in recall – which Stendhal describes as 'large gaps in the fresco where only the brickwork of the wall is to be seen', the nature of all memory over time – he means the deliberate adding of detail. But I don't think there's any real intention to deceive in the elaborating of what happened. It's as if we can't help ourselves; it's in service of the story, it has to be embroidered, shaped, added to. Perhaps St Denis' hands involuntarily jerked outwards as he was decapitated by the Roman soldiers and the severed head brushed his fingers as it fell. By the end of the week the story was that he had caught his head in his hands and by the end of the next he had carried it over Montmartre. After a few months it was recounted as fact that he had preached a sermon as he went.

When we came out of L'Entr'acte it was still light, the sky was clear and the air was fresh with that clear electric feeling after storms I remembered from childhood. Out on the farm it had meant momentary relief in a drought and the pleasure of finding destruction: branches torn off, a water tank rolling across the paddock, a brown flood in the usually dry creek. Here in the rue de Montpensier there were only puddles of water and buildings that had been standing solidly for hundreds of years.

Not long after, I went to an exhibition of self-portraits at the Luxembourg museum. I had seen the poster for it in the Metro, '*Moi! Autoportraits du XXème siècle*', which showed a Norman Rockwell portrait – he was back-on as he looked in a mirror sketching his own face. I liked the 'infinite mirrors' idea of it: the artist who paints self-portraits can never really be outside the frame, but it also reassured that the self was a fit subject to consider; it has always felt like a slippery slope.

The museum was on one side of the Luxembourg Gardens in the sixth arrondissement not far from Metro Odéon but, not yet knowing my way around that *quartier*, I came in through the opposite gate off the boulevard St Michel and walked up the gravelled path. Somewhere in these gardens, perhaps on this pathway, Simone de Beauvoir bowled a black hoop in childhood. The gardens where she had played were formal with paths and smooth lawns, statues and massed beds of Japanese windflowers, azaleas, amaryllis and lisianthus and, in the middle, a pond with green iron chairs scattered around it. People sat there and read and sunned themselves like cats but no-one lay on the grass; lawns were for beauty's sake, not for lounging about. Seated around the pond they looked as if they were in *Miss Brill*, my favourite Katherine Mansfield story about a woman watching the world go by in a park in Paris.

Up a side alley I came upon a group of people gathering around beehives near a summer-house. They were wearing white overalls and netted hats and gloves, as if they had stepped from a science fiction film or a Sylvia Plath poem. 'I stand in a column/Of winged, unmiraculous women,/ Honey-drudgers.' I was puzzled – what on earth were beekeepers doing in the middle of Paris? The sight stayed with me: the loose, relaxed arms of the apiarists, their 'moon suits and funereal veils', the wooden boxes like the bee-hives along Bushrangers Creek Road, the white gravel under their booted feet, the bright blue lavender and the pink roses behind them. Perhaps this was where the honeycomb in the rue Mouffetard had come from.

I headed back towards the museum. On one side there was an elaborate Italian fountain with marble statues and balustrades and a narrow pond, built in the seventeenth century by Marie de Médicis, the widow of Henry IV. The Luxembourg museum had been her home, modelled on a palace in Florence, her hometown, and these were her Italian gardens. This was where nineteen-year-old de Beauvoir sat and argued about 'pluralist ethics' with Sartre, who took her argument apart until she exclaimed, 'I am no longer sure what I think, or if I think at all.' It was the beginning of her accepting Sartre's opinions as more valuable than her own. I looked at the fountain for a while, mesmerised by the statue of the fearsome Cyclops looking down at two lovers and the atmosphere of drama and myth, shady and mossy in the middle of summer.

In the exhibition there were self-portraits by Van Gogh, Duchamp, Matisse, Magritte, Monet, Degas, Léger, Kahlo, Miró, Picasso, Mondrian, Klee, Hockney – and nearly everyone else I'd ever heard of. I studied them for much longer than I normally look at paintings, and took notes. They were memoirs in paint, observer and subject in the same tangled relationship.

What I remember most clearly is the two portraits by Matisse. One was drawn when he was young, detailed and precisely shaded, the other years later, by which time his portrait had become just a few spare lines. I was struck by the way his drawing became less detailed, more pared back to essential shapes, as he grew older. Disturbingly, when I checked the exhibition notes online recently I couldn't find a record of two pictures by him. But I remember them, and I have my notes which describe both portraits. I can see myself standing there on the polished wooden boards gazing at the small portraits and I remember the white Chinese-style dress I was wearing.

The other thing I remember is a sentence in the exhibition notes: '*Jamais je n'ai vu mon visage*', 'I have never seen my face'. There was a sudden shock of realisation; it was both blindingly obvious and a startling revelation. Of course we never see our own face, only a reflection. And a reflection, of course, is the exact opposite of the way others see us. Those angles, that imbalance, they are all the other way around. I can never see what others see. Stendhal, in his memoir *The Life of Henry Brulard*, put it even more precisely: 'The eye cannot see itself.'

Any truthful portrayal of the self probably has to be a multiple and messy reflection rather than Matisse's few spare and beautiful lines. How can it be anything else when the mirrors we gaze in are tinted, cracked, murky, overlit, fragmentary, reflecting infinitely? And the one who gazes is just as disjointed. Montaigne said that trying to see himself was like a drunk examining a drunk: 'I am unable to stabilise my subject: it staggers confusedly along with a natural drunkenness.' The observer and the mirror are both disunited and unreliable.

I have never seen my face.

FOUR

SEPTEMBER

While we are doing nothing the days pass, and our poor lives are made up of those days, and we grow old and die.

Madame de Sévigné

One day in September, needing to be amongst trees, I walked in the Luxembourg Gardens and again saw the bee-boxes, but not, this time, the beekeepers. I wasn't puzzled anymore as I had since found out about the Rucher École, the beekeeping school. It was founded in 1856 and apparently the honey the school collects is richer and better than anywhere else in France because of the many different flowering plants in the city. The bees love the chestnut trees in the Champs Élysées and the linden trees of the Palais Royal and the lavender and geraniums in the window-boxes and gardens of Paris. What is beginning to puzzle me is why bees seem to be skimming into my mind as I turn over my memories of the year in Paris.

I don't remember bees as being significant at the time. I can see they come from Montaigne and his metaphorical bees making 'honey which is entirely theirs; it is no longer thyme nor marjoram honey', but I don't know why they have started multiplying. I do know that Napoleon had chosen them as his symbol. They had represented immortality for the Merovingians, the first line of French kings founded in the fifth century by Childeric and his son, Clovis. Engraved golden bees were found in Childeric's tomb a thousand years after he died, although some sources say they were actually cicadas. Either way, Napoleon was connecting himself to the origins of France. He wove himself into the story of his country, stamped himself into the fabric, an indelible bee. Even without Childeric, bees are an image of devotion to the common good; they store riches for future need, they are armed with a ferocious sting to defend against intruders. I can only hope the bees flying into my head are intent on making honey rather than stinging.

*

It was the evening of my first meeting with the *choeur,* the choir. I liked that *choeur* was the word for heart, *coeur,* but with an 'h', like a breath, in it. I felt nervous, but not too jittery. I had been in a choir before, after all, and survived. And I knew Montaigne, whose good opinion I already wanted more than anyone else's, would approve. He wrote that there was nothing more striking about Socrates than his taking up music and dancing in his older age, to make himself vulnerable by becoming a beginner again.

I arrived early at the hall in the Marais, up a flight of wooden stairs in one of the narrow streets running off the rue de Rivoli, the spine of central Paris. There were dozens of confident, well-dressed people milling about and chatting to each other, mostly in French, although I did hear a couple of English voices and a couple of Italians. They all knew each other already. The choirmaster arrived, a slender, grey-haired man in a linen shirt, well groomed, with a leather case under his arm. He put it down and looked around the group, nodded at me and said, '*Bonjour Madame.*'

'*Bonjour.*' I nodded back, suddenly sure he knew I was from the backblocks without a note of music in me. He talked to the group for a few minutes about term dates and a performance, and then the warm-up began. The choirmaster stretched and wobbled his face, pursed his lips, rubbed his face and we all followed suit. I could do this, it was just like my choir in the Mountains.

Next were the vocalisations. 'Ee ee ee oo oo oo ah ah ah.' Up and down the scales he went. Powerful tenor and soprano and alto voices burst out around me, producing and projecting the notes in full bel canto mode. They had proper voices! This wasn't a Blue Mountains community choir with a motley collection of people who liked singing. What on earth was I thinking? My squeaky little voice trembled in shock.

I looked around surreptitiously – perhaps I could slip out. But I was in the middle of a knot of people and couldn't have walked out without excusing myself several times. A deep breath. I tried to follow the notes in a low voice. The woman next to me looked over. She already knew I was a pretender.

The choirmaster opened his leather case and sheets of music were handed out. There was excited conversation. Someone's *Requiem*. I couldn't read the music so I looked at the words, trying to make them save me. The group reshuffled into parts. I looked at one woman and raised my eyebrows. 'Soprano,' she said. I stood next to her. My voice had slightly more high notes than low.

The choirmaster tapped with his baton on a stand that had been produced from his case. I breathed out. He will sing the parts and I will copy him the way I did in my choir back home. Then he counted, *un, deux, trois, quatre*, flicked with his baton and without one note from him, the choir burst into powerful song. Voices soared out around the hall, rising, floating on notes and descending with enormous grace, sopranos as pure as bells, dark honey altos, rich tenors and basses. I tried for a couple of lines – I have to give myself some credit for pointless courage – my voice squeaking more and more with embarrassment until I gave up and simply mouthed the words. I don't think I've ever felt more out of my depth in my life. I mouthed the words for the next two hours until I could safely slip back down the stairs and into the warm September evening.

If I had been with someone I would have burst out laughing. It was absurd, stupidly naive. Just the kind of thing a country bumpkin would do. We could have laughed immoderately and then had a glass of wine in the Café des Philosophes nearby and not care that we were talking loudly in English. But I was on my own, so I slunk home, my face still burning. I wasn't Socrates enjoying being the fool at all, just a middle-aged woman hauling the burden of wanting to be good at everything.

'How was it?' asked Anthony. He has a good voice, not trained but he could sing anything in tune, even songs he last heard when he was a child.

'Terrible,' I said. 'They can sing.'

'Well, they are in a choir.'

I made myself a cup of tea and sat in the shadowy courtyard. The evening pooled around me, different from the deep darkness of the evenings in the Mountains, but still returning memories as evenings will. I thought of Dina singing to Theo, and performing in a country rock band, although that was before I met her. It was a long way from requiems, but then, maybe not. Her songs wailed of loss and longing, of grieving for people who are gone; times that have vanished. I glanced down and saw the beginnings of wrinkles on my arms, a faint terrain of cracks. It looked like a new geography on my body. I'd always found wrinkled arms disturbing, even as a child. I didn't mind wrinkles on the face, that seemed natural, but on the arms they were frightening. Skin drying up, shrivelling, not fitting the body anymore. I wished I had a cardigan to pull over my arms even though it was still warm.

'Guess who I think I've found?' Anthony said. He had joined me in the courtyard, and squatted against the wall. 'Jean-Jacques.'

'Really? How? He's here in Paris?'

'No. He's in Switzerland. I somehow remembered in the back of my brain that his father owned a driving school in Lausanne and I looked it up on the net. And there he was, Jean-Jacques.'

'Are you going to contact him? Was there an email address?'

'Yeah, I think I will.'

People always come and go from life and after a long enough time, it seems some people won't come back ever again. Some die and others just disappear. Maybe it was best to leave them where they were. We both sat in silence for a while.

'Why does anyone, me, want to be good at everything?' I asked into the shadows.

Anthony shrugged. 'So our mothers will love us the best?'

We sat for a while in the warm dark. In early September the evenings were still long enough to sort anything through, even making a fool of myself, long and quiet and just the right pace for reflection. I wondered what I did without a long twilight back home.

*

I lay in bed one night when I was seven and my mother counted the freckles on my nose. Forty-seven, she said, or fifty-two, I can't remember, but I haven't forgotten the delicious glow I felt at the attention showered on me, me alone. It is the sole memory I have from childhood of being the only one in my mother's gaze. Every other time, I was one of many – four of us washed in the bath, eight of us fed, three of us told to get some 'chips' for the wood stove, five of us doing homework at the kitchen table, two of us yelled at for squabbling about who was supposed to do the washing-up, six of us ferried to Mass. I liked being one of many, proud our family was so much bigger than nearly everyone else's, and even after the pleasure of the freckle-counting night, I didn't realise that I longed to shine in my mother's eyes. There was no conscious competition for her love and in my memory she treated all eight of her children equally, but I did have the feeling that I wasn't really her sort of person. Writing that now all these decades later, I still feel my heart fall away. She was secretly rebellious, someone who didn't like the rules, whereas I wanted to fit in, to look and act 'right'. I suspect now that I got on her nerves – just enough for her not to acknowledge it to herself. It was only when I was older and found we shared a passion for ideas and reading that I felt I had some credit; I was almost conscious by then of giving her the novels I was reading at university to win her over, to make her see that, underneath, I was worthy of her love.

When my mother finished counting my freckles, in the midst of my warm glow, she told me I was going to have another baby brother or sister. I didn't mind; I already had a younger brother and sister and three older brothers and another sister. It was just what happened.

When I look in any mirror, there's always my mother standing in the background. I don't think it can be any other way, although I suppose for some it's the father. I wanted, still want, her gaze. Montaigne argued that the bond between mother and child is not so deep, that it can be broken by giving the child to a 'wet-nurse or a nanny goat'. He explained that two of his manservants were suckled on nanny-goats, a common practice when the mother didn't have enough milk, and it was well-known the nanny-goat would come running as soon as the baby cried. I don't like to argue with Montaigne, but to me, that only shows that the bond is developed in the smell and sight and sound of nourishment – and that must begin when the baby is still in the womb. The knowledge is not remembered consciously, but it is there, shaping our longings and the desire to please. Couldn't it be that many great achievements and many terrible ones were born of the desire to regain a mother's gaze?

I went back to the Marais one afternoon to the Carnavalet, the museum of the history of Paris and, in the seventeenth century, home of Madame de Sévigné. Long ago the area had been a marsh, *marais* means marsh, but by the seventeenth century there were Italianate mansions, convents and grand gardens stretching between the elegant place des Vosges at one end and the Cimetière des Innocents at the other.

In those days the Marais was where the aristocracy lived and where the idea of Paris as a literary city was born. Women like Madame de Sévigné and her friend Mademoiselle de Scudéry, who wrote *La Princesse de Clèves*, a popular novel in the seventeenth century, held the first salons to talk about books and ideas with friends. Now it's a *quartier* dedicated to fashion boutiques and cafés with tourists and locals bumping into each other on the narrow footpaths.

I criss-crossed the streets, passing an office for the French Association of Beekeepers, a small gallery selling globes of the world and skulls, a synagogue and, in the rue des Rosiers, shops selling Jewish food and religious objects. Then I saw a sign on the wall of a school: '*165 enfants juifs de cette école déportés en Allemagne durant la Seconde Guerre mondiale furent exterminés dans les camps nazis. N'oubliez pas!*'; 165 Jewish children from this school were deported to Germany during the Second World War and exterminated in Nazi camps. Do not forget! A chill crept over my skin at the exact number. 165. I couldn't imagine millions being exterminated in camps, but I could imagine that many children. Their arms as they were grabbed, their terrified cries. The skin on my skull tightened. History was not something far away and a long time ago; it was right here in front of me in living memory. I felt bereft and then, disturbingly, a pang of envy. I walked away trying to shake my reaction.

I backtracked through the narrow streets of the Marais until I came to the wrought-iron gates of the Carnavalet on the rue des Francs Bourgeois. I sat for a while in the garden with its gravelled paths and low box-hedges clipped into the shape of fleurs-de-lys. I didn't think I'd like its severe control, but, sitting there for a while, I felt myself quieten.

I remembered *Rue Ordener, Rue Labat,* Sarah Kofman's brief memoir of being a Jewish girl in Paris during the Nazi occupation. Because she was blonde she was able to live with a Gentile woman as her child while her mother lived separately and sometimes, carefully, visited. In one of the many smaller stinging tragedies of war, Sarah grew to love the woman who looked after her more than her own difficult and emotional mother.

It was no longer hot, but a warm and still September noon. It was calm in the garden with few visitors, that lull as people leave to find somewhere to eat. Even the bees were quiet, ferrying their nectar back to the hives, perhaps the ones on the top of Opéra, where the props man kept his bee-boxes. Twenty-five years ago, he had been waiting to move into his house in the country and put his boxes on the roof of the Second Empire glory of the Palais Garnier opera house as a temporary measure – he got the idea from his friend who also worked at Opéra and bred fish in a pond under the building. The bees were happy in Paris and the props man's honey became famous, the honey from the roof of Opéra.

There were cone-shaped trees on the other side of the Carnavalet garden and low roses between the clipped hedges, all perfectly ordered. In the quietness I started to recognise my reaction to the terrible events recorded on the wall. I had felt it before; it wasn't a desire for pain or suffering, it was story-envy, a hungry desire to be in a story, no matter how dreadful. Growing up on the raw and sunny side of the world, I had no such stories of my own. It was almost as if I felt having such stories could compensate for such loss. I was outside these horrible tales, watching where they had flooded by, the bodies of ghostly children tumbling past me.

Sarah Kofman wrote: '9th February 1943, eight in the evening. We are in the kitchen having some vegetable broth. There is a knock. A man enters: Go into hiding immediately with your six children. You are on the list for tonight. And he hurried away.'

What can be done with the pain of other people's stories? And why do I seek it?

I had creeks to play in, German soldiers in comics, straggling eucalypts to swing from, wheat fields, our horses Flicka and Beetlebomb, a well with a corrugated- iron cover, almond trees to climb, long droughts to dream of rain, arguing brothers and sisters, flies and bees and ants to watch, Baron Rock, a rocking chair for reading books. My mother and father never had their children snatched from them at school one day, never yearned until their last breath to see us again. The sun shone, my father came home when the sun went down, we ate lamb and potatoes and peas with tomato sauce at tea-time, and we slept through the night. In the morning we heard magpies and kookaburras and the sun was shining again.

By the time I got up to go inside through the museum entry in the rue de Sévigné I felt the slow drift of calm. Perhaps I was condemned to be the powerless witness of other people's stories. Had I travelled from the other side of the world to accept that I could only say, 'Yes, I see what has happened here to you'? It wasn't resolution, and it could have been only the result of warm sun and an ordered garden; in these ways it becomes possible to continue.

Inside the museum there were hundreds of rooms and corridors with displays of street signs, maps of sixteenth-century Paris, gilt furniture and paintings, historical documents. I looked longest at the paintings of Montmartre in the seventeenth and eighteenth centuries. This was where I lived! A steep wooded hill, windmills, orchards, vines, a fountain, a crooked village street, a stone fence. I read gallery notes, slowly. The people who lived there were uncouth, rural, dirty. Later, criminals and revolutionaries hid out on Montmartre and gangs known as the Apaches roamed about kicking in a head or two. I wondered how many years had to pass before violence and horrors became dramatic and romantic tales.

I stood in front of the original Declaration of the Rights of Man, and to my surprise, tears of admiration welled. People sticking up for their rights, however dodgy it becomes in practice, has to be a good thing. The museum guard noticed my tears and talked to me about the Declaration with pride. He showed me the rope ladder used to scale the Bastille on that fateful 14 July in a nearby glass case and I gladly believed it was the very rope.

I saw the cork room of Marcel Proust, cork to keep out annoying sounds and smells – he was a sensitive type – and the desk of Madame de Sévigné. It was a dainty black and gold Chinese lacquered writing desk in a light and airy room with a parquetry floor. I imagined she sat with a quill pen and creamy paper, writing in her clear but not excessively neat hand to her beloved daughter and friends.

In the painting above her desk she is a pretty woman with full lips, large dark blue eyes and an aristocratic nose. She looks sweet-natured, but judging from her *Letters*, I don't know if I'd trust her after I'd left the room at one of her salons. She had a sharpish eye on everyone around her. After one evening at a friend's gathering she wrote, 'A pyramid [of pastries] wished to come in – the sort of pyramid that makes people have to write to one another from one side of the table to the other (not that one grieves that over here, on the contrary one is only too glad not to see what they hide) – that pyramid, with a score of china dishes, was so completely knocked over in the doorway that the noise silenced the violins, hautboys and trumpets.'

I was drawn to her though. I liked her humour and directness and her admissions about herself, especially her intense love for her children. She seemed obsessive about them, but then, I wonder if she was only trying to be honest about a love that most women know is too terrifyingly deep to reveal. Don't let the Fates know how much my boys mean to me.

*

What do I know about her? Madame de Sévigné was born Marie de Rabutin-Chantal, at 1b place des Vosges in Paris in 1626 and died seventy years later. She arrived in the world after Montaigne, whom she read, and before Rousseau, whom I suspect she would have given the sharp edge of her tongue. Her father died when she was a baby and her mother when she was seven. She married at eighteen, had a son and daughter, and was widowed at twenty-four when her husband was killed in a duel over another woman. Her husband and, years later, her son both took the same woman, Ninon de L'Enclos, as a lover. She was friends with many writers, such as Mademoiselle de Scudéry and Rochefoucauld, and political figures like Nicolas Foucquet, Louis XIV's finance minister, and Madame de Maintenon, the king's mistress. She became famous for the thousands of letters she wrote to her daughter about cultural and political life in Paris. And infamous for her 'excessive' devotion to that daughter, who had married and moved to Provence, which, in those days, meant de Sévigné only saw her every several years. She was religious but had a sharp and witty eye for the absurd and for foolishness, and had a streak of melancholia. She went to see the plays of Molière, Corneille and Racine – she didn't think Racine would last – and loved to talk about books. She had many admirers but, apparently, she never took a lover after her husband died.

I was in de Sévigné's house several centuries later but it didn't feel like a house. It was too vast and too grand and I found it hard, even with her portrait in front of me, to see her as a thinking, feeling person. The elaborate silk gowns and jewellery and even more elaborate hairstyles of the time made women seem like ornate objects. It was only in her words that I could see who she really was. Or at least, see her version of herself.

She admits to occasional depression in her *Letters*: 'When one goes to bed one's thoughts are only dark grey … and in the night they become quite black: I know how true it is.' I was startled by her honesty, especially in a time when wit and style were all that mattered. Depression and anxiety run through my family; my solid peasant-farmer father suffered from it. His way of life out on our few dry acres in the bush was as far from the mannered rituals of the Sun King's court and the literary salons of seventeenth-century Paris as possible, but he would have known exactly what de Sévigné meant if he had ever read her. Inheritance is a chancy thing, it dances like a bee, bestowing or skipping over at will; depression stung some of my brothers and sisters and flew past others. I was one of the ones who escaped its grey miasma; I'm more inclined to blind optimism and I'm drawn to sunny dispositions, but I've always both feared and been attracted to the shade and angles of depression.

Montaigne suffered from depression after his dear friend, Étienne de la Boétie, died, but he was essentially at ease, enjoying the pleasures and delights of life without anxiety; Rousseau worried about everything, was disturbed by everything, including his own passions; de Sévigné was, I think, simply sad.

When I looked again at the portrait of de Sévigné, a woman of beauty and intelligence, wealth and influence, I could see some hooded wound in her eyes. She once confessed to wishing she had died in her nurse's arms so as to have avoided the many sorrows of her life. Perhaps the wound was because, like Rousseau, she lost her mother when she was only a child. And like Theo too, whose mother died when he was three years old. It felt as if I was being given pieces of the mosaic I was making about him and his mother at home in my studio. A beautiful, gifted boy with panicked eyes trying to hide infinite loss.

The last time I saw Dina she was lying exhausted in the Blue Mountains hospital, only her eyes able to move as her gaze followed Theo's chubby body around the room. Then Theo came over and climbed on my knee and fitted his body comfortably into mine. Dina's eyes filled with tears and Theo patted her stiff hand lying on the bed cover.

Outside in the streets of the Marais, people lingered over a late lunch with a final cup of coffee, their purchases in shopping bags on the chairs beside them. I wondered if they knew about the 165 children taken from the school around the corner. Or about Madame de Sévigné missing her daughter so much she felt she would jump from the window of her grand house nearby. Perhaps they felt no absence in not knowing the stories surrounding them; perhaps they were fully immersed in their own rich weave and had no need to knot and tie themselves into other people's tapestries.

*

I arrange to meet Madame de Sévigné for a coffee in the Marais so she can see how much it has changed. 'The Café des Philosophes,' I text, 'on the corner of the rue Vieille du Temple – you can walk through place Royale where you were born, but it's called place des Vosges now.'

'Let's sit outside so we can watch everyone walk past,' she texts back.

She orders a long black with Narbonne honey and then, seeing mine, wishes she'd ordered a *café au lait*. As far as I know she was the first French writer to mention coffee with milk. She is striking with her creamy skin and dark hair – everyone looks at her – but she takes no notice. She talks about members of parliament including government ministers, she knows them all, and various actors and artists. These days she writes well-informed and entertaining analyses of politics and social mores; she's always being asked to be a guest on various television programs. No-one feels safe from her clever and amused eye. She unsettles me at first – her beauty gives her an unnerving power – but she has a genuine warmth and also a sadness and I begin to feel that we are women together. She makes me laugh with her observations about people walking past and she listens to my stories with attention. I can tell she wants to win me over, that she does that with everyone, and I *am* won over.

*

In the Marais there are the ghosts of the Knights Templar tortured in the fourteenth century, wandering medieval streets past art nouveau synagogues. There is the shadow of Evelyn Waugh drinking at Au Père Tranquille, Balzac as a child in the rue Vieille du Temple, Victor Hugo magnificent in the place des Vosges, Rousseau and Madame Rousseau living simply in the rue Plâtrière. Here are the smells of silvery fish, oysters, runny cheeses, cabbages and the noisy yelling and arguing of Les Halles market echoing under a suburban shopping mall, and here is the dusty late-Gothic splendour of St-Eustache towering over the *quartier*; and there the coloured pipes of the Pompidou Centre shining like a giant plumbing works.

Over there, bikes bump on the cobbles along narrow streets, lines form for the best falafels in the world in the rue des Rosiers, pretty place du Marché St-Catherine looks like a village square, bees buzz in the hidden gardens of the Hôtel de Sully and Jardin des Rosiers, and a few metres of the twelfth-century wall of Paris protect kids playing basketball. The homeless camp with their eiderdowns under the arches in the place des Vosges, the hooded monks chant in St-Gervais, and in the rue des Mauvais Garçons, the Street of Naughty Boys, the name makes everyone smile.

*

It was mid-September. I had been in Paris for three months and it had to be faced: immersion as a way of learning French was not working. If it was supposed to soak in like dye into cloth, then I was an impermeable substance. The final evidence came when I was still in the backstreets of the Marais and a young woman said, '*Excusez moi.*'

I stopped. '*Oui?*' I said. I noticed she was staring straight ahead.

'*Blah, blah rue, blahenblah?*' She was looking over my shoulder.

I suddenly realised she was blind – and I had no idea what she'd said. What should I do? She was blind and I was deaf and dumb. She said '*rue*' somewhere in there, maybe she was lost, but even if she was, I couldn't tell her where she was. I didn't know where I was myself and the words would not come and arrange themselves in the right order to explain any of this. I reddened and felt hot.

'I'm sorry,' I burst out in English. She looked puzzled and worried. I think the sound of my voice was harsh. She was young, no more than twenty, and looked vulnerable. I turned and rushed away. I glanced back before I turned the corner and the young woman was still standing there, bewildered.

I told Anthony when I got home that I'd abandoned a blind girl in the street and that was it. No more wandering about thinking the words would soak in to me. I was going to go and enrol in French classes.

The following day I went to Alliance Française in the boulevard Raspail to ask about class times. The efficient girl, who seemed annoyed with people who couldn't speak fluent French, told me to sit down and do a written test to see what level to enrol in. It was late in the afternoon, I was tired, but I sat down as instructed. There were multiple-choice questions with a confusion of verb conjugations, but I recalled as much of Mrs Berman's French as I could and then waited while it was marked. After half an hour I was given a slip of paper saying I could enrol in an intermediate class, which started on the following Monday.

I knew Simone de Beauvoir had lived in the boulevard Raspail when she was 'a happy and somewhat opinionated child' and a 'dutiful daughter'. It was not difficult to imagine her pressing the *porte* button to unlock her apartment building door and walking along the street to school, immersed in her own sense of self, her sense of being a separate individual. I was a student in Paris too, carrying my books and the desire to know alongside Simone in the cool morning air, smiling happily at no-one.

I swung through the gates of the language school and into a building of corridors and classrooms. In one of those doublings of time, the chalky hot smell of my high school classroom and the glaring summer light and the feeling of being caught forever in a desolate town trembled under the cool Paris morning. All those years ago Mrs Berman came and took our small class to the library and we had our French lessons there, surrounded by books before present-time existed.

I found the classroom and sat down. All the other students were at least twenty years younger than I was.

'*Je m'appelle Didier*,' said the teacher. My name is Didier. That was easy. I could do this.

It didn't take long after that to realise my written French had betrayed me into a class higher than I had a hope of understanding. I couldn't answer any of the questions, I had no clue as to what I should be doing. The young Indian next to me chatted and asked Didier questions. Teacher's pet, I thought. *I* was the clever student; I was the one who could answer all the questions.

The two pretty Japanese girls in the next row stumbled through their answers and Didier smiled at them. I kept my head down and tried not to catch his eye.

The two hours were up. I waited until most of the students had left and approached Didier, who was packing up his books and papers.

'*Cette classe est trop difficile pour moi,*' I said. '*J'ai besoin d'une autre classe.*' This class is too difficult for me. I need another class.

'It's only your first day,' he said in accented English. 'Take some more time.'

'No, it's too hard,' I said, relieved to understand something again. 'I need an easier class.'

'Okay, I have another class that is more easy. You come to that. I speak a little English there. Tomorrow.'

I turned up the next day, a little less jauntily this time, but relieved when Didier greeted me with a smile and a clear, '*Comment allez-vous*?'

I sat down with another mix of travellers and migrants from Poland, Japan, India, the USA and the Middle East. As promised, Didier used some English and two- or three-word French instructions, which I could follow. He handed out a sheet of paper with conversation topics and lists of vocabulary and asked us to practise a short conversation with the person next to us.

We began halting, laughing exchanges, helping each other out with words and guessing what might be being said. Didier walked around the class, listening to each conversation, correcting grammar and pronunciation and providing the right French word when we looked at him helplessly. The woman I was speaking to was a doctor from Istanbul, nearer my age than any of the others. We laughed together, recognising each other's embarrassment at failing to be good at everything. Then we changed partners and I talked to a Japanese teenager who worked in IT and who was serious about his sentences. I felt pressure again, the desire to say everything perfectly. I wanted to have all the words in the right order, the tenses correct, before I even began the sentence. I told him the same things that I had told the Turkish doctor.

I went to class each day for a few weeks. As we relaxed with each other we spoke more and more in a *Franglais* in a variety of accents – Japanese, American, Hindi. Didier tried to correct us, but the urge to communicate was starting to overcome the desire to speak correctly. If I kept coming, in a few months I would be able to talk to all the people in the class easily, but not to anyone speaking actual French.

On the last day I gave Didier a card I had found in a shop which sold Australian postcards off the boulevard Raspail. I'd bought an elegant black-and-white image of the Sydney Opera House and wrote on the back, *chez moi*, my house, and *merci*. Didier smiled when he saw it. I had made a little joke in French.

On the way home from classes I sometimes got out of the Metro at Pigalle and walked up the steps to rue des Abbesses. There was often a transvestite street-worker in a mini-skirt and fishnet stockings on the corner of the rue André Antoine, the narrow alley below the steps. She was stockily built and looked Tahitian, with a broad nose and thick black hair. Every time I passed her she said, '*Bonjour Madame*,' and I answered, '*Bonjour Madame*.' The first time I was startled as I hadn't been greeted by a prostitute in the street before, but after that, it was the same as any polite exchange with people you see regularly but don't really know, acknowledging each other sharing the same space. It made me feel at home for that moment. In fact, I began getting out at Pigalle, just to greet her. To her I was part of this place, just like the two little boys who often played in the alley and the beggar with the smelly overcoat and swollen legs who sometimes rested there. One day I saw her talking to a young mother who had a baby in her arms and a boy standing in the folds of her skirt. I looked at the boy, bored and swinging the skirt, and felt envious of all of them. There was nothing any of them needed of me.

With the aid of my *Larousse*, the French bible of verb conjugations, I constructed a note asking for a conversation partner and put it on the wall of our building, outside on the street.

That afternoon the telephone rang, a young woman named Cosette. 'Have you read Victor Hugo? Like that,' she said. Meaning, I guessed, like Cosette in *Les Misérables*. She lived in the same apartment block and suggested we go to the *piscine*, swimming pool, together the next morning. Apparently she had some children whom she had promised to take to the pool.

The next day I turned up at her apartment, hiding my towel and cossie in my bag in case that wasn't the arrangement we had made. A woman in her early twenties came to the door, curly blonde hair, short and slim. Inside was a teenage girl sitting at a table and a younger teenage boy half-lying amongst the sheets of a sofa bed watching television. I was confused. There was no way Cosette was old enough to be the mother of either of them and, besides, they were both African looking. I was introduced to Ornella and Augustin, who greeted me politely. In a garbled way I gathered that Cosette looked after them, but it appeared they lived there as they were still in their pyjamas.

The kids dressed and we all piled into Cosette's car and headed south right across Paris to Portes de Sèvres pool. I smiled a lot and pretended I knew what Cosette was chatting about. I learned that she was a mathematics *professeur*, which at that stage I thought meant professor. So young to be a professor! Finally at the pool, we changed into our cossies then walked out into the brilliant sunshine. The blue sky and water, the concrete, looked and felt like summer in my hometown in Australia. Cosette stripped off her bikini top, revealing sturdy shoulders and tanned breasts, and dived into the pool. I looked down at the loose skin on my arms and decided not to undress.

Ornella and I chatted laboriously and I understood that she was waiting to go to university where she wanted to study English literature. '*J'adore l'Anglais*,' she said. Whew! Now there was something I could talk about. We spoke for several minutes before the effort embarrassed and tired us both. Cosette, out of the pool, chatted to a couple of young men. She was so at ease, so French, in her nakedness that I wanted to be her.

I had several more conversations with Cosette. I found out she was from Normandy, that she was doing a PhD in mathematics, and that she had a dream to live in Cairns in tropical Australia because she wanted to be warm all year round. I wondered aloud if everyone longed for elsewhere, and Cosette smiled. Most of the time I left with a headache from the strain of trying to listen. The two teenagers were with her each time, which meant it was mostly noisy, and there were just too many voices to follow. I needed quiet conversation with one person if I was to get anywhere at all.

Although Cosette lived in the same building as I did, in one of those random mismatchings, I didn't even bump into her in the hall or courtyard or street after that. I sometimes wonder if she ever got to Cairns.

By the end of September it was noticeably cooler. The days were still warm but in the mornings and evenings the air was fresh. I'd never been much of an early riser, but I enjoyed getting up in the mornings and walking down to the *boulangerie* with the morning city smells of coffee and hot bread and old motor oil on the cobbles. The twinges of pain in my shoulder and arm had become an occasional dull ache, especially at night – I thought it must be the hard futon – and a walk in the morning helped ease it out.

Anthony arrived back from a week in Jordan talking to students and it was the weekend. We headed for the Parc des Buttes-Chaumont, in the north-east of Paris, not far, as the crow flies, from Montmartre. It's a hilly park with grassy slopes where, we noticed, people were allowed to lie about. There were oak-filled glades and paths lined with chestnuts and clusters of cedars and pines and beeches. There was also a lake with a sheer cliff rising from it, on the summit of which was a temple, the Temple de la Sibylle, and further around, a torrent falling over an abyss into a cave. It didn't take long to realise that everything, the lake and cliff, the torrent and even the cave, was fake, the artfully arranged rocks and waterfalls puzzling the eye for a moment before the artifice was revealed.

The park was constructed in the mid-nineteenth century on a bare hill near the gibbets of Montfaucon where the corpses of criminals were left hanging until they rotted. The area was notorious for the smell and the carrion birds and the sheer terror of dozens of human bodies decomposing in the midday sun. The Age of Romanticism reclaimed the hill for a version of natural beauty, the park designer trying to imitate Rousseau's drama-filled version of wild nature: 'Never does a plain, however beautiful it may be, seem so to me. I need torrents, rocks, firs, dark woods, mountains, steep roads to climb or descend, abysses beside me to make me afraid.'

I thought of the Blue Mountains where our boys had grown up, the sandstone cliffs and rocky streams and waterfalls, so different from the plains and undulating hills where I was raised. I was used to subtle changes in form and colour, long stretches of grey-green eucalypts, yellowing wheat paddocks, gradual inclines. I wondered how much landscape shapes longings and even stories, whether my boys needed wilder country than I did, more dramatic tales?

'A good place for kids to play,' said Anthony.

'I was just thinking of our boys,' I said. We were stretched out on the grass by the lake looking up at the cliff, me propped on my elbows, Anthony leaning with his back against my knees. 'Not kids anymore.'

Anthony nodded, his eyes shut. He reached his arm backward and I took his hand.

'I wonder if Patrick has heard about his application for Amsterdam?' I said.

'He would have told us. If he does get in Matt will be the only one left back home.'

We were going to talk about our boys. It was a recurring conversation, a reweaving of the pattern of our lives with them. It wasn't woven every day, not even every week, but once we started there was a deep pleasure that both of us extended as long as we could. It was not done in front of other people, it was a private weaving, not fit for others to see. At the same time, there was fear that the gods might hear us. Don't let the wanton gods know, speak in low voices. Don't let them know of the older boy who made a sculpture of string and Christmas baubles in the back yard, don't let them hear of the younger who whistled 'Ode to Joy' on the veranda, don't let them see both boys sitting around a campfire watching sparks disappear into the night, don't let them smell their soapy after-bath-in-pyjamas bodies.

None of the memoirists except Madame de Sévigné writes of the visceral absorption in one's children. Montaigne says he doesn't like babies and de Beauvoir's disdain is famous: to have more children 'was to go on playing the same old tune, *ad infinitum*'. I thought of Madame de Sévigné, criticised over the centuries for her outpouring about her daughter: 'Do you think I don't kiss with all my heart your lovely cheeks and bosom? Do you think I can embrace you without infinite affection? Do you think affection can ever go further than mine?'

It's not how I would ever talk to or write to my children; it's too dramatic for me, like the fake Rousseau landscape, and yet, I know it speaks to the unsayable depth of my feeling. And Anthony's. Today, when the boys are on the other side of the world, love and some nostalgia well up and there is a tone in our voices that no-one else ever hears. It's over now, the daily care of small bodies and tender minds, and although they no longer orbit around us, we can't yet let go being the centre of their lives.

FIVE

OCTOBER

I entreat the reader, should I ever find one, to remember that I have no pretensions to truthfulness except in what concerns my feelings; as for the facts I have never had much memory.

Stendhal

By early October the days were a couple of hours shorter than they had been when we arrived. I missed the long evenings, the feeling of endless ease that had been so enticing. In the mornings I awoke on the hard futon to an airless chilliness. The sky was often overcast, creating flat grey days where nothing seemed to move and, even when it was sunny, the studio didn't get any direct sunlight so the chill deepened. I noticed it more because the arm that had been aching seemed to get colder than the other one, as if the blood wasn't circulating through it. And my back was starting to ache. Apart from the occasional twinge from sitting hunched at the computer, I had never really had problems with my body before and simply expected it to go away. I had to admit that it had been getting worse for a while now.

'It's not severe pain,' I tried to explain to Anthony. 'It's more like someone hit me with a baseball bat a week or so ago and it's still aching.'

'You should see a doctor,' he said.

'Yeah, but it'll be right.' I was operating under the unsound belief that if I ignored it, it would go away – and, as it happened, I was more or less right, it wasn't anything life-threatening in the end but it did still have several stages to play out. I tried to ease out the ache with hot showers but the thin spray of the dodgy camp shower ran out in two minutes, barely enough time to even wash. I needed a proper shower, a proper bed and sunlight. I wanted to be able to stand up in my bedroom, not crouch on my knees, and I needed to be able to see further than the two metres across the courtyard. I had to find another apartment.

I had taken to sitting on the kitchen stool at the windows in the one spot where, if I gazed upwards, I could see the sky. I hadn't ever noticed it before, but not being able to see far made me feel cramped, more than that, trapped. I sat on a bench in the square at the bottom of Sacré-Coeur with my manuscript and soaked in the weak autumn sunlight and watched children on the carousel, but even out in the streets I couldn't see far enough. In the afternoons after writing I took to heading to the Seine to stand on the bridges so that I could see farther and feel the sense of release it gave me. I didn't know why at first, I just liked standing on the bridges gazing up or down the river, but one day I realised it was because I'd been used to being able to see a long way since the plains and low hills of earliest childhood. A long field of vision; it's odd the things you find you need.

There were practical reasons to move too. One of my travelling nieces was coming to stay, several friends were visiting later on, including Theo and his father, Kit, and both our boys might be coming. And now that it was getting colder, Anthony needed an office to work in and an internet connection at home. I couldn't keep sending him out to Camille's every day. He had put the idea to the international studies office at his university and they agreed to pay part of the rent of a two-bedroom apartment as it was cheaper than renting a separate work space.

It still seemed difficult to act. I wondered if it was the lack of light, or the endless silence when Anthony was away, or was it just that my body was changing? I'd not had a period for several months and my body felt as if it were drying out. Sometimes when I was sitting or walking I was conscious of my vagina as an inverted dagger, cold and empty, and my libido had started to disappear too, for a couple of weeks at a time, leaving me to feel as if a light had gone out. One evening I walked over the pont des Arts and saw laughing people in their twenties picnicking on the bridge with champagne and beer, baguettes and cheese, dining in the middle of the Seine, and I felt a stab of envy. Why couldn't I have been young in Paris and not a middle-aged woman groping for something that was long gone?

'There's no age limit to being in Paris,' said Anthony. He came and went and when he wasn't there I felt as if I might be a nun in an enclosed order, silent and separated from the whole world. 'You feel the same to me anyway. In my arms.'

'Well, I'm not,' I said.

It wasn't just to do with the lack of desire; it was an everyday arid absence. As if sexuality had been central to my personality and without it I was voided. Then it came rushing back, wildly strong, seeming more intense than it ever had been, as if to doubly make up for its absence.

I studied the memoirists, looking for clues about this new flux. Montaigne wrote about his sexuality with extraordinary openness: 'I yielded as freely and as thoughtlessly as anyone to the pleasure which then seized hold of me: making it last and prolonging it however, rather than making sudden thrusts' – which must have made his sixteenth-century lady readers quite interested in more than his literary technique. Sexuality, he believed, was the steady rhythm under everything: 'The movement of the whole world tends towards copulation', but then his own virility began to fade: 'I have been struck off the role of Cupid's attendants' and 'It is certain that my organs may now be properly called shameful and wretched.' But, of course, he writes nothing of women's organs, the changes in our bodies that are far more radical than they are for men, the end of a rhythm of rich bleeding month by month since childhood, the final loss of the ability to grow entirely new human beings within our own.

The strange fluctuations, the thoughts of lost blood, blood flowing where it shouldn't, blood drying up, started creeping into the story about Theo and his mother – two different kinds of life ending. I wrote a series of pieces about blood: menstruation, the weird sisters in Macbeth, Theo's nose bleeding, a vein bursting in the brain. One night I dreamed there was an explosion in my own brain and I woke up with my heart thumping and lay in the dark wondering if my time had come. Lists of small losses accumulated. I dreamed about Dina, that I was her sister and had bought her a pale-green linen dress. I dreamed it so exactly that I got up in the morning and drew it – 'But,' I said in the dream, 'she never had a chance to wear it.' I woke up with tears still wet on my face.

I started searching for a new place, somewhere on an upper floor where I could see out. It didn't take long to find an apartment nearby in the rue Simart on the north side of

Montmartre. It was on the fifth floor, without a lift admittedly, but that didn't matter because it was high and on a crossroads. It must surely have a long view in four directions, and sunlight. It was owned by Susie Laporte, who turned out to be a cheery Australian from Ballina in northern New South Wales.

'Is the shower good?' I asked.

'It's the first question Australians always ask. Yes, it's good. I used to live in rue Simart,' she replied. 'After my children left home.'

'I'll take it,' I replied, before I'd even seen it.

The choir in the Marais ought to have been the beginning and end of singing in Paris, but I regained courage and found a booklet, *Chanter à Paris*, listing all the choirs in Paris. I studied it carefully, limiting my choices to those open to beginners, and picked the one that was easiest to get to. It was past enrolment day, September was the *rentrée*, the beginning of the year for schoolchildren, universities, community classes and even for new book publications, but I thought if I turned up on the evening of the first class I would be allowed in. I wrote in my diary: *Choeur, 6 pm jeudi*, Choir 6pm Thursday, *rue des Amandiers, Metro Ménilmontant.*

I set off in plenty of time the following Thursday, catching the Metro at Anvers on the line that took me directly to Ménilmontant. I had begun to love the Metro, the constant and changing flood of other people's lives passing mine. It was an underground labyrinth where the whole world might cross paths, a streaming set of stories seated next to each other for a few minutes; a beautiful young Muslim mother in a blue robe with a white veil looking like the Virgin Mary; two middle-aged Indians with a beat-box singing a rap song; an accordionist playing 'Those Were the Days'; two Americans anxiously wondering aloud who might steal from them; an African girl with hair like Diana Ross's in the 1960s; the man whose skin was patched black and white like a Dalmatian dog, a pure black patch on one cheek and over his nose, the rest of his face pure white, his neck and arms dappled. I wanted to step inside them, to know the shimmer of their consciousness as they looked out at the world.

I had a sense of hunger at first, of need, but then it induced a tender reverie, a kind of daydreaming with physical warmth, a pleasurable loss of urgency about anything. I thought of Rousseau who said he 'preferred to dream awake than asleep' and Proust who said reverie was his favourite emotion, a dreaminess that came paradoxically from a momentary insight into the nature of things. And Stendhal too wrote, 'In Paris I was an impassioned dreamer, gazing at the sky and always on the point of being run over by a cabriolet', and, better still, 'I am witty no more than once a week and then only for five minutes; I prefer to daydream.'

I liked Stendhal right away. He's a curious cup of tea; he tells the truth, but he pretends to hide. For a start, his memoir is called *The Life of Henry Brulard*, one of his many pseudonyms. He claims on the title page that it is a novel and adds, 'To the messieurs of Police. There is nothing political in this novel. The scheme is a hothead of every kind who grows weary and slowly sees the light and ends up devoting himself to the cult of luxurious town-houses.'

None of that is true, it's all a sardonic screen. Behind it he writes with sharp honesty so it's unsurprising when he says his two pet aversions are vagueness and hypocrisy. He says he has no pretensions to truthfulness except where it concerns his feelings because he's never had much memory for the facts, an escape route of course, but I'm inclined to believe him. He reveals more of himself in hiding; he has more actual truthfulness than Rousseau, who protests his honesty so passionately. Rousseau's claim that he bares his soul as God has seen it makes me squirm; can't he see? Fooling yourself is worse than fooling other people.

I like Stendhal when he says near the beginning of his memoir: 'I ought to write my life [...] The idea appealed to me. Yes, but the terrible quantity of *I*s and *Me*s. That would be enough to put the most well-disposed reader's back up.' Indeed. It's always the first problem for any writer who won't go to the bother of constructing a fiction. Not everyone can be as bold as Montaigne and say, with a shrug, 'Therefore, Farewell dear Reader.' Stendhal puts his case without argument or defence: 'I ought to write my life, perhaps in the end, when it is finished in two or three years time, I shall know what I've been, cheerful or sad, a witty man or a fool, a man of courage or fearful, in sum happy or unhappy in fact ...'

It sounds simple enough, not too ambitious, but it doesn't take long to realise Stendhal is nothing if not ironic. In the end he puts aside his fear of egoism: 'My confessions won't exist thirty years after they are printed if the reader finds the *I*s and *Me*s too tiresome; all the same I shall have had the pleasure of writing them and of conducting a thorough examination of my conscience.'

I didn't even notice that phrase of Stendhal's when I first read it, 'the pleasure of examining my conscience'. It was what each member of my family did every day when I was a child. We were taught to ask ourselves in the evenings, had we been good, which mostly meant had we obeyed our parents and not argued with our brothers and sisters, or at least not gotten into an all-out brawl with them. Kneeling on the lino next to my bed, making a sign of the cross, praying for the salvation of the Communists, promising to be good. It was earnest and dogmatic, but by the time I was a teenager it had become a habit of self-examination that has lasted a lifetime. Did I speak to the prostitute on the corner with an open heart or was I secretly judgmental? Was it pride that made me flee from the choir in the Marais? I'd never thought of it as a pleasure before Stendhal, but he's right. It's the careful spreading out of what actually happened, not accepting the self-serving version that is instantly manufactured; it's the pleasure of seeing what the heart is made of, a multi-striped thing of light and dark.

It means that Stendhal can admit, for example, that despite his passion for the rights of the common people, his tastes are aloof and aristocratic: 'I love the people, I detest their oppressors, but it would be a constant torment for me to live with the people', because 'the people are always dirty'.

Not just, it would be trying, but rather a 'constant torment' for him to have lived in the disorder of my childhood: encrusted tomato sauce bottle on the table, a mountain of unironed clothes in the corner, a broken fibro and tin lavatory in the back yard, coats on the bed at night in winter when there were not enough blankets. I'd like to be able to tell Stendhal it wasn't harsh or difficult, it was just the way things were. *C'est la vie.* I would admit to him that when I reached adolescence and realised how other people lived, it became embarrassing, but I didn't feel disadvantaged, because my mother had ingrained in us a disdain for people with money. We looked down on the rich.

*

What else can I report about Stendhal?

His given name was Marie-Henri Beyle. He was born into an haut-bourgeois family in Grenoble in south-east France in 1783 and died in 1842. He detested most of his family except his adored mother, his refined Aunt Elizabeth and his generous, cultivated grandfather. His mother died when he was seven years old making him yet another motherless writer. He was a lonely and unhappy child, kept separate from other children most of his childhood, but finding them noisy and rough when he was finally allowed to mix with them. He didn't like crudeness and vulgarity: 'I avert my gaze and my memory from anything low', a confession that made me feel let off the hook as I have a similar prissiness – no fart or poo jokes for me. He called it his *espagnolism*, his 'accursed Spanish character', a refinement he inherited from his aunt. He joined the army for a period, loved Italy, loved many women but had sex with only six of them and wrote novels, *The Red and the Black* and *The Charterhouse of Parma*, for which he became famous – but not until the twentieth century. He was a man of sardonic wit who liked Montaigne, but thought Rousseau bombastic, although when he was a boy he was in 'raptures of delight and voluptuousness' reading one of Rousseau's love stories.

I want to select an elegant café for coffee with Stendhal. He would wrinkle his fastidious nose at Camille's with its cigarette butts and lotto tickets on the unwashed floor, and the cool, relaxed Zebra à Montmartre in rue des Abbesses would be too easy-going. I decide on Angelina's in the rue de Rivoli, understated white with gilt trim, but when we arrive there's a queue. He makes a few disparaging comments about the tourists in the rue de Rivoli as we wait, and I laugh, revealing our shared aesthetic snobbery. When we are seated he orders a short black – he loves coffee, but if he drinks too much of it, it brings on neuralgia. I'm nervous at first, hiding my dirty fingernails in my lap – I always have dirty fingernails at important meetings – because I know he can't bear dirtiness, but there's an unexpected humour and gentleness in his expression, which helps me relax. We talk about reading and writers we admire. 'I'm a great fan of Montaigne,' I say, knowing we have that in common.

'Know Thyself?' Stendhal replies. It's the inscription on the Delphi Temple, which Montaigne liked to quote. His tone is sardonic but also yearning as if he equally doubts and hopes it's possible. He changes the topic, suddenly claiming that he couldn't love Paris because it had no mountains, and worse, it had pruned trees. The conversation darts from his family to politics to gossip and back to writing. I confess my own lack of ribald humour and he shrugs. 'This *espagnolism* prevents me from being a comic genius,' he says, but again his voice is ironic. He confesses his sensitivity to his writing being criticised when he was young, and his wait for genius to arrive: 'I wish someone had told me just write for two hours every day, genius or no.' I realise I like him but I'm unsure whether he likes me – he is difficult to read. We end up arranging to meet again, but somewhere we don't have to wait in line.

*

Because I was early on the way to choir, I got out of the Metro at Belleville, a couple of stops before Ménilmontant. I was in the twentieth arrondissement, a traditionally working-class neighbourhood. In the 1930s de Beauvoir came up here when she was a young woman to teach literature to the workers. It's where many migrants from France's former Southeast

Asian colonies have settled, mainly Vietnamese; the cafés and *épiceries* and greengrocers sell Asian meals and spices and vegetables, bok choy and lemongrass and Vietnamese basil. It's also the area where artists and writers live, the current bohemian *quartier,* because the rents are cheaper. It looked rundown, untidy, bustling, not at all like the studied bohemian kitsch of Montmartre.

In the butcher's there were rows of ducks, yellowish and naked, and large chunks of dark red meat marked '*cheval*', horse. There were many cafés but they were not funky or cool; the floors were a bit grubby and everyone smoked. I saw a few people in track pants; an old Vietnamese man wearing a beret, the first I'd seen in Paris; an African woman in a long dress of swirling red ochre and sea-blue with a baby in a matching sling on her back; Algerian men in groups, lounging and smoking. I wandered up the boulevard de Belleville, absorbing a new sense of Paris. There were no 'sights' in Belleville, just people living their lives. Here nothing was for show. I started to think I might just be able to slide under the rough surface here.

I turned up rue Ménilmontant and found the community hall in rue des Amandiers. It looked familiar, like a community centre built in the suburbs in the 1970s in Australia, brick with a glass front. I found the office, enrolled and paid my fee. Then I wandered hesitantly along corridors, peering through doors where people were doing yoga or pottery or painting, until I found a room with a loose circle of people still milling about, some of them holding sheets of music. They hadn't started yet.

'*Choeur?*' I said.

A young man in jeans and waistcoat nodded. He was handing out the sheets of song music. I greeted him and he smiled and gave me a small sheaf of pages.

'Je m'appelle Marc. Tu t'appelle quoi?' he asked. My name is Marc. What's yours? I was startled that he had used *tu*. I had been carefully saying *vous* in every situation for the past three months, obeying Mrs Berman's rule that one only used *tu* for children or people in your family.

'My name's Patti,' I answered in French.

'Bonjour Parti,' he said, mispronouncing my name. 'Welcome to choir.'

'Merci,' I answered and stepped back, hoping the exchange was over.

I looked around the rest of the group. There were fifteen or so women and four or five men, ranging in age from thirties to fifties and looking strangely like the choir I'd been in at home in the Blue Mountains, the same mixture of personalities and even of looks: the busy, neat, curly-haired woman, the tall pretty one, the barrel-chested bloke. They were still introducing themselves to each other, smiling and chatting. Everyone seemed to use *tu*. Several asked my name, and then, when they heard my accent and where I was from, I quickly became 'Partie d'Australie'. It was a joke, which I didn't get for several weeks. To their ears, my name sounded like the word for 'part of', so my name was, roughly, 'A little piece of Australia'.

I looked at the half-dozen song sheets. The first two were '*Petit Poucet*', 'Little Thumb', and '*Qui a tué Grand-maman?*', 'Who Killed Grandma?', which I figured must be traditional folk songs, and then one in Spanish, '*Ai Linda*,' and a choral section from a Bach cantata and another song in French called '*La Paysanne*', 'The Peasant', and '*Asikatali*', an African song I had already learned.

'I know this one,' I said in French to the woman next to me.

'Oh really?' she said, smiling. Her name was Marie-Louise and I liked the look of her intelligent gaze. She could see I was near the deep end and would keep an eye out for me.

We started with warm-ups, chanting up and down the scale using each of the vowels and then exercising the mouth and lips with the delicious word *pamplemousse*, which turned out to be the word for ordinary sourish grapefruit. Then we started with '*Petit Poucet*'. The French rhythms were odd to my ears and hard to remember and the long, muttering phrasing left me dashing over syllables to reach the end at approximately the same time as the others. Next we tried '*La Paysanne*', which resembled '*La Marseillaise*' with lots of patriotic sounding '*Marchons, Marchons*'. In both the chorus was easier to sing, the strong beats more like English song rhythms. Then we started learning the first couple of lines of the Bach. The others in the choir grumbled about the difficulty of the German but to my surprise I found it easier than the French, the longer phrasing easier to fit in. I loved the sound of it too, the slow richness of it compared to the rushing French songs, but I didn't dare say so.

The two hours were over sooner than I expected. A few more people asked my name and where I was from as I put my song sheets in my bag. What was I doing here? Was I going to stay? I felt shy but at the same time realised I was enjoying being an object of interest. At least someone other than Anthony knew I was here, would notice if I turned up or not.

Marc said, '*À jeudi?*' See you next Thursday?

'*Oui*,' I said.

I walked out of the Centre d'Animation with the other women, chorusing '*Au revoir*' and '*À jeudi*' and swung my bag along the street to the Metro and surged down the steps with all the other people in the cool dark evening.

The weekend before we moved I received another phone call about the French conversation notice I'd put on the wall. It was Sylvie, whose mother lived in my building. Even though I'd started to pack, I arranged for her to come to the studio that evening.

At the appointed time there was a knock and I opened the door to see a young woman who looked Indian. To my shame my first thought was a disappointed 'Oh, she's not French!' It was the Mrs Berman effect again.

'*Bonjour,* Patti?' she said with a shy smile. She was pretty with wide cheekbones and long black hair and was wearing a short skirt and jacket, almost looking like she was going to the office, but somehow not quite.

'*Entrez, s'il vous plaît.*' She stepped in and we sat opposite each other on my couch, both smiling nervously. We exchanged information about ourselves in French and English, her English as halting as my French. She suggested we speak French one week then English the next so we could help each other. She said she used to practise with an Englishman for a year, but he went back home and there was the shadow of something in her eyes that made me wonder if he had been her lover.

'*Quel est votre métier?*' I asked. What is your work?

'*Consultante financière,*' Sylvie said.

That was easy to understand even with my limited vocabulary. I had never met anyone who knew anything about money. What would we say to each other?

'*Et votre métier?*' she asked.

'*Je suis écrivain,*' I said. I'm a writer.

Sylvie burst into a wide smile. 'You have written some books?'

'*Oui*.' I got up and grabbed the books I had carted in my suitcase from Australia, and put them in Sylvie's lap, aware that I was 'showing off' like my mother said never to do. She picked them up one by one, examining the covers and turning them over to slowly read the back cover blurbs. She looked up, her eyes alight.

'I love books. I love to read. It's the most important thing in the world,' she exclaimed. She loved books and reading more than anything – and I had found her by posting a note on a wall! We looked at each other, delighted. I told her we were moving to the other side of Montmartre during the week and didn't know anywhere there we could meet. She said she lived in the sixteenth arrondissement just on the other side of the *périphérique*, the ring-road around Paris, too far away, but suggested we rendezvous at Le Relais Odéon on boulevard St Germain in central Paris next Sunday morning. It was on the Left Bank in the sixth, easy for us both to get to and opposite a Metro stop.

'Ze café on ze corner, zis is white,' Sylvie said. She sounded just like Mam'zelle.

It was easy to move to the new apartment as we had no furniture, only clothes, a few books and laptops. The only real effort was getting our things up the five flights of stairs. We hadn't seen the place, except from the outside, but my faith in Susie Laporte was vindicated. A short hall opened into a large room with French doors on all sides leading on to a wraparound balcony – the light poured in and, because it was on a corner, I could see all the way down two streets. From one position on the balcony we could even see the cupola of Sacré-Coeur. There was a desk for Anthony in one of the high-ceilinged bedrooms and space for a desk in the other. I went into the bathroom and turned on the shower and the room quickly filled with steam.

The only thing that was needed was a desk for me. A few weeks earlier we had passed a market selling second-hand household goods at place des Abbesses and wandered around looking at bits and pieces of furniture, appliances, stacks of old linen and lace, children's toys. I had wished aloud that I could buy something for the studio so I could feel like I really lived here.

'Buying furniture doesn't make you belong,' Anthony said.

But I thought the opposite. How could I not feel at home if I was hauling a table or a bed up the street to my apartment? Don't things weight us to the ground, stop us floating away? I thought about the Wiradjuri and how they'd had no need of apartments or furniture to feel at home. It made me suspect that I knew I couldn't belong in this place and had to weight myself to the ground with anything I could find.

In fact I didn't have enough money to buy a desk, I was living on my savings, so I made one from two metal trestles that Anthony bought at a hardware shop, and a piece of building board I found in passage Ramey around the corner. The passage was one of those places where people left furniture or appliances they didn't want. Whatever was left there – a table, a fridge, shelves – was always gone in a day or two, someone always wanted what someone else had finished with. After carrying the board up the five flights with the help of Anthony, I put it on the trestles against the wall where, when I was seated, I could look sideways out the French doors and see the balcony and chimneys of the buildings opposite. Then I arranged the desk-light, my laptop and printer and notes. I was ready again.

The ritual preparation of a room for writing is a long tradition, the making of a space for thinking and imagining. Montaigne wrote of his writing room in his chateau near Bergerac:

> It is on the third storey of a tower […] a large drawing room. It was formerly the most useless place in my house: now I spend most days of my life there, and for most hours of each day […] If I feared the bother as little as the expense – and the bother drives me away from any task – I could erect a level gallery on either side, a hundred yards long and twelve yards wide […] Every place of retreat needs an ambulatory. My thoughts doze off if I squat them down.

I'd like to think that it makes no difference where the writing desk is, but I can't help believing the third floor of a tower in the south-west of France might have its uses – especially with a hundred-metre ambulatory above the chateau gardens. My thoughts too tend to doze off if I squat them down.

And then, on the beams of his tower writing room, Montaigne carved 'I decide nothing. I understand nothing. I suspend judgment. I examine', the words of the Skeptic philosopher Sextus Empiricus. I imagine him walking up and down in his room – in the absence of the ambulatory which he never got around to building – glancing every now and then at the words just in case he should ever fool himself into thinking he really did know something. One day I will go on a pilgrimage to his tower, run my fingers over the words and let them roughen my fingertips and seep in through my pores.

He also wrote about the part of writing that happens outside the tower – the part of the reader or listener who receives the words. He said, 'Words belong half to the speaker, half to the hearer.' Without the speaker or listener it is as if nothing is written – the tree falling soundlessly in the forest. It means every word is completed in a different way, every reader reads a different book. But until the book is read, each word belongs to the writer.

I was nearing the end of the draft I was working on and the words still belonged more to me. I kept writing every morning, trying to create the place where Dina had lived and died, conscious that one of the people reading my words would be Theo. He was almost fifteen now and however carefully I chose, he would finish the story in his own way. He and his father were coming over to Paris in a few months and I wanted to make sure I had a draft finished by the time they arrived. There is so much of the thief even in writing one's own experience of being because it always involves other people – and even if it didn't, it is still a kind of thieving of the flesh and blood substance of everyday life in order to create it in a parallel reality. I didn't want to thieve from Theo while he was with me, even though Stendhal says that the instinct to steal comes from what he called 'a reverence for what is true'.

I want to believe Stendhal is right, that the constant thieving *is* a search for what is true. Proust wrote about the urgent task of his narrator 'recalling exactly the line of the roof, the colour of the stone' that offered to yield a secret revelation if only he found the words. The daily blue of the sky in childhood and the pearl grey in Paris, the restless longing of a freckled girl on the veranda of a farmhouse, a baguette and cheese on a kitchen stool at twilight, the ripple of unease as a woman envies a story of annihilation on a wall-plaque in the Marais, the bewilderment in the heart of Rousseau and de Sévigné and Stendhal and Theo whose mothers never came back into the room. It's what I search for and find so rarely; it's so fine and transparent, like a tiny dagger made of crystal, it's easily lost. I've never been able to hold on to it for long. It means I have to keep ransacking, trying to find it over and over again.

*

Anthony and I set out to explore our new *quartier.* Our apartment was on the corner of rue Simart and rue Eugène Sue with a *boulangerie* diagonally across from us and a *tabac* and a *crèche* on the other two corners. Although it was still the eighteenth arrondissement it was a different world from the rue des Trois Frères, a borderland between the bourgeois area around Metro Jules Joffrin and the African *quartier* on the other side of boulevard Barbès-Rochechouart. In our street there were hole-in-the-wall places with sewing machines offering clothing repairs and an internet café selling phone cards, an African restaurant and a tea-house with couches and large hookahs, and up the road, a bar called Le Temps Perdu – although I doubt it was referring to Proust's Lost Time. In the streets there were tall Senegalese and Malian men in long robes, peacock blue and emerald green, and women in brilliant scarlet and azure and ochre dresses carrying babies in matching slings on their backs alongside pale-skinned and soberly suited businesswomen and men going to their offices.

I discovered that rue Eugène Sue was named after the novelist who wrote *The Wandering Jew*, that the street at the top was rue Labat where Sarah Kofman had lived as a child hidden from the Nazis, that rue Goutte d'Or further up towards Metro Chateau Rouge was where Émile Zola set his most famous novel, *L'Assommoir*. It was inscribed, but it wasn't romantic Paris, there were no monuments and no tourists and it wasn't especially tidy and clean and life was going on in full view all the time. I found myself becoming addicted to watching the street life below and looking into other apartments from my fifth-floor eyrie, a sticky-beak pleasure that I'd never had before.

One afternoon after finishing work for the day, I went to see an exhibition of masks at the Musée d'Orsay. It presented masks mainly from nineteenth- and twentieth-century artists but there were some from Roman times and medieval Africa and Europe and from Asia and Polynesia as well. The program said, 'Revealing while concealing, serving both spiritual and worldly pleasure, the mask goes back to the dawn of time.' It struck me that almost every culture had wanted to make a representation of the human face that could be worn over the actual face. I wondered who first thought, let's make another face for myself. And what did they want to reveal in their mask-face? Forbidden thoughts and feelings? Or was it to hide what was too fragile to reveal? Montaigne said, 'We must remove the mask' but perhaps it was more useful to study the mask.

On the walls and in the cabinets of the d'Orsay there were death masks and Noh theatre masks from Japan, stone grotesques from Roman gates, ceremonial masks made of feathers and mud and grasses from Africa and New Guinea, plaster artists' masks for studio drawing practice and a Medusa mask with snake hair.

I thought of Jean-Jacques' masks at home on our mantelpiece, the ferociously beaked bird-man made of papier mâché. He had moved to Sydney and was enrolled at art school by then and one day when he was visiting, he had shown Matt and me how to make masks using torn-up paper pasted on inflated balloons. We had spent an afternoon making a mask each; mine was a friendly-looking witch with a hooked nose and Matt's was a happy moon-face. We left them to dry for a few days and then painted them, mine blue and his pink, both of them in sunny contrast to the bird-man mask.

It wasn't long after he moved to Sydney that Jean-Jacques started using heroin again. He had been a junkie before he came to Australia, but he'd been clean for a couple of years when we first met him. I don't know why he started using again – perhaps it was the break-up with Olive which came soon after they moved to Sydney, or perhaps it was just that he liked living near the edge. He reminded me of a moth flying at a flame, a kid who can't help going too far out on the branch.

Each time Anthony visited Jean-Jacques in Sydney he came home with increasingly worrying tales. He had stopped going to art school, he was living in a squat in Darlinghurst, he was dealing drugs, he had sores on his body, he was too thin, dangerous people had threatened him with iron bars. Every now and then Jean-Jacques came to stay with us in the Blue Mountains to withdraw but each time he would return to Sydney and pick up the needle again. He still had the sweetness of heart that had drawn us both to him, but there was violence in him as well. He talked about standover men and police bashing him and stealing his money. He sometimes brought a girl, Shayla, with him who was also a junkie and worked as a prostitute. My clearest memory of her is her sitting thin and damaged on our veranda, painting baby Patrick's fingernails with pink nail polish.

All these years later Anthony had heard back from Jean-Jacques. The email address on the driving school website had reached him. He wrote, 'I am very exciting', which made us both laugh. He had always said that and we had never corrected him. Over the years we often repeated it to each other when we were looking forward to something: I am very exciting. He told us that he and Ana – he was still with his Spanish girlfriend, Ana! – had three children and they lived in Lausanne. Anthony wrote back, saying we would come and visit them, but Jean-Jacques replied immediately, insisting they would visit us. He wanted to see us in Paris, he said. It was already late October and getting cold – they might come in November if they could, but otherwise it would be some time early the following year.

Writing was making my shoulder and back pain worse; it was difficult to sit at my laptop for more than a few minutes at a time. When I was out, even my small daypack felt like a sack of stones and at night it took a few hours of tossing and turning before I could go to sleep. I didn't want to admit that I was in pain; I was ashamed. I wrote in my diary: 'Here I am in Paris with dreams fulfilled and I whinge because my back hurts! But it bloody does.'

I looked up the word for pain, *douleur,* and went to see a doctor who, I checked online, spoke English. He turned out to speak less English than I spoke French, so we tried to work out the nature of the *douleur* in simplified French. He told me to take codeine and gave me the contact details of Tristan de Parcevaux, a physiotherapist with a clinic not far from our old studio. The medieval name alone was enough for me to make an appointment as soon as I got home.

When I turned up a couple of days later at the *cabinet* of Tristan de Parcevaux in the rue Durantin, part of me was surprised that he wasn't a twelfth-century knight on his way to Jerusalem, but a good-looking young man about the same age as my older son. Later, when I got to know him better and I confessed that I had imagined him as a knight, he said that he was in fact from a noble family. I thought of his ancestors in their chateau with their fine stables and lands and battles and Crusades and wondered how ordinary or extraordinary our lives would seem to them.

SIX

NOVEMBER

The memories of place that one has within resemble a palimpsest.
Annie Ernaux

I like the idea of memory as a palimpsest, a parchment where remains of earlier writing or drawings can be seen through the present text. At times older memories float up and are read before the later ones. Months and days and years are interleaved. I could try to establish dates more accurately – and I do try, making alignments with weather, with political events, who was president in France at the time – but that's not really the point. It seems more accurate to try to make the layers and fragments that form memory. And then stories already told, already written, float in and repeat themselves, the details changing a little, told and retold down the years until the repetitions darken like layers of glue and paper.

I do remember Anthony was in Jordan in early November and I had been alone all week. Although I had joined the choir and made an arrangement to meet Sylvie, I still didn't have anyone else to talk to. Now that I was in a new *quartier*, the shopkeepers didn't yet recognise me either, so I often had that floating sense of being, if not quite invisible, then negligible, as

I'd been that hot summer day on the rue St Jacques in the early months. No-one knew I was here, I could disappear for days and it would make no difference to anyone. I began scanning faces when I was out in the lonely hope of accidentally seeing someone I knew from Australia.

One morning I went out to Café de la Place opposite the town hall of the eighteenth arrondissement and sat in the window, out of the cold, to watch the passers-by. They looked back, cool and appraising. They made me feel as if my gaze didn't exist, as if it wasn't enough to make them avert their eyes. I had lost my sense of 'Here I am'. I returned to the apartment and wrote in my room on the fifth floor, constructing another time and another place: Dina who had died and seven-year-old Theo who had said, 'What I really want is to see my mother just one more time.' It was clear that he knew the endless futility of his longing. I had realised then how much of knowing who you are and where you belong is created and shaped in the gaze of others. If no-one sees you, then do you exist? I closed the document and wrote to Matt and Patrick instead, the same email to both. I told them about our new apartment and that there was a spare room with two beds waiting for them in Paris.

Susie Laporte had given me the telephone number of Vicky Cole, who had been a friend of hers when she lived in Paris.

'You will like her,' she emailed, 'she likes books.'

Vicky lived in the rue Labat, a couple of minutes' walk away. I stared at the phone number for days until one afternoon my need to be seen and heard overcame shyness and I sat down and rang it. Vicky, who was born in England but had lived in France most of her life, invited me around for 'supper' the next night. I had never been invited for supper before – it sounded like a nursery meal from Enid Blyton – and Vicky had a posh voice, but as soon as she opened the door I felt at home; the walls of her entrance hall were covered with books, right up to the ceiling.

She smiled a welcome and greeted me in English. She was about the same height as me, slightly older, and was wearing jeans and long-sleeved t-shirt and a silver and amber necklace. She invited me into her lounge-room where there were more books on tables and on the mantelpiece, and, on a low Afghani coffee table, a tray with cheeses, gherkins, *saucissons* and wine. After it was vacated by an indignant cat, I sat down in an old leather armchair – in the sort of disrepair only the English gentry would have in their living rooms – and we began talking about books.

A couple of hours later we were still talking about books and we kept on talking. I stayed much longer than the acceptable time for an evening with a new acquaintance, but words and ideas were firing between us as we exchanged our stories. Vicky told me that when she was a child at birthday parties a nanny stood behind every child's chair – but she had come to France to escape all that and had brought up her children as a single mother in a village in the south-west of France. She had done all sorts of work: packing cold and smelly crates on a fish farm, sorting tourists' complaints about their showers in rented village houses, and had eventually set up her own holiday accommodation business. And she loved books. She read as easily in French as in English, but seemed to have more English books scattered around. We had read all the same women writers in our youth: Simone de Beauvoir and Violette Leduc, Anaïs Nin, Doris Lessing, Jean Rhys, Alice Walker.

I walked back home late that night with the airy feeling and glow on the skin that comes after a passionate exchange about books and ideas. As de Beauvoir said, 'As long as there were books I could be sure of being happy.'

Before I left that night, Vicky invited me to another rendezvous, a performance at the place des Vosges in the Marais. It was billed as an 'Evening of Poets and Tigers' – I had already seen a poster for it and thought I'd go. At the end of the same week, we met at her place and walked down to the Metro Marcadet-Poissonniers together. Between us there was the slight uneasiness of a second meeting after an intense first connection. Was the passion really shared? Or were we too open too soon? Like Montaigne, 'I am able to make and keep exceptional and considered friendships, especially since I seize hungrily upon any acquaintanceship which corresponds to my tastes,' and I was sensitive to the rhythms of making a new friendship. We talked about ordinary things, what we had been doing, the weather.

The 'Evening of Poets and Tigers' didn't live up to its exotic title. The gates of the square in the place des Vosges had been shut and temporary fencing installed, presumably to keep the tigers in, and by the time we arrived, there were crowds at least four or five deep all around the fencing. I am short and so is Vicky, which meant neither of us could see much. We managed to wriggle forward and spotted a couple of bored-looking tigers lying on a gravelled pathway in the distance. Nothing happened for quite some time. Some French was read aloud but I couldn't tell if it was poetry or an announcement and I didn't want to ask. After another long while, white horses did a display of precision stepping, crossing their hooves this way and that, trying to make up for the poets and tigers not living up to their dangerous names. The crowds stayed although there was little to see except shadowy shapes in the square.

'I've read that French people will come out and look at a wall if it was rumoured there was something happening on the other side of it,' I said.

Vicky shrugged. I thought of the desire for danger and for something different to happen, even the desire to see destruction. Madame de Sévigné had waited on Notre Dame bridge to see Madame de Brinvilliers, the poisoner, burned on a pyre after being executed: 'Well, it's all over, Brinvilliers is in the air: after the execution her poor little body was thrown into a very large fire and her ashes scattered to the winds; so we shall inhale her [...] no-one has ever seen so many people, nor Paris so excited and engrossed in anything.'

We shall inhale her! Present-day media vultures have nothing on Madame de Sévigné and the Paris crowds in the seventeenth century! I don't know what the excited and endless need for catastrophe means – or what hunger it feeds – but there seems something like primitive witchcraft in it; if I eat enough of other people's tragedies then I will be protected. I will be the child to run with the valuable news of a disaster, I'll watch the planes fly into buildings for days on end. The crowd rocked the temporary fence, daring it to fall, daring the tigers to care and leap forward and tear someone – someone else – to pieces. It was the same crowd feasting at the guillotine in the place de la Concorde, or standing on Notre Dame bridge watching Madame de Brinvilliers burn. Breathing in the ashes of the poisoner's body.

As we walked back to the train Vicky apologised for the evening as if it had been her responsibility. I said it wasn't her fault that the tigers had not rampaged, nor even stalked around the square.

*

In my zigzagging across Paris, in and out of streets and parks and galleries, gathering a strange mix of nectars, I found '*L'Abeille*', 'The Bee', by the Symbolist poet Paul Valéry.

'So deadly and delicate your sting,' he begins. He longs for the sharp quick sting of the bee to wake him up. He says that without it, love will die or sleep, and, in my reader's half of the words, he doesn't mean romantic love, but the loving intensity of being awake to life; the bee is a bringer of awareness. I am no great believer in the necessity of pain, but mostly there is no choice in the matter. Since that year in Paris, friends have died – cancer, motor neurone disease, heart failure – and others are suffering ills or loneliness. None of us are old yet, but still, the harvesting has begun. I remember the yellow wheat paddocks of my childhood, the ripe ears, the grain bins filling, the bare spiky stalks left in the ground; I never thought the harvest was sad then.

I dreamed my mother died a few days before her birthday in November. I was showing her around a house, but I knew she had already died. I had a severe pain in my chest and could hardly breathe. In the dream I thought: the pain of someone you love dying is a real physical pain. When I woke up I worried all day that the phone would ring with bad news from Australia. It didn't come then nor for several years, but when it did, the pain I had dreamed was accurate.

I don't know why I'm thinking of death; it seems a long way off for me, although even when I was a teenager I thought about it often. It wasn't with fear, and certainly not with longing – I wasn't a dark teenager – but with a consciousness that it would happen. De Beauvoir said she was terrified of death, sometimes utterly panicked by the thought of it, but for me it was more of a puzzle. I stood in the heat of the day on the veranda of our farmhouse and tried to imagine not being. It would happen, but the texture of nothingness is impossible to imagine and so the day would ripple and resume.

Montaigne thought about it a great deal when he was young too, but he thought the slow death of youth was more dreadful than actual death. He says, 'Death is one of the attributes you were created with; death is part of you; [in running away from death] you are running away from yourself; this being which you enjoy is equally divided between life and death.' I wonder if he did feel as calmly about it as he sounds. Non-existence, non-being, has to be a bit confounding whenever it is considered.

Instead of non-existence, other elaborate worlds have been created to live in afterwards – Heaven, Paradise, Valhalla – populated not just by those who have died but also by gods and a hierarchy of heavenly beings. And then ways to communicate with those who lived there had to be developed. Dreams could bring messages from the dead, and so could angels, and certain creatures, birds and cats. In ancient Aegean cultures, bees were the sacred messengers from this world to the dead.

Bees were also messengers from the gods to us. The messages were passed on in honey so that truth could be expressed in scholarship and poetry. Honey-voiced. Honey-tongued. The Oracle at Delphi, the one who had 'Know Thyself' carved above the temple door, was the Delphic Bee. The priestesses of Artemis and Demeter were known as bees and even Apollo was given his gift of prophecy by the Thriae, a trinity of pre-Hellenic bee goddesses.

Bees were seen as truthful messengers because the ancients thought honey was incorruptible and pure, that nothing was added to the nectar for it to become honey. Pure and incorruptible Truth. Of course, science has discovered that the bees do add enzymes from their own mouths, chewing it for half an hour or so to break down the complex sugars into simple sugars and then, after they put it in the honeycombs, they fan it with their wings for hours to evaporate water from it. It takes quite a bit of work, really. Making honey.

*

It was cold by mid-November and often grey. When I woke on the fifth floor I could see the orange chimney pots on top of the building across rue Eugène Sue. All the buildings in the street were Haussmannian, built after Baron Haussmann demolished most of medieval Paris in the nineteenth century, cream-coloured limestone, each six storeys with long balconies on the second and fifth floors, the only differences being the colour and design of the iron balcony railings. Ours were blue fern whorls, the building directly opposite, black ovals. As I opened my eyes I could tell what kind of day it was by the light on the chimney pots on the *chambre de bonne*, maid's room, above the black-oval railing: if the orange of the pots was flat it was another grey day; if it was light and golden, then at least the day had started off sunny. I don't normally mind grey weather; in the long drought of my childhood, cloudy, rainy days were longed for, welcomed, but here the low light was wearying.

I had a rendezvous with Tristan de Parcevaux three times a week. I looked forward to the visits, not just because of the massage – which didn't make much difference to my sore shoulder – but because we had begun to talk to each other. He practised his English and I practised my French. I learned that he was a musician in his life outside the physiotherapy rooms, and he learned that I was writing about my friend who had died. For practice, he gave his instructions to me in English and one day when I was lying on my stomach, he said in correct English, 'Now put your feet to your arse.' I laughed. He was embarrassed when I explained that 'arse' was not the word a health professional would use. He was more careful in the way he related to me for a while afterwards.

I didn't say much about the pain, even to Anthony. I think I inherited my mother's impatience with whingeing, but it was more that being in pain undermined my sense of self – and self-respect. There was too much suffering in the world to even mention aches and pains. It wasn't me; I didn't have neurotic, undefined problems, and I didn't get depressed. The firmer the ideas one has about oneself the harder it is to see the truth.

Montaigne says, 'We are entirely made up of bits and pieces, woven together so diversely and so shapelessly that each of them pulls its own way at every moment.' But I was still trying to see myself made of one enthusiastic piece. And in fact some days I felt fine. The tiredness and pain came and went in a periodic fashion, three or so bad days, then one good day, just enough relief to create the cheering illusion that it would all be better soon. The days of pain were not so much the short sharp sting of a bee as the dull ache that comes afterwards, which sounds as if it would be easier to bear, but it felt like a slow grinding down. The dull weather felt like an image of my inner flatness – if the light on the chimney pots was flat it took a lot more effort to get out of bed.

One day I lay there thinking about my boys, about their childhood. As Ernaux said, 'a palimpsest' of memories floated through my brain: Matt looking for a lost lake called Paradise at the bottom of a cliff, Patrick swimming in the dark water of Gollum's Pool and catching yabbies in a cold stream, a birthday party where boys played hide-and-seek behind blue gums and apple gums and grevilleas and banksias, ten-year-old Patrick instructing me when I was halfway up a cliff, frightened and unable to move, how to edge my foot to the next ledge. And images from my own childhood came: sitting in the wheat bin with wheat showering all around me, scraping my legs on the giant pepper tree in the back yard, riding Flicka bareback, reading all Sunday on my bed. I had a happy childhood – poor and loved, which sounds like a sugar-coated fairytale but it can be said truthfully – and so did my sons, but here in Paris I could feel something finally slipping out of my grasp. Leaving forever.

I remembered a moment near the end of long-ago childhood, at the beginning of adolescence. I was standing in the scraggly front yard near the veranda – I can see the exact spot in my mind many decades later – when I was suddenly lifted – I don't know how – out of immersion in the moments of my existence, and saw that there was a future stretching out for numberless days and that it wouldn't fill up by itself, that it would be up to me to fill in the hours and days and years. Simone de Beauvoir wrote that one morning when she was a child, 'Suddenly the future existed; it would turn me into another being, someone who would still be, and yet no longer seem, myself.'

I wondered whether all children have one moment when they are torn out of the eternal present, the moment when time and space no longer formed a closely woven cloak over the gaps and holes of existence.

When I finally got up in the rue Simart and looked in the mirror in the bathroom, I was shocked to see the shape of my face had changed. I had always had an oval shape, which I quite liked, but now there were jowls on either side making it rectangular. When had that happened? I held the skin of the jowls back with my fingers and I immediately looked five years younger. So that's why people have plastic surgery! I looked down at my arms, the faint geography of age appeared only when my arms were bent. My skin was dry, like my mother's. Not yet loose and papery like hers, ready to bruise at every touch, but one day it would be.

I made myself sit at the trestle desk but gazed sideways out the window. I saw a woman in a wheelchair in the apartment opposite, quite a bit older than I was, with soft, well-cut, grey hair. There was a younger man looking after her, not young enough to be her son, definitely a younger lover, laying her clothes out on the bed: a pink satiny slip, a bra, a red skirt. I stood up to see them come out of the door into the street below, he angling the wheelchair carefully through the door, and she dressed in the circular red gypsy skirt and a jacket and scarf. He thought she was the most wonderful woman in the world and she took it as her due.

I saw them nearly every day after that and thought about them a great deal. Had she always been in a wheelchair? Or did they meet when she could still walk and now he had to take care of her? Not that it was a burden; he was always so tender and so proud of her. Anthony had noticed them too, although coming and going as he did, they hadn't become woven into his daily life. But he knew I was referring to them when I asked him, 'Will you dress me in my favourite red skirt when I'm sixty-four?'

He stood behind me putting his arms around my waist. We were standing at the French doors in the bedroom, both looking down towards the street.

'And will you still love me when I'm sixty-four?' I asked. Pushing my luck.

'Will you still love me?' he said. He turned me to face him in front of the glass doors and we kissed and then made love, the half-drawn Venetian blinds letting in slices of light on our bodies.

Peering into other people's apartments became one of my main pleasures in the rue Simart. In the apartment on the opposite corner there was an Algerian family – a mother with dyed red hair, a grandmother and two girls, one about nine and the other a baby, a toddler. I wondered where the father was, whether he had found work in another city and only came home every few months. They sat on a brocade sofa and watched television in the evening, the blue glow flickering in the room. Once, I saw the girl hold the baby over their balcony, not to frighten her, but to show her their flame-haired mother approaching in the street below. I wondered if the baby would ever remember the moment, high in the air, seeing her mother from above.

Most of the time the window of the only bathroom I could see into was shut. On the occasions when it was open I sometimes saw a woman about my age washing her son's hands. An older mother. She had a beautiful face, brown-skinned and dark-eyed. She looked as if she may have been Tahitian and because I never saw a man through the window, I thought she was a *fille-mère*, a 'girl-mother', as the French call unmarried mothers, although she was in her forties. On Saturday mornings she washed her woollens at the hand basin with the window open and hung them on the railings. The boy's two pullovers hung there every Saturday, their tiny arms dangling in the sunlight, and I realised I missed not just my boys, but I missed that they were no longer little boys. I could neither hold them in my arms nor gaze at them for as long as I wanted, but only for brief seconds.

It gave, still gives, me such pleasure to watch people unseen that I wonder if I'm a kind of voyeur. I meant no harm though, and it arouses tenderness to see a hand reached out, a neck stretched, when there is no consciousness of being seen.

*

Simone de Beauvoir liked looking into apartments, even when she was a child: 'I would be deeply moved to see my own life displayed, as it were, on a lighted stage. A woman would be setting a table, a couple would be talking [...] I didn't feel shut out; I had the feeling that a single theme was being interpreted [...] repeated to infinity from building to building, from city to city, my existence had a part in all its innumerable representation.'

She also liked watching people in the street from her balcony in the boulevard Raspail: 'Their faces, their appearances and the sound of their voices captivated me; I find it hard now to explain what the particular pleasure was that they gave me; but when my parents decided to move to a fifth floor flat in the rue de Rennes, I remember the despairing cry I gave: "But I won't be able to see the people in the street any more." I was being cut off from life, condemned to exile.'

Oh, the watching of people's lives from above! One day I watched two ancient, wrinkled women, both white-haired, one with a cane, walking slowly arm-in-arm, helping each other along. One woman was black and the other one was white. Another day I saw a boy with a first beard, walking with neat straight steps, his arms folded above his waist like a young girl unsure of her blossoming breasts.

And another day an accordion player walked down the middle of rue Eugène Sue, playing and collecting coins as people threw them down from their balconies. Some of the coins rolled under cars and he had to get down on his hands and knees to retrieve them. I thought it must be a hard way to make a living when most people were out at work and apartments were empty during the day. My choir had started to learn a new song, '*L'accordéon*' by Serge Gainsbourg – we sang about how cruel life was for the street musician, how his only friend was his accordion, but this accordionist was cheerful. When I threw him down some euros from the fifth floor, he stopped and played a whole song for me. I didn't recognise the song, but it made me feel like I was in a French film from fifty years ago.

Then one day there was a teenager in army fatigues fighting his own private war, knocking over bins and ripping down posters as he loped along the street. Drawn out by the noise I stood on the balcony looking at him from above. He scooped up the real estate magazines from the stand outside the *boulangerie* and threw them in the first bin he came to. He had a roving gaze, as if he were not going to miss anything that needed his attention. He was about the same age as Patrick, perhaps two or three years older. He kicked the rolled-up carpet used by the African street-sweepers to direct water along the gutters, he punched cars, he yelled obscenities. Then he looked up, a raging, crazy, unloved boy, and saw me watching him. I looked away quickly, ashamed.

'*Salope*,' he yelled. '*Va te faire foutre*.' Fuck off, bitch.

The rue Simart was a kind of littoral, I suppose, a shore between privilege and disadvantage, often delineated by race instead of class. The raging boy was white, and so were most of the *clochards*, the down-and-outs, but all the *sans-papiers*, refugees without legal status, and many of the poor were Africans or Arabs from former French colonies: Mali, Senegal, Algeria, the Sudan. Algerians have been in Paris longer, most of them coming to escape the civil war in the 1960s, and are more likely to have jobs and small businesses – *allez chez l'Arab* means 'go to the corner shop'. When shonky apartment buildings burn down and lives are lost, most of the names of the dead are African. Most live in wretched state housing towers, called HLM, in the *banlieue*, outer suburbs, but there is a large African *quartier* on the other side of boulevard Barbès. They are 'the people' now, the disadvantaged and the oppressed.

Montaigne, Stendhal, Rousseau, de Beauvoir all wrote about 'the people', Rousseau especially: 'An inextinguishable hatred grew in my heart against the oppression to which the unhappy people are subject and against their oppressors.' And Montaigne lived in a peasant household until he was weaned because his father wanted him to have sympathy for 'the people'. Stendhal, in an age of revolutions, defended the people but was honest, more than once, about his distaste: 'I loathe to have dealings with the hoi-polloi while at the same time under the name of *the people*, I long passionately for their happiness.'

Madame de Sévigné – I'm sorry to say because I did come to like her over coffee – wasn't sympathetic even in theory; she describes the punishment of the leader of a people's insurrection in Brittany where she came from:

> The day before yesterday, a ruffian who had called the tune and begun the thieving of the official stamped paper, was broken on the wheel; when he was dead he was quartered and his four quarters put on view at the four corners of the town [...] Sixty burghers have been arrested: tomorrow the hangings begin. This province is a fine example to the others, and particularly that they should respect their governors.

In case the details of seventeenth-century justice are not clear, 'broken on the wheel' means being tied to a large wagon wheel and then beaten with wooden or iron cudgels until your body is bashed through the spokes. 'Quartered' means the body is then cut into four. I am sure it did make them respect their governors.

It was several centuries later and I was from the other side of the world, standing on a balcony, God-like, watching. Like Annie Ernaux, I had come from 'the people', as much as that applies in Australia. Neither of my parents had any education past primary school; my father's parents were a farmer and a housemaid, my mother's, a house painter and a barmaid, all hard-working and quiet people. My father owned a farm but it was a small patch of dirt to support a family of ten – eleven counting my grandmother lying in her dark room with no windows to the outside. The house was shabby: boards rotted on the veranda, in one of the bedrooms white ants had destroyed the walls, and cement, which made do as plaster, was falling off the walls in the kitchen. We had no heaters, no indoor toilet – *The Land* newspaper for toilet paper in the cracked fibro lavvy outside – and no hot water unless it was heated in a kettle.

For most of my childhood I had no shower and no bath, ineffectually washing in a small tin dish. In my first few weeks of high school in town, I was drinking at the water-bubblers one lunch-time and realised the girl next to me was looking at my arms. I noticed for the first time that both my arms from wrist to past the elbows had several 'high-tide' layers of dirt on them, dirty, dirtier and dirtiest. I had not realised I was dirty until I saw myself through her astonished gaze. Stendhal was right, the people are dirty – 'dirty, damp, blackish' – but I think I spent the following decades hiding evidence of my grimy body. I succeeded well enough; I'm not 'the people' anymore. I'm one of those who can talk about them, watch them, from a balcony in Paris.

*

Annie Ernaux came from 'the people', which for her meant a small town in Normandy called Yvetot. Her mother and father moved up from being a farm labourer and factory worker to run a café. Her mother had 'ideas' – and so did Annie – so she was sent to a convent school where the other girls were middle-class. She tells a story in *Retour à Yvetot* which is almost a copy of my dirty arm experience, although in reverse. At home, her family used bleach to wash everything: sheets, curtains, even their hands. Annie didn't think anything of this, didn't even notice it, until, in the first French class, Jeanne, a girl whose parents were 'chic', exclaimed: 'It stinks of bleach!' and 'Who smells of bleach? I can't stand the smell of bleach.'

Ernaux writes that she wanted to sink into the earth. She hid her hands under her desk, filled with shame and terrified one of the girls sitting next to her would know it was her. In that moment she realised it was the smell of a 'cleaning lady', an inferior. She hated Jeanne but, even more, herself.

It was a secret humiliation, no-one outed her, and as far as I know, the girl next to me at the bubblers didn't reveal my secret – although I don't know why not because I would have been an easy target – but I felt the shame and the fear just as Ernaux described it. To be uncovered, not just as different but as inferior, was a terrifying thought. I already knew what happened to girls who were judged as different and inferior.

In that small town, apart from the Wiradjuri who lived on the edge of our lives, almost everyone was of English and Irish descent, fair-skinned and utterly certain there was no other way to be. Cathy Dantrinos, who sat near me in class and whose only crime was having a Greek father, had olive skin and black hair and was belittled and mocked every day. Her thick plait was mocked, her thick legs were mocked and her mother, who also, oh how embarrassing, wore a thick plait, was mocked. For the first few days when I arrived at the school I talked to Cathy, until a stream of girls came up to me, making it clear it would be the same for me if I continued along this dangerous path. I abandoned Cathy to her fate.

Annie Ernaux broke with her past, with her ancestors, saying at the end of the chapter, 'I had just broken with generations of women who washed with bleach.' Reading that sentence, I felt the sting. It was a small enough break in a world scarred by ruptures, but on opposite sides of the world the dirty girl and the bleached-clean girl had both submitted to the rule of their betters and made it their business to slip by unnoticed.

I've just begun to think that my writing life may have been a journey back to that grubby girl before she knew what other people thought of her.

*

Anthony and I were both robbed in the streets within a week of each other. I was getting into the train at Anvers Metro on the way to choir with my folder of songs tucked under my arm and shoulder bag slung on my back as usual. The crowd surged onto the train and there was jostling as the signal for closing the doors sounded, but people were smiling and good-humoured as we were pushed up against each other. I felt the push of the man who had leapt in behind me and turned around to see that he had got in safely, then turned away and reached in to hold the centre pole so as I wouldn't fall. As the doors shut I looked out and was surprised to see the same dark-haired man walking away along the platform. I realised instantly what might have happened and slipped my bag off my shoulder to check. The wallet was missing. There were sympathetic noises from the other travellers and several pointed at the man we could still see walking away on the platform, but the train was pulling out. It had been well executed and we were all too late.

I told Marie-Louise and three or four others at choir about it and they were upset for me, taking it personally that one of their own had robbed a visitor. Strangely though, it made me feel less like a visitor and I felt pleased to have a story to tell them. Marie-Louise offered me money for my fare home, but I said it was okay, I had a weekly Metro ticket still in my pocket.

I thought about going to the police to report it, but it seemed pointless and there hadn't been much money in the wallet anyway, no more than twenty euros. I cancelled my credit cards and wrote it off to experience. But within a couple of days Anthony was mugged down at place des Abbesses, pushed over and his wallet taken. He had gone down there one evening to see if he could buy some marijuana from the teenagers who were always kicking a soccer ball around the square – the same boys we had seen on our first day – but they had knocked him down and expertly slipped his wallet out of his pocket. He wasn't hurt – and I wasn't overly sympathetic – but we decided two robberies were worth the bother of reporting so we went to the police station in rue Clignancourt near our apartment.

We sat and waited for a few minutes, watching entranced as two groups of police officers greeted each other with three kisses each in the bare foyer.

'We must be in Paris,' Anthony said.

I nodded. The only other time I'd been in a police station was the small police-cottage in my hometown when Matt's bike had been stolen from my mother's back yard. No-one had kissed anyone there.

We were allocated one of the policemen who transcribed the events as we explained them in simple French: *voleur*, thief, and *portefeuille*, wallet, but not *marijuana*. He didn't ask many questions, just let us tell the two stories, although he did ask if my thief was an Arab. It seemed a leading question and I was surprised.

'I'm not sure. He could have been. He had black hair.'

'No. If you are not sure, I can't write anything.'

It was an odd exchange, which I didn't know how to read. I thought it was a racist question but then his refusal to write any details of the thief's appearance on the grounds of my uncertainty suggested that it wasn't.

I wanted to think that the French were not racists; they had welcomed black Americans, musicians and performers, most famously Josephine Baker, in the 1920s. It wasn't until after I got to know Sylvie that I realised it was another romantic illusion.

There was a mix-up on my first rendezvous with Sylvie. She had told me the awnings of the café were white, but the awnings on the café named Le Relais Odéon were green so I was unsure whether I was in the right place. I was a few minutes late, so I rushed back into Metro Odéon and out again at St Michel to check another café near the Metro station there. I eventually and literally bumped into Sylvie coming out of the Metro. I was hot and bothered and Sylvie was embarrassed at having described the place incorrectly, but we both settled down inside the quiet elegance of Le Relais Odéon. It had wrought-iron railings and painted ceilings and perfect waiters. We sat in the window and Sylvie told me it had been her favourite place to watch people when she first came back to Paris.

'I watched the women because I wanted to learn how to be a true French woman.'

She smiled a little self-consciously, aware of her naivety, but I wondered what she had looked at. Was it their clothes – dark, well-cut, with intriguing details – the way they walked, the tilt of their heads, the movement of their mouths as they talked to each other? It seemed to me that French women looked different in all those ways when I sat and watched, especially in this *quartier*, the sixth arrondissement. This was literary and intellectual Paris, near the Sorbonne and the Latin *quartier* and surrounded by publishing houses where words and ideas are still currency, where the student uprising of May '68 raged, where my conception of Paris had been born and was nourished every day.

The sixth arrondissement stretches from the Seine to the other side of the Luxembourg Gardens, bordered on one side by boulevard St Michel and crossed by boulevard St Germain. In between, there are nests of narrow streets crammed with shops and galleries and crêperies where I always lost my sense of direction. Around the corner from where we sat, in the rue de l'Ancienne Comédie, François Procope had opened the first coffee shop in Paris in 1689 – we could go in and bump into Voltaire and Rousseau, although they probably wouldn't be speaking to each other. After Voltaire read Rousseau's *Of the Social Contract* he sent a note to him saying, 'I have received your new book against the human race and I thank you for it [...] One longs, on reading your book, to walk on all fours. But as I have lost that habit for more than sixty years, I feel unhappily the impossibility of resuming it.' Ouch. It was a most civilised way of drawing blood. We might be safer in Le Relais Odéon, watching from behind glass.

I ordered a coffee and Sylvie had a hot chocolate and a croissant. We sat, both of us a little shy, and tried to tell our stories.

Sylvie was born in Paris, but her mother and father were of Indian '*origine*' as the French so exactly put it; she was dark-skinned, dark-eyed, dark-haired. But she had not come from a disadvantaged background. Because her father was a diplomat, she and her brother had grown up in Brazil, Senegal and the French Congo with visits back to France until she moved permanently to Paris in senior high school. I felt the envy of the exotic that only someone relentlessly Anglo-Celtic who had lived on the same few acres all her childhood could feel. How dull, unchanging, homogenous my life was. This, I thought, was exactly why I had come to Paris. To see and touch difference.

'I grew up on a farm in Australia and never knew anything else every day of my childhood,' I admitted. It was a dreary story with not even a change of scenery to hold attention.

'How lucky you are to have a home, a landscape that knows you,' she exclaimed. I felt a jolt of surprise when she said that. How did she know that secret truth when I had hardly articulated it to myself?

She tried to explain how living in so many countries had created an uncertain identity, which was further complicated by the fact of her dark skin. When she was in South America or Africa, she said to those who asked, 'Of course, I am a French girl,' and as she repeated it to me, her voice was indignant. How dare she be questioned about her right to be called French. She felt completely French even though she recognised that she physically resembled the people in Senegal and Brazil more than she did the other diplomatic families.

'But when I came back to Paris, I didn't know who I was. I felt like I didn't know how to be French. I was confused and felt like an outsider.'

I know it sounds improbable that with my limited French we could have articulated such things, but we did. We were strangers but there was something happening between us. A few times in my life I have had an instant intimate connection with a stranger, as I did with Vicky, but never before in another language. For the first time, I threw a few words of French into the air with the feeling they would be caught and put together. There was something brilliant about the way Sylvie leapt towards meaning from my fragments.

'*À dimanche*,' we said as we parted. See you on Sunday. We were friends already.

*

Jean-Jacques and Ana couldn't come in November. It would be more like March or April the following year. But plans for visitors from Australia were falling into place, the Paris magnet exerting its endless pull: a new friend, Camilla, had already arrived – she was an actress and director who had worked with Matt when he was younger; Theo and his father, Kit, were coming in March; our friend Phil who had drawn the cartoon of us in Paris was arranging to visit early in the New Year; Peter, who heard music in his head, and his wife, Libby, were calling in; my niece Hannah, travelling in Europe, was staying for a day or two as she passed through to somewhere else. And Patrick had been accepted into the University of Amsterdam, starting in the New Year. He was coming to stay for a few weeks in late December and would be with us for Christmas before going on to Amsterdam. I emailed Matt, hoping he would find a way to join us. He was waiting on funding to make a film and lived hand-to-mouth, although he always seemed to get by. I had no income and everything extra in my savings had gone on Patrick's studies, but Matt had always been one of those people whom the world likes and looks after.

I waited on the fifth floor in the rue Simart. Each visitor must climb the narrow staircase and, out of breath, knock on my door. I would bring them along the hall and stun them with the glimpse of the cupola of Sacré-Coeur and the sound of the accordionist playing '*Les Temps des Cerises*' in the rue Simart below and then serve them camembert and *vin de pays* from the Arabs on the corner. Other people must see my dream, otherwise it might be said that it did not exist at all.

SEVEN

DECEMBER

Nor is any learning so arduous as knowing how to live this life naturally and well.

Michel de Montaigne

The pain in my right arm and shoulder was constant now, and had spread to my back and between my ribs. When I breathed, in and out, it hurt between every rib.

'Go and see the physio,' Anthony said.

'I already go three times a week.'

Most of the time the ache was dull, but if I moved my arm suddenly a sharp pain shot through it. Because the autumn leaves on the footpaths were wet and slimy, I often skidded on them and instinctively shot my arm out for balance. There was an instant of calm, and then the searing pain hit and doubled me over, breath held. People looked at me in astonishment. '*Qu'est-ce qu'il y a?*' What the matter? What's she carrying on about? There was nothing to see.

One day when Hannah was staying for a week on her travels around Europe, she stood with me at traffic lights and I went to step out onto the pedestrian crossing. She saw a car run the red light and grabbed my arm – the pain shot through me as I bent double in front of her startled face.

Sleeping had become difficult; there was no position that didn't make the pain worse after a few minutes so I lay this way and that for hours. Worst of all, self-pity was creeping damply in to match the cold, grey weather.

I went to another doctor who gave me stronger codeine and an anti-inflammatory. I swallowed as many of both as I was allowed a day; the codeine made me sluggish and the anti-inflammatory gave me ulcers all over my tongue and gums so that I couldn't smile or eat or kiss without it hurting. I knew there was nothing seriously wrong with me, none of it was life-threatening, not even enough to justify calling it suffering. I thought about illness and pain being good for the character and wondered why it was dissolving mine.

Montaigne suffered a variety of illnesses: 'rheums, fluxions of gout, diarrhoeas, coronary palpitations and migraines', and 'the stone' or 'gravel', which sounds like either kidney stones or gallstones, both extremely painful, which is perhaps why he said 'nor is any learning so arduous as knowing how to live this life naturally and well'.

But he was not one to seek pain as a way of learning; in fact he thought pleasure was both a guide for what we should choose – 'I have never been bothered by anything I have done in which I found great pleasure' – and our aim – 'we ought to have given virtue the more favourable, noble and natural name of pleasure'. For him, the only use of pain was the pleasure that came when pain was lifted; the contrast heightened the experience of pleasure.

He did say too that 'we must learn to suffer what we cannot avoid' and that 'experience has taught me that we are ruined by impatience'. That struck home. Each time the pain eased I thought, now I'm better, but the next day when it returned, I was consumed with impatience.

Rousseau was often sick as well, even as a child: he 'was born almost dead and they had little hope of saving me'. As a young man he had long and mysterious illnesses, which he was certain each time were fatal. He knew he was a hypochondriac: 'There was not an illness of which I read the description that I did not imagine to be mine [...] I believed I had them all.' He appears to have had depression when he was young and suffered later on from paranoia and from almost continual maladies including painful 'urine retention', which meant he had to use a catheter every day.

None of these are romantic illnesses, just painful, and embarrassing to talk about, and they must have shaped his thinking, at least in that they meant he was sidelined and had to observe society from the edge. It meant he also observed himself from the edge; he may have been 'maddish' as Hume said, intense in his passions, fanatical, but he was also self-aware in some aspects: 'I have a passionate temperament, and lively and headstrong emotions. Yet my thoughts arise slowly and confusedly, and are never ready until too late.' Oh, mine neither, I need a day or two to think of the quick reply!

I have been judging him too harshly, I realise. He was just another struggling human being. I had judged against his weaknesses too quickly, a flaw in my own character which has always been there. Even when I saw Proust's cork room in the Musée Carnavalet, I wasn't sympathetic. Marcel Proust was asthmatic, allergic to all kinds of dusts and pollens, and couldn't bear noise; he spent much of his life shut away from the world, convinced that he would otherwise die. Instead of compassion, I felt impatience, even faint scorn. There was something in my then robust health that found his sickliness and oversensitivity irritating. I felt the same when I read the interminable – that word conveys my attitude already – pages in *In Search of Lost Time* where the narrator – I can't help thinking it's Proust himself – is waiting for his mother to say goodnight. Just get on with it, for heaven's sake. I'd always been impatient with others' illness, and now with my own obscure ailments.

In the middle of one afternoon I was feeling more than sorry for myself. I was in pain, exhausted from lack of sleep, my mouth was entirely coated with ulcers, it was cold, and Anthony was away in China, in Shanghai. I had a sudden longing to have his comfort, a longing for the phone to ring and to hear his warm voice which was never impatient with illness. I even thought for a second of ringing him, but remembered it was 3 am in China and he always slept like the proverbial log and it was unreasonable to disturb him. And then, within a minute, the phone rang, and of course it was Anthony.

'How did you know?' I stood there, disbelieving, tears stinging.

'I woke up suddenly with the thought that you needed to talk to me. So I rang.'

In a way, I don't want to say anything else about that phone call, but there is so little ever said about long marriages – apart from being a source of tedium and disillusionment – that, at the same time, I want to shout out from the rooftops. Communion might be quieter and nearly invisible – tempestuous affairs are given all the good lines – but it is as fine and rare and worth as much as stormy weather. Our connection had always been strongly physical – both of us wondering aloud at times how long we would stay together without sex – and strongly intellectual, dependent on decades of conversation about books.

I sometimes wondered if there was anything else between us. Sex and books. And our sons too, of course. And wasn't that more than enough anyway? But the yearning thoughts of a sceptic had travelled across high mountain ranges and cities and seas all the way to Shanghai to wake one man amongst millions from a sound sleep and caused him to make an international phone call to a self-pitying woman in Paris. When I put the phone down I couldn't stop smiling.

It was only a week to Christmas and both the boys were coming from Sydney. Matt in his impetuous way had decided to buy a ticket on his credit card and deal with it later. He would arrive first and then, a few days later, Patrick, on his way to his year at university in Amsterdam.

The weather was cold and damp but Paris sparkled as each *quartier* tried to outdo the other with Christmas lights. There were garlands strung across market streets, moons and shooting stars and mandalas and nativity scenes dancing in the sky above the crowds of shoppers, glittering in the darkness.

When Anthony got back from China we spent an evening going from *quartier* to *quartier*, holding each other's gloved hand and admiring the transformation of the gloomy evening into sparkling fantasy. The strings of small windmills made of lights, gold and red and blue and green, in our old neighbourhood in the rue des Abbesses, were the most beautiful to our loyal eyes, but we didn't go and see the most spectacular in the Champs Élysées that night because we wanted to see them with Matt and Patrick when they arrived. Sylvie had told me it was the custom for parents to take their children to see the Champs Élysées lights in the week before Christmas each year. Carollers wandered down the streets singing to people as they sat in cafés and parents and children drank hot chocolate and watched the lights.

'*Papa* and *Maman* took us every year when we were back in Paris,' she said.

I thought of children too young to properly remember, but recalling glimpses of singing and cold and stars fallen to earth. One New Year's night when we still lived in Sydney and Matt was a baby, about two years old, Anthony and I took him sleeping from his bed and carried him down to the harbour and climbed onto a ferry. It was nearly midnight. The New Year's Eve fireworks began and Matt woke up to see the sky exploding with red and gold and silver and green stars. The water lapped on the side of the ferry and the cool dark wrapped around him and fountains and bees and dragon's eggs and falling leaves sparkled in every colour. He would not remember the midnight journey from his bed, but underneath conscious memory he would always have the idea that extraordinary things might happen in the dark of night. It seemed to us that it was the beginning of his education. At that time I hadn't read more than the two or three essays of Montaigne's that Mrs Berman had given me in high school, but I know he would have agreed. Education was to enrich the inner being, and ought to be pleasurable, a delight. Waking to the sounds of a spinnet or the sight of golden stars filling the dark, 'to educate the soul entirely through gentleness and freedom'.

*

I went to concerts every Sunday: sacred music in St-Louis on the Île St Louis, choir at the American church, a chamber concert in St-Jean de Montmartre at place des Abbesses, pianists playing Brahms at St-Merri near the Pompidou Centre.

Sometimes my lack of musical background meant I couldn't understand the blur of sound and I became restless and sat in my overcoat – the churches were always cold – wondering why I was still trying to join a club where my ignorance held me back at the door of grace and beauty, trying to see in.

Then I met an opera singer, an Australian woman, Trish. I'd gone to an exhibition of paintings at the Australian Embassy and she had turned up, as I had, in the hope of meeting new people. I don't remember any of the paintings at the exhibition or even who the artist was, but I have a photograph of myself there in a pink and green dress, which, in the narcissistic hierarchy of memory, I remember I bought at Porte de Clignancourt, the flea markets in the north of Paris. I talked to Trish about my manuscript, how I had taken singing lessons back home, and that I had joined a choir in the twentieth arrondissement. She told me she had come from Adelaide to study singing in Strasbourg in her twenties and had never gone home. She had married a Frenchman and had two sons, but she couldn't sing while she was married and ended up leaving him. It wasn't that her husband prevented her from singing, she just lost her voice.

She was sexy-looking, with green eyes and long brown hair, and had an earthy laugh, and I liked her right away. She said she was currently performing in a concert of songs from Mozart operas – she was a mezzo-soprano – and asked me to come and see it.

'It'll be fun,' she said. 'We don't take ourselves too seriously.'

The following week I turned up at the theatre, which was down a lane in the eleventh arrondissement. I climbed up narrow stairs leading to steep rows of seats that looked as if they might tip me over onto the stage if I tripped. The dusty red velvet stage-curtains appeared to have been there since the nineteenth century at least.

A series of sketches unfolded: a man in a loud shirt sitting in a striped deckchair, a nurses and doctors surgery scene with everyone in clinical white, Roman soldiers, Trish as an Italian housewife wearing a headscarf and glasses – each with glorious songs from *Don Giovanni, Cosi Fan Tutte, The Magic Flute, The Marriage of Figaro.* The singers fell about with slapstick humour, acting as if their soaring voices were effortless, accidental. The program explained that they wanted to explore Mozart's *gout de l'espièglerie,* his taste for cheekiness and his childish spirit. I relaxed. It didn't have to be solemn, reverential. Their voices were rich, powerful; they could do somersaults at the same time and still sing. Trish's dark earthy mezzo reached effortlessly low and skimmed the high notes as she clowned around on the end of a telephone acting the gossipy fool.

Afterwards we had a drink in a nearby bar. The waiter hovered around Trish and asked if she was free later. A couple of men at the next table started flirting with her.

'Like bees to a honey-pot,' I said.

She laughed. It was an everyday dance for her, the stepping forward and back of attraction. She smiled at them and returned to our conversation.

'I'm trying to compose a set of songs about Australia,' she said.

'Even though you've been living here for twenty years?'

'Proabably because I have. I'm working on a series, the whole piece will be called *Terre Rouge,* Red Earth. But I need to listen to Aboriginal music, didgeridoo and sticks and chanting.'

'But what kind of songs are you writing?'

'I'm writing them to perform myself, so I guess you would call them arias. It's not folk or rock'n'roll or jazz anyway.'

'And you want to combine that with didgeridoo?'

We continued talking, both of us offering bits of our work. I envied Trish her voice, her capacity to make music, her entry into a world of sound that seemed to me beyond words. Like Stendhal I had come from 'an essentially unmusical family'. Like him I was trying to sing, but as he said, there was little that could be done about it. I could only respond with more words. I told Trish that Dina in the book I was writing had sung in a rock'n'roll band for a while and that when I wrote about her tragedy, a beautiful young mother leaving a little boy forever, I had thought someone should write a sad love song about it.

Because stories keep going, a couple of years later when I gave Trish a copy of the book about Dina, she did write a song for her, a sad love song, and sang it when I did a reading of my book at The Red Wheelbarrow bookshop in Paris. That was in the future, but I like the way stories thread back and forth over time, connecting things that might otherwise have been lost or left flapping in the wind. It makes time past and time present seem to be, not a line, but arcs of a spiral. Trish finished writing *Terre Rouge* after I left Paris and performed it for a season on a nightclub barge on the Canal St-Martin. I didn't see it, but Camilla, who had also become a friend of Trish's, directed it. I heard the Paris audiences loved it.

*

Days and weeks had found a rhythm. I wrote each morning, immersed in life after Dina had died, the long slow connection with Theo, trying to stitch it together. I had begun to think of it as a kind of song and that I was trying to find the pattern of notes. I wrote pieces and arranged them as if they were notes: four or five short pieces, a run of quarter beats, and longer pieces, whole beats, or longer still, a note held as long as a breath would allow.

While I was writing, I listened to bellbirds and magpies in the Blue Mountains, to the sound of Theo's near-silent crying, to Dina's breath gargling in her throat as her weak lungs struggled to draw air. As I tried to re-create those sounds, those days, I felt as if they inhabited me, that my body and heart were living there and not in Paris. My body felt warm while I wrote, but afterwards, I was cold. I finished about two o'clock each day and when I lifted my head the sound of police sirens and cries from the street rose to my room on the fifth floor.

In the afternoon I returned to the present where there were ordinary tasks: I had my new trousers taken up at the Nigerian sewing shop across the street, I bought bath cleaner at the supermarket and ginger and honey at the African shop, I had massages with Tristan de Parcevaux, and studied French verbs on the internet. In the evenings I had a drink with Camilla or a conversation with Sylvie, and went to choir every Thursday night.

At choir I had learned that '*Qui a tué Grand-maman?*' was an environmental protest song and I was getting the hang of muttering through the wordy lines of a *chanson*. We had added a few more to our repertoire, '*J'en ai marre*', 'I've Had Enough', which I understood was a general angry complaint about poverty and hard work and lack of love, and a folk song, '*J'ai vu le Loup, le Renard et la Belette*', 'I Saw the Wolf, the Fox and the Weasel'. They were fun but the Bach cantata,

No 11, Choral 6, I loved and was now brave enough to say so. I didn't understand any of the German words, but the slow rich sound and rhythm reminded me of the swing of the incense crucible in the Friday night Benediction service of my childhood, the comforting weight of a belief I no longer had. The priest chanted and the faithful responded, incense filled the air. Here in the room in the rue Amandiers each note felt like a solid step underfoot, and each one inevitably led to the next one.

'*J'en ai assez de Bach*,' the young woman next to me grumbled. I've had enough of Bach.

'*Non, j'adore Bach*,' I defended. Marc nodded approvingly.

We started learning an English song too, Janis Joplin's 'Mercedes Benz', one of my all-time favourites. I had sung it when I was sixteen walking up the middle of the road one night on a weekend away from boarding school, my first time in Sydney without my parents, the first time I'd had a beer or two. I was with a school friend who had introduced me to Janis Joplin's torn soul, and we sang loudly in the quiet street. 'Oh Lord,' we yelled into the night.

'For Parti,' Marc said, and asked me to read it out loud with the correct English pronunciation. I read it, delighted to be the one who was the authority on a song for the first time, but when we sang it, I couldn't help but blend in with the French accents: 'Ma fren orll drive Porchez, Ay muz make amen.'

Marie-Louise had taken me under her wing and invited me home to practise French with her. She told me she loved French with all her heart and wanted to protect it – I understood – from my murdering ways. There was a kind of intensity in her that made me nervous though, and made me fear doing violence to her language. I had started to see that the passion to communicate mattered more to me than sounding perfect; I improved more with Sylvie because we wanted to understand each other more than we wanted to be correct.

I still practised French every day, listening to the news with a dictionary open on my knee. The words I learned weren't ones I could often use in daily conversation – *naufrage*, shipwreck; *sinstré*, disaster victim; *ravisseur*, kidnapper – but I could understand what was going on in the world. I liked listening to President Chirac in particular, not because I agreed with any of his politics, but because he enunciated so clearly. '*Français et Françaises*,' he would always start solemnly. French men and French women. I wanted to sit to attention, be one of the patriotic French women he was addressing.

I learned more useful words from Tristan de Parcevaux as he massaged my sore body. *Allongez-vous*, lie down; *l'hanche*, the hip; *la boite*, slang for nightclub – he sometimes told me about his weekends. It was an odd way to have French lessons, a young man and a half-naked older woman. I suspected there was more warmth and gaiety in the way we corrected each other's pronunciation than might have been the case if we were both sitting at a desk in a classroom. And then, on my second-last appointment, a 'thing' happened between us. It was unspoken and, if anyone had been watching, unseeable, but it was something. We were talking, I think it was about his desire to be a musician, and then there was a silence, but not because we had run out of things to say. It's strange that I can't remember our words but I can remember the quality of the silence. It was warm and there was a current of understanding or acknowledgment exchanged, a kind of energy. It wasn't sexual, not on my part and most likely not on his, but there was a tenderness, a knowledge that we had, for some brief moments, connected. There was something exposed in it, a vulnerability. We both hastily resumed our professional selves and pretended it had not happened, but I think of it sometimes. The way human beings can touch each other isn't something to forget.

*

Rousseau and Stendhal often wrote about their passionate feelings, but not about the delicate and transitory. They both seem to have lived most of their relationships entirely in their own heads – or is that what we all do? Perhaps every relationship is imaginary in that we construct a version of the person in our heads to fall in love with. Proust said that the loved person is 'a person most of whose constituent elements are derived from ourselves', but Stendhal and Rousseau both went as far as falling in love with women who were entirely imaginary, Stendhal with a fictional character – 'I went absolutely berserk, the possession of a real life mistress, then the object of all my desires, wouldn't have plunged me into such a torrent of voluptuousness' – and Rousseau with women he imagined himself: 'I created for myself societies of perfect creatures, celestial in their virtue and beauty [...] I spent countless hours and days, losing all memory of anything else.'

De Beauvoir wrote of her feelings for her friend Zaza when she was a teenager: 'I allowed myself to be uplifted by that wave of joy which went on mounting inside me, as violent and fresh as a pounding cataract, as naked and beautiful, and bare as a granite cliff.'

To my Anglo-Celtic soul, it sounds extreme – violent, naked, pounding cataract, cliff – and I want to shrug it away as excess. But just as I do, I suddenly remember the long-forgotten years as a teenager when every night I unfolded an imaginary love affair in fine detail in my mind. It's curious that I didn't think of it when I read of Stendhal's and Rousseau's imaginary lovers. Each evening I could hardly wait for the solitude of my bed to imagine the next intricate instalment of love and passion. There were jealous scenes, passionate reconciliations, slow kisses, piercing glances from dark eyes. Cliffs and pounding cataracts; I've had a few in the endless landscapes of the mind.

Still, still, I want to insist, what of the subtle and transitory? A boy's smile as he plays 'Flight of the Bumblebee' on his violin, a wordless conversation in a physiotherapy clinic, two elderly women helping each other in the street below, the accordionist and his song, beekeepers inspecting hives in a park.

*

I told Sylvie that my sons were coming to Paris. She smiled and said I always glowed when I talked about them.

'Do I?' I blushed as if she had found me out in some sentimental nonsense. I hadn't thought I was a woman who centred her life around her children; like Simone de Beauvoir, as an adolescent I had wanted to write, not beget children. She famously said that to have children was to keep playing the same old tune, 'but the scholar, the artist, the writer and the thinker created other worlds, all sweetness and light, in which everything had a purpose'.

I can remember saying something similar as a teenager: why be born simply to give birth in turn? But somewhere along the years I had realised that nothing mattered more. Writing mattered, of course it would always matter, but if I couldn't write again it wouldn't annihilate me. Probably.

'Sorry, I guess I'm like Madame de Sévigné.'

'Ah my dear,' she had written to her daughter, 'how I would love to see a bit of you, hear you, embrace you, watch you go by …' A familiar longing. But I thought of de Beauvoir and how she never found out that feelings as fundamental as disinterest, and even distaste, could be transformed into an adoration filling every cell of the body. I had not been interested in babies either when I was a teenager – I couldn't imagine what it was people saw when they exclaimed 'what a beautiful baby'. To me they looked red-faced, squashed, bald, and they smelled of milk and poo. I scorned women in my country town who didn't want to go anywhere or do anything except have babies. My mother had observed my lack of interest. After I told her, when I wasn't quite twenty-one, that I was pregnant, she dreamed that I got off the train in my hometown alone, blithely saying I'd left the baby behind in another city.

'*Non, non,*' Sylvie smiled. 'But anyway, it's the most important thing for children that their parents believe in them, don't you think?' she said.

I knew she wasn't talking about believing in their brilliance or beauty and I felt reassured. I had looked at them and recognised them and that was worth something.

Years later I lay on a small camp-bed alongside my dying mother. We, all her many sons and daughters, had been taking turns to stay with her in her last days and that night it was my turn. It was the middle of the night in winter and because the winters are cold in my hometown I had the blankets up to my chin. Her hospital bed was higher than mine so I couldn't see her face but I still lay with my face towards hers. It was quiet, not even the rubber-soled pad of nurses' feet checking other patients could be heard. My mother had not spoken for several days and I thought I would probably never hear her speak again.

Suddenly in the dark I heard her voice, low but quite clear. 'Kathy,' she said, 'Peter, Barney, Tim.' I held my breath. 'Patti, Kevin, Mary, Terry.' They were the names of all her children. All my brothers and sisters. She started again. 'Kathy, Peter, Barney …' All the way through to the last. And then again. And again.

She told me once that she used to chant our names to herself every night and if she stopped on someone's name she knew something was wrong with that one. One last safekeeping chant of the name of each child before she died.

*

On the day Matt was due we arranged to meet him at Gare du Nord. It's a vast station on the RER, the Île-de-France lines, and the national train lines as well as the Metro, and was being renovated at the time. We tried to give instructions by text.

'Outside ticket barrier, near Lafayette poster.'

'Which barrier? There's lots.'

'On stairs leading up to main concourse then.'

'?'

'Stay there, at top of stairs – can see u.'

And there he was, with his open face and warm energy, bounding towards us. His reddish gold hair had darkened as he'd gotten older and it was shorter, no more luxuriant curls, a grown-up man. He was taller than both of us, and more outgoing, more confident and at ease. He had been the sort of child who made friends in a moment and kept them for life, never doubting that he wouldn't be received with the same openness. He had always been ready for adventure, jumping off cliffs into mountain pools and riding his bike along fire trails *and* doing well at school, delighting teachers with his enthusiasm. I often thought, he likes the world and the world likes him. He put his arm over my shoulder as we walked.

That evening he went out after dinner and found Café Oz, an Australian-style café with corrugated-iron walls near the Moulin Rouge. Each evening afterwards he went out to chat to the Australian dancers who met there after performing at the Moulin Rouge and came home in the early hours of the morning.

Patrick arrived a few days later, slipping in from the airport and making his own way to rue Simart. He came in smiling shyly, trying to hide his delight as he had when he was a child and first realised how vulnerable it made him. It was a smile from a better world, I'd often thought, and it made me realise there was such a thing as a pure heart. He had been a child who loved knowledge, the kind that explained medieval trebuchets and how the pyramids were made and the history of architecture. He wandered the student *quartier* in the fifth arrondissement on the first day and went to the Museum of the Middle Ages on the boulevard St Michel. In the evening he drank wine with us. His narrow face and dark hair and his dark-coloured, understated clothes made him look typically French. I wasn't surprised when, a few years later, he went back to Paris by himself and came home with a French girlfriend.

The first night we were all together we played Scrabble in Camille's, but there were letters missing – someone had taken most of the 'e's – and we didn't get far. In the next few days both boys explored all over Paris, walking from Montmartre down to the Seine and all the way up to the Eiffel Tower, but when they were back at rue Simart, they took up all the available space with their bodies and backpacks and clothes and youth. I bought a coat-stand to shift the small mountains of hats, gloves, scarves and coats off the lounge chairs. It fell over with the lopsided weight nearly every time either of the boys hung their coats up.

I announced we were going to take them both to see the lights in the Champs Élysées.

'Okay, but I'll just go myself,' Patrick said.

'No, I want you to come with us.'

'Why? I can work out how to get there.'

'It's traditional. Parents take their kids to see the Chrissie lights in the Champs Élysées.' I knew how I sounded before I'd finished the sentence.

'You want us to be like little kids. Swinging hands.' Matt grinned. They were ganging up on me.

'Yep. That's it. Indulge me.'

We did go, rugged up in gloves and hats and scarves, and there were children everywhere, bundled up in woollen coats or parkas, their faces shiny in the cold. We walked up from Concorde towards the Arc de Triomphe with thousands of others, a stream of sightseers enchanted by pretty lights. The roundabout near Concorde had a halo of lights in the middle like a vast swarm of bees, and the gardens – where Proust's narrator played and chased his friend Gilberte – were festooned with golden shapes and patterns, and the chestnut trees all the way up the avenue glittered, a glorious silvery-gold blaze. Near the top we sat in a café on the terrace and had extraordinarily expensive hot chocolate. Up close in the chestnut tree in front of us we could see the lights strung along each branch.

'Is this what you imagined, us all together in Paris at Christmas?' Matt looked at me quizzically. 'It's not bad, is it?'

Patrick didn't say anything. They were both used to my attempts to make life fit a perfect imaginary version. A couple with three children walked past, one of them crying to be picked up. The father carried a large parcel and the mother was carrying the baby but they both looked down and made encouraging noises. A white terrier hopped around the child, trying to be of use.

'To our boys,' said Anthony, and lifted his cup of hot chocolate with one hand and, under the table, held my gloved hand with the other.

'It's cold,' said Patrick after a while. 'Let's go.'

'I've booked a proper house for Christmas,' I said. 'It's in Languedoc in the south-east. La Livinière.'

'Are we going to have a Christmas tree and presents?' asked Matt.

'If you are good children. A Christmas tree and a turkey and an open fire,' Anthony said.

*

Christmas on the farm was always hot. A branch was lopped from one of the tired pines in the top paddock and put in a bucket full of rocks to hold it up. There was anticipation and sticky-taped presents and Mass in the town church and a hot Christmas dinner in the hot middle of the day. Sweat on the vinyl kitchen chairs, roast chicken and roast potatoes and pumpkin and tomato sauce, wrapping paper and cards still lying about, the old plaster nativity scene with the paint chipped off Mary and Joseph, Christmas stockings from Coles. And then the long, slow afternoon. One year someone was given a plastic slide viewer of Switzerland and at first I thought it was magical. Snowy peaks and grassy meadows and chalets.

But there were only eight pictures and once I'd clicked through them a few times, that was it. It wasn't enough to transform a flat Christmas afternoon.

*

Even though it was in the south, it would be cold in Languedoc, which meant I needed a book for days around a fire. Perhaps a novel – I could leave the memoirists to themselves for Christmas. In WH Smith's bookshop I pulled out novels I had always wanted to read but not got around to and ones I thought I ought to read one day. None seemed what I needed. As I stood there in front of tens of thousands of books, there was a sense of looking for exactly the right tincture for some wound. I felt stiff, heavy. A sense of grief had been with me the whole time in Paris and I couldn't quite see what it was. The painful shoulder seemed an obvious metaphor; I was carrying something heavy that I needed to put down. I had to be quiet and still, let the right book come to me.

I moved over to the memoir section but still didn't see anything. Then just as I was about to give up I pulled out *My Father's Glory and My Mother's Castle* by the film-maker Marcel Pagnol. I turned it over – the back cover said it was about his boyhood exploring the wild hills in the south-east of France. Before I even opened it, I knew this was the book, that there was some revelation waiting for me. I started reading it as soon as I got back to the apartment.

We set off for Languedoc four days before Christmas, the boys' backpacks and our bags and presents stuffed in the boot. It was sleety when we headed off and there were two snowstorms on the way. Snowflakes blew towards the windscreen from a single, ever-disappearing point and snow powdered my head and shoulders as I ran with Anthony and Matt and Patrick into auto-stops for hot coffees and toilet breaks. I remembered photographs of us standing in the snow in the Blue Mountains, Matt in a cardboard box sled, Patrick not quite born yet. Snow on gums and bottlebrush and banksias.

It was evening by the time we reached the medieval steel crucifix marking the turn-off to the village. It wasn't snowing anymore and I could see La Livinière ahead along a winding road through the vineyards, its milk-coffee stone buildings and orange slate roofs looking like a perfected French village. It was lit by the golden light that comes sometimes after the sun has gone down, '*entre le chien et le loup*' – between the dog and the wolf – the light between two worlds. We bumped over a walled bridge and suddenly dropped back at least two centuries into cobbled lanes between stone houses, each with brightly painted shutters.

The house on the corner of the rue de la Républic and the rue Vieux Pressoir had three whole bedrooms to spread out into, a huge fireplace, and a kitchen with everything you could want including Scrabble and a pile of books. It was cold though, and the air had a faint stony shut-in smell of past human lives, sweet and sour traces of other meals, other habits. I pushed newspaper into the cracks around the windows and pulled the shutters tight. Anthony tacked a blanket over the door, and Matt lit the fire with pine-cones and roots he found in a basket next to the grate.

Next morning we ventured out, rugged up like bears. It took minutes to layer on the coats, hats, gloves and scarves, all tucked in tightly with no chinks to allow the cold air entry. Just up the hill behind our house was a Romanesque church, twelfth century, with arched buttresses joining it to the surrounding buildings. Nearby was a square with a medieval covered market and fountain and on the edge, a cemetery with its gravestones sinking into the earth. Back in the house I read that La Livinière had supplied wine to the Romans and the name had originally been Cella Vinaria, Latin for 'wine cellar'.

Although there were bare vineyards all around the village, with no resemblance to the wheat paddocks of my childhood, I kept thinking of the farm. The girl I was on the farm. Proust says the 'better part of our memories exist outside us, in the blatter of rain, in the smell of an unaired room or of the first cracking brushwood fire in a cold grate'. At the edges of rows of vines, bushes clung to the dry soil and the crumbly texture of the dirt brought the memory of walking barefoot in a wheat paddock, the wheat as high as my chest. The smell of wood smoke gave me my father chopping wood. The cold air on my face in the morning when I woke in the whitewashed bedroom brought back a winter's morning walking up the lane to school, frost on the grass. The sharp sweet eddies of lost childhood washed through me in a foreign place.

In front of the pine-cone fire we drank local red wine and played Scrabble. And read. Pagnol kept pulling me into the *garrigue*, the stony hills he roamed as a boy and, strangely, I was that boy as well. I breathed in rosemary and lavender and chalky earth and scraped my legs on a thorny bush, but it wasn't until I was almost finished that I came upon the sentences I had been waiting for. I went upstairs and sat on the bed and cried. Later that night, after I had gone to bed, I recalled the sentences and again cried. Anthony started reading Pagnol as soon as I finished – not because I cried, he didn't see my tears, but because I'd said it was the right book to read in this part of the country.

I went out the next afternoon and bought some holly and arranged it along the mantelpiece. I understood for the first time what it was really for. The fierce green leaves and red berries had only ever been Christmas kitsch before seeing them here in the bare coldness.

Anthony finished reading the book the day after he started. He has always been a passionate reader and will sit and read until he is finished whereas I like to take my time.

'Did you cry?' I asked.

'No,' he said. 'Why should I cry?'

'Because of these sentences,' I said. I opened the book and read them out: '*Such is the life of a man. The long childhood of joy is obliterated by unforgettable grief and sorrow. But there is no need to tell the children so.*'

To my surprise I started crying again. I had thought before it was the cumulative effect of the story, but even on their own the sentences pierced the pleasant surface of things. Patrick and Matt sat by the fire, reading, taking sips of wine, pretending they didn't notice.

Somehow Pagnol's words untied the amorphous sadness. Nothing can ever be turned back; childhood was long ago, and now my children's childhood was long ago. Sun, wind, the smell of harvested wheat, the caw of crows, bees in the almond blossoms, the peppery smell of rosemary – a child's heart knows and sees everything. In every life, the kingdom is lost again and again, it must be lost, and nothing will ever bring it back. But there is no need to tell the children so.

The next day was Christmas Eve. Anthony and I tried to make a traditional French Christmas dinner according to the instructions Sylvie had given me before we left Paris. We drove across the bare countryside to the markets in Narbonne, an ancient seat of Roman government, and found *dindes*, turkeys, staring balefully at us from dead eyes. They were too big for four people to eat so we selected a chicken instead and watched the woman hack its legs and head off and stuff them inside the body cavity. Then we found *marrons*, chestnuts; *moules*, mussels; and an extravagantly iced and decorated *Bûche Noel.*

I cooked the mussels in wine, Anthony prepared the chicken and roast potatoes and green beans, then we sat around the table on Christmas Eve and ate our Christmas dinner in a village in the south of France. Afterwards, at midnight, we toasted each other with champagne and then, in the middle of the night, I rang my mother in Australia. It was already a hot Christmas morning there.

EIGHT

JANUARY

I, too, was taking part in the effort which humanity makes to know, to understand, to express itself: I was engaged in the great collective enterprise, which would release me forever from the bonds of loneliness.

Simone de Beauvoir

Back in Paris it was cold and still, the light flat, the kind that robs everything, even Paris, of beauty. The sky was whitish-grey, without the drama of distinct clouds. Buildings looked grim, the chestnuts and plane trees in parks were leafless, people hurried by dressed in black or dark grey, rubbish overflowed from public bins as if the garbos thought it wasn't worth picking anything up in this light. I remembered Degas, 'Light is my consolation', and thought, it's more than consolation, it's salvation. I tried not to long for a hot Australian summer day: soaring blue sky, bare arms, sweat, squinting eyes, dancing sunlight on waves.

And then on the night before the year changed, it snowed. During the day clouds had started to form out of the white blur, clouds with the tell-tale brownish hue I recognised from winters in the Blue Mountains. I stood at the balcony doors with Patrick in the late evening – Matt and Anthony had gone to see a film – as the flakes started to fall. At first the snow was sparse, dotted over the buildings and the night sky, but it soon filled the air with soundless, moving whiteness. When we looked upwards, the snow seemed to be coming from a point of infinity, when we looked downwards, the *tabac* neon sign over the road gave the flakes a reddish glitter. We watched the Great Silence as it drifted like poetry or grace through the dark, and then we stepped outside onto the balcony in the sharp cold and saw the crossroads below become whiter and whiter until the roads were smooth, and parked cars, a fire hydrant and rubbish bins became simplified, essential shapes. We stood shoulder to shoulder on the cold balcony, neither of us speaking. The snow fell more thickly still, it was midnight and there was no traffic and the streets in either direction were perfectly white, flawless.

'I'm going to make the first footprints,' said Patrick. He went inside and grabbed his coat and ran down the five flights. I stayed shivering on the balcony and watched him walk across the crossroad, once and back again, making clean sharp footprints. They were distinct even from five floors up, human footprints in the snow, the brief trace of a journey, clear just for those moments until more snow or other traffic obliterated them.

I don't understand the mysteries of the human heart and why it reacts the way it does, but I can't imagine the day I will forget my son's footprints in the snow.

*

Something had shifted in La Livinière. The weight on my shoulder had a clear outline, which didn't mean that it had gone, just that I could see it. Childhood had disappeared forever and I had been too immersed to grieve it when it happened and, in our culture, there are no rituals to acknowledge it. When

I had watched, in Matt, and then seven or so years later in Patrick, the slow ending of childhood, I felt each time not just the loss of being able to hold them endlessly in my arms, the physical delights, but the loss of daily actions whose necessity I couldn't question. It wasn't until after they were gone that I realised there is a deep assurance in actions that don't need to be questioned; I never had to ask myself if I needed to feed this child, or keep him warm, or stop him from running across the road. I understood then that initiation ceremonies – incisions, separation, secrets – were as much for the mother to let go of the assurance of necessary action as for the child to step through into his own world.

Pagnol and de Sévigné are the only memoirists who had anything much to say about it. 'I confess that the rest of my life is covered in shadow and gloom when I think that I shall spend so much of it far from you,' de Sévigné writes to her daughter, Françoise. And, 'Three years ago today I experienced one of the deepest sorrows of my life: you went away to Provence, and you are still there. My letter would be long if I wished to unfold all the bitterness I have since felt in consequence of the first one.' I have to admit it starts feeling manipulative. She's clingy, and truthfully, I have too strong a sense of my own separateness to hold on so tightly to someone else, even a child.

Montaigne wrote at length on educating children but he had little to do with his own child because – it pains me to say it – she was a girl. We know Rousseau abandoned his. Stendhal didn't have children and didn't like them, even when he was a child himself, writing of his companions at school, 'I hadn't met with the gay, friendly, noble companions I had pictured to myself, but in their stead some very selfish young brats'. De

Beauvoir didn't have children either and, at least in her memoirs, had both an ideological and innate distaste for them.

I don't mind about Rousseau and Stendhal, but in Montaigne and de Beauvoir, because I love them both – Montaigne more than de Beauvoir – their lack of insight into what it means to love and to bring up a child bothers me. I don't want to admit to limitation in either of them, and yet to not value through experience or imagination the poetry of a teenage son making footprints on a snowy crossroads at midnight seems a serious lack.

*

The following day was New Year's day and Patrick was leaving for Amsterdam. His university course had not started yet, but he wanted to find his accommodation and his bearings in Amsterdam first. He had to go out to Port de Bagnolet on the edge of Paris to catch the bus, so Anthony decided to go with him on the Metro to the bus-station, just to make sure he found his way.

Matt and I walked down the five flights of stairs with them. When we reached the street there was still snow on the edges of the road, slushy and dirty, and light snow was falling and dissolving as it landed on our heads and shoulders. Patrick carried the large Kathmandu backpack we had given him for his eighteenth birthday and was wearing an overcoat and scarf and woolly hat. He had the beginnings of a beard, a smudging down his cheeks and chin, and his eyes were alight with the beginning of an adventure. He looked like any traveller down through the ages, rugged up against the winter cold, carrying his possessions on his back. As I hugged him goodbye I felt the rough woollen fabric of his coat and his slight body underneath.

He and Anthony walked away and then, at the corner, Patrick paused and turned, his backpack swaying. The snow was starting to fall more thickly.

'The scholar trudges off through the snow to continue his studies in Amsterdam,' he said, and grinned.

He turned back and continued down the hill to the Metro with Anthony, and Matt and I ran back inside and up the stairs. By the time we had got to the French windows, they had both disappeared.

Matt had a video camera with him in Paris and one day he shot Anthony and me as we sat on the couch talking. As soon as I realised the camera was on, I could feel my lips moving in strange shapes. I said I was frightened of cameras. He turned the camera on himself and said wryly, 'Why is she afraid of cameras? I am not afraid of cameras.'

When he played it back I saw how distorted I looked and how natural he was, his mouth and eyes smiling, his face open to anyone's gaze. I wondered if I knew only how to look, not how to be looked at.

Matt was the next to leave Paris. The film funding that he had been waiting on had come through and he had already shifted into production mode, sitting in front of his laptop for hours, sending emails and writing notes. I remembered when he was a child how he tried to organise Anthony and me, sitting with his arms out on the table; okay, so what time are we leaving? What do we need to take? Let's make a list. He caught a flight back to Sydney and then there were only the two of us.

In the quiet of no more boys, we lay on the couch in each other's arms. I could see the buildings across the road over Anthony's shoulder and I thought, there is a gap in each of us but we have started to grow around it, like gum trees carved for a bora ceremony grow back around their cuts. This new shape with its ridges and hollows is part of us now.

Then Anthony left for a couple of weeks' work back in Australia. I was in Paris alone. I settled down to writing the first morning with a sense of limitless time, a rare experience. I have hardly ever been alone in my life, born into a family where there were already three brothers and one sister, and then another brother in twelve months, then a sister and finally another brother. Five boys and three girls, and we all knew our place in the order. A few years after living in Paris, when my mother died, after her night chant of our names, we all stood at the altar at her funeral, shuffling into the correct order with unspoken knowledge and we all laughed at our private coordinates.

I'm fifth from the top. There are not a lot of roles left for the fifth. I wasn't particularly good, meaning I wasn't inclined to serve others, and I wasn't pretty – freckles and red hair were both disadvantages – but I was considered 'brainy' as it was called then.

De Beauvoir too thought her future lay in her love of knowledge rather than in being good or pretty, both of us influenced by Jo in *Little Women* whom de Beauvoir considered 'superior to her sisters, who were either more virtuous or more beautiful than herself, because of her passion for knowledge'. I didn't think I was superior, and both my sisters were also brainy – and pretty – and it didn't make me want to be a scholar. Even as a child I knew I wanted to write books. I remember thinking one day out on the farm, I want to do for readers what writers do for me; make a world in their heads.

The patterns of family, or lack of it, formed all the memoirists as much as time and place. Neither Madame de Sévigné nor Rousseau had brothers or sisters and both lost their mothers as children; Stendhal had a younger sister but he too lost his mother as a child; de Beauvoir had a younger sister, and Montaigne, I've just discovered, was one of eight! He doesn't mention them, except to say he has four brothers, but I can see now that he understands the difficulty of knowing who you are when there are so many other opinions about that. And the difficulty of knowing what makes you part of the family and what makes you distinctive amongst so many.

There is such a strong desire to be like other people – I listen to teenagers walking past my building from their school at the end of the street saying 'Same, same' eagerly as they listen to each other's lives – but equally, a need for difference. Sometimes I wonder if writing, especially memoir, isn't just a way of doing that: noting similarity and finding distinction. I'm thrilled to find Montaigne one of eight; I'm relieved to have Stendhal share my prissy reaction to crudeness; I recognise I don't have the quick wit and sharp tongue of de Sévigné; I recoil from sharing Rousseau's self-deceit; and with de Beauvoir, it's 'same, same' all the way through as I read her childhood.

As children and teenagers, Simone and I both liked embroidery but not sewing, couldn't sing in tune, loved reading above all else, suspected the existence of another parallel reality, were 'no good at jobs requiring finicky precision', were thrilled to join a library and were overcome by the endlessness of books to choose from, wanted briefly to be a nun, had an existential experience of 'Here I Am', dreaded Hell and often imagined how terrible it would be, identified with Jo as clever but not good or pretty, had detailed sexual-religious imaginings based on public humiliation and degradation – hers involved being a half-naked royal slave stepped on by a tyrant, mine being a half-naked martyr tied up in a square and taunted – experienced a sense of pride in having our first monthly bleed, wanted to be a writer, had 'a happy disposition', disliked loud voices and coarse language, liked to make public everything that happened to us, were transported by beauty, especially the beauty of Nature, lost God at thirteen, fantasised long romantic stories with fictional lovers, felt sorry for adults because they led 'a monotonous existence', had an insight that the future was for our own making.

Nothing in this list is remarkable, only that two women born at different times in different cultures and classes shared the same collection of traits. I imagine that millions of others do too.

*

What else needs to be said about de Beauvoir? In my twenties, I thought of her as part of my generation, a contemporary, but she was much nearer to my grandmother's age. She was born in 1908 and yet when she died in 1986 it felt as if one of us had died. She was brought up in a bourgeois family in Paris, a family with money at first, but they came down in the world. She had a sister, Hélène, known as Poupette, and they attended a Catholic school. She was devoted to her faith until she was thirteen, when she stopped believing in God. In June 1929 she met Jean-Paul Sartre, with whom her name would be forever linked. She loved other men – and women – but he was always central. She wrote in *The Second Sex*, 'one is not born a woman, one becomes one', and in the 1970s her star rose as a heroine of feminism and Sartre's faded – at least with women – but she always put him above her. She wrote her most famous novel, *The Mandarins*, the year I was born.

Although I was raised in an uneducated family on a poor farm in Australia and she grew up in a bourgeois apartment in boulevard Raspail and then rue de Rennes in Paris, when I read *Memoirs of a Dutiful Daughter*, it felt as if I were reading my own story. It could sound absurdly vain to say that, but I only mean my inner life was so similar to hers as a girl that it makes me think there must be 'types' who resemble each other closely despite vast differences in background, education and class.

I decided to meet Simone de Beauvoir for coffee at Les Éditeurs in the Carrefour de l'Odéon, because it's lined with books. She wouldn't like her old haunts, Les Deux Magots or Café de Flore, these days as they are more likely to be the haunts of tourists than intellectuals, and anyway, I want to be somewhere *I* feel at home. I'm nervous enough as it is. She walks in wearing a stylish grey suit, self-possessed and unsmiling. I feel as if I have to establish my credentials, that she will have no patience with me if I try to connect with her emotionally. She orders a short black and asks me about the book I have on the table.

'It's Annie Ernaux's *Une Femme* – about her mother's death. I liked your book *A Very Easy Death* about your mother as well – and of course, *Memoirs of a Dutiful Daughter.* You might think it strange – I'm from a different class, totally different family patterns – but I recognised so much of myself in you as a girl.' I blurt out as much as I dare, not wanting to annoy her.

But she's interested in the fact that so much of my inner life as a young woman was the same as hers and points out there were similar cultural influences of Catholicism and, of course, being women. I want to say that our ways parted when we became adults, that I had babies and continued to study and write more slowly, but that I didn't feel disempowered bringing up children. But she is the woman who said, 'Women should not have the choice [to stay at home and care for their babies] precisely because if there is such a choice, too many women will make that one.' If I admit anything I will be relegated to the ranks of the misguided.

'May I ask about Sartre – how much did admiration underpin your love for him?' I ask instead.

'He was my double in whom I found all my burning aspiration raised to the pitch of incandescence,' she responds. It's what I thought she might say but it still sounds unexpectedly intense. Although I admire him deeply, I can't imagine speaking of Anthony in that way, not aloud at least. I show her a photograph I'd found of the two of them, Simone and Jean-Paul, working together in Café de Flore. She picks it up and smiles with real delight. I'm bowled over by the way her face changes, all the severity is gone, her eyes crease and she looks girlish. There's a certain closeness between us, but still a sense that de Beauvoir is in control. She is more friendly now, but I will not be one of her chosen ones, I suspect because I have nothing to offer her that she doesn't already have. We say we must meet again, but no date or time is set.

*

I made a balcony garden when I first arrived at the rue Simart. A tiny plot of earth. I had never lived in an apartment before I came to Paris so I wasn't sure how it was done, how to just live indoors. I recalled that de Beauvoir as a small child had loved creating a world under the table in her family's apartment, but I wasn't used to enclosure. The childhood farm, even though it was the smallest in the district, still stretched out in every direction, so that every time I looked out, stepped out, there was earth and sky.

My mother tried to make a garden on the farm, to make the world smaller, prettier. The yard was bare dirt during droughts and overgrown with marshmallow grass when it rained, but over the years my brothers dug flower plots for her. She planted stocks, pansies, poppies, sweet-peas and geraniums and we all helped bucket water to them in the long summer. We knew the flowers were some kind of talisman against harshness, we could see it on her face as she gazed at the sweet-peas in the evenings and exclaimed about their scent and their delicate colours, mauve and pink and white.

The yard in the Blue Mountains was mostly native bush, gum trees and grevilleas, bottlebrush, banksias, ti-tree, and there was a creek at the bottom, but near the house there was a rough lawn and garden beds. In breaks from writing, I wandered around with a cup of coffee in one hand, pulling out weeds, and after a while realised I found it soothing. I planted the same old-fashioned flowers as my mother, and raked endless gum leaves and pinched laterals in the tomatoes and, in the spring, picked pansies and stocks, but the weed-pulling was more satisfying than anything else.

Voltaire said at the end of *Candide*, after all trials and foolishness, the only useful thing to do was 'to cultivate a garden'. In Paris I bought window-boxes and hooks and dirt and geraniums and hung my garden on the balcony railing. I felt as if I were planting myself as I put the soft-leaved cuttings in the dirt. I like geraniums – they were the only flowers in my mother's garden that lived through droughts when everything else had died. When I read the bleak Henry Lawson story 'Water Them Geraniums', telling of a woman living in hardship in the country, I knew what it meant. Keep one thing alive at least, resist the forces of desolation.

Here in Paris, geraniums were simply pretty. Mine weren't flowering yet, I had to wait until spring, and because my garden was so high up, I worried at first that the bees might not find them until I found out bees didn't like geraniums anyway. I tended the plants with care, watering them once a week and turning the soil over with a kitchen fork. Because it was a garden on the fifth floor and with fresh-bought dirt, no weeds appeared. I wondered if the geraniums would survive the cold, but in January other balconies had pots out so I left mine out as well.

I still missed the bush though, especially in the cold. I remembered the coastal bush in Sydney, foreign to me when I was a young student as everything is when you haven't known it in childhood. There were ruffled paperbark and lilli pillis and Moreton Bay figs with dangling buttress roots clinging to sandstone. A country almost impossible to imagine in Paris. I thought of the child Stendhal saying to his aunt, 'So there's a country where orange-trees grow out in the open?' He was talking about Provence, not Australia, of course, but it's the same astonishment that there are places where nature does unimaginable things. Fig roots melting onto sandstone as they spread out to find enough nourishment on rock, wild fruits that I didn't dare taste, seed pods shaped like devils.

In rue Simart, I had the photograph of Baron Rock on my writing desk – it is always within sight when I write. Years ago

I had written on the back, 'This is a photograph of my heart.' When French film-maker Agnès Varda said, 'If we opened people up, we'd find landscapes', I knew it was true. Inside me, even on the outside, it feels sometimes that there are the low hills and plains and dry creeks of the central western country, Wiradjuri country west of the Blue Mountains. It doesn't feel as if it is located in my mind, but in my body, imprinted as if pressed on wet clay, and when I look at that country it is as if I am looking at myself. And yet I don't, and probably couldn't, live there. I found myself thinking of it often in the rue Simart and I had to wonder then, what am I doing here, so far away from my own landscape?

*

When I was a teenager I went for long walks across the countryside, sometimes with brothers and sisters, but more often alone. It was my only chance to be solitary, not talking or walking with anyone, with only paddocks and scrubby gum trees around me. I climbed over boundary fences, carefully lifting the barbed wire, and walked across foreign paddocks and up into the hills owned by a neighbouring farmer. Sometimes I found things: a buzzing swarm of bees hanging in a wattle tree, fossils embedded in stone in a creek bed, a goanna, but mostly I just walked. My mind roamed, I saw a kookaburra on a fence post, felt the wind in my hair, listened to the soft shirring of she-oaks, learning that most of life happens on the inside.

Montaigne says we should have family and home and health if we can but 'we should set aside a room for ourselves, at the back of the shop, keeping it entirely free and establish there our true liberty, our principal solitude and asylum'. I think I was starting to make that room then as I walked across the paddocks, but before I was twenty I had met Anthony and lived with him and our babies and a dozen others in large share houses. Montaigne argued we don't need to live alone to have a room for ourselves at the back of busy lives, but I think I didn't have enough time to put up the framework for mine or find its shape. I lived for a long time out the front in the shop, which was full of delights. Here in Paris was the first time I was alone again since wandering across the paddocks in my childhood.

The threads connecting me to others were still in place. The row of hand-made Christmas cards from friends hung on string across one wall in the rue Simart. There was the drawing from Phil, the cartoonist, and the note from Theo and his father, and the cards from Jean-Jacques and from Camilla, and the tiny plastic Christmas tree with a present for Vicky when she arrived back from seeing her family, and one for my niece when she came back through from Germany. Outside, the women in the *boulangerie* across the road knew me and we had a chat each time I went in there. I only had to say '*comme d'habitude*', the usual, and they would carefully wrap my *framboiserie* in a paper pyramid each day. A vegetable-seller at one of the stalls in the markets knew me too, and the waiter at Café de la Place.

At choir, Marc offered another English song, David Bowie's 'The Man Who Sold the World'.

'*Pour Parti*,' he said again, and asked me to explain it to the choir.

I had no hope of deconstructing Bowie lyrics in French so I told them it was *surréaliste*, that it didn't really make sense at all. Marc smiled and everyone nodded thoughtfully. I had become the authority on English song lyrics.

Each week we tried the Bach cantata, which I still loved and which everyone else still grumbled about. Its yearning richness stirred some longing in me and I could feel my voice giving in to the notes. One evening as I sang happily, I suddenly realised everyone was leaning in and following my voice. I was the one keeping the tune! In my chest and throat the rich notes rose and held, reached down again, held. For the first time in my life I felt the notes and their unfolding inside me like soft round fruit, plums or peaches, in my mouth. For this one glorious song, '*Nun lieget alles unter dir*', I was necessary. I looked up the words: 'Now everything is subject to you.'

I still met with Sylvie every Sunday morning, always sitting in the same place in the window at Le Relais Odéon and we smiled with delight when we saw each other. Sometimes we talked politics and one day I told her of the shameful refugee camps in the desert in Australia. Then she told me that when she'd had a job interview at a finance firm, the employer, seeing her dark skin, said the criteria had changed and she was no longer suitable. She explained that because her name was French, they hadn't realised until they saw her that she was not white. Other applicants with African or Arabic or Indian names would have been screened out already.

I said I had thought that Paris was not racist, that it had welcomed the African-Americans right back in the 1920s and 1930s and later, when they were still segregated in their home country – what about Josephine Baker and James Baldwin and Nina Simone?

'It's different if you are a singer or dancer or musician or painter. Or writer. All the rules are put aside in Paris if you are an artist,' she said, 'but for everyone else it's the same as anywhere. There are more racist places than Paris, but we are not immune here.'

Other times we talked about our families. I told her my father did not even get to high school and missed half of primary school helping out on his father's farm, but he always believed I could do anything I wanted. Sylvie told me her father, the diplomat, had directed her to have a sensible job so she had become a financial consultant, although this was not her dream.

There was a rhythm to our rendezvous, we were part of the scenery of Le Relais Odéon, and the young waiter knew us. I wondered what he made of it, the way I stumbled along in French one week, then chatted away in English the next. At times Sylvie would get carried away and speed up her French and I'd grasp maybe three or four words per sentence. Leap as I might, I'd fall flat in the gaps between. Sometimes I had to wait until the English Sunday to check what it was exactly we had been talking about on the French Sunday.

One afternoon I arrived first at Le Relais Odéon and was startled to see that it was closed and the interior looked sooty and disordered. There was a handwritten note on the door which said there had been an '*incendie*'. I waited until Sylvie arrived and we both exclaimed over the misfortune. We stood in the cold street at a loss, wondering where else we could meet. I suggested Les Éditeurs, a café nearby on the Carrefour de l'Odéon that I had visited with Anthony a few weeks before. We had both been drawn in by the name – 'The Publishers' – and inside the walls were lined with books, which customers could take out and read if they wanted. Sylvie liked it straight away and we settled in under the bookshelves and ordered our coffees.

It was French Sunday so Sylvie started. She talked about her brother who wrote poetry and how she admired his sensitivity. He too had been influenced by their father to choose a sensible career, but poetry was his love. Then we discussed writing songs as poetry and then singing and I talked about my choir. I said that this week I realised I was carrying the Bach song. That somehow I had slipped inside the song and let it come out of my heart and soul instead of standing outside it fearfully. It seemed like a kind of magic to me, not just my singing, but that human beings sang at all, that we had an instrument inside our bodies.

Singing and music were still something I knew so little about and were so powerful that they seemed like the activities of the gods. I had been to a musical exhibition at the Cité de la Musique during the week, where, as I walked around the museum, performers played musical instruments from different cultures and periods. I heard the harpsichord as Montaigne might have heard it, the instrument beautifully inlaid with mother-of-pearl, and the thrumming of African drums and tambours, and two violins singing Mozart. I'd thought as I had many times before that music was the highest gift. To me there was no doubt.

'Music is the highest art,' I said to Sylvie, 'the greatest gift.'

'But no, it's literature, of course. You remember when I first met you, I said it's the most important thing,' said Sylvie.

'No, you know I love books but I can accept music is the best. Music is the most mysterious – the effect, I mean – and it crosses all languages,' I replied.

I thought I had won the argument but Sylvie launched into a passionate defence of writing as the highest art. She said all writing could be translated, so it too crossed all boundaries of language and then she talked about her teenage years in Brazil and how she was always a stranger, how confused she felt, how her sense of self had been dissolved. The characters in books were her friends, their experiences, their conversations, were hers. Her thoughts, her awareness of her emotions, her sense of being in the world, were all detailed and shaped by reading. She spoke intensely, her dark eyes holding mine.

'*Je me connais quand je lis*,' she said.

I know who I am when I read.

Stendhal said 'a novel is like a violin-bow and the soul of the reader is the violin-belly which gives off the sounds'. It means that the words of a writer are only given their sound, their richness and fullness, in the soul of a reader. The vibration enters the chamber and amplifies and diffracts and reverberates according to the shape and size and texture of the violin-belly soul so that every reader, reading the same book, reads a different book. I would have liked to say that to Sylvie, but it was too complicated for me to say in French.

*

I wrote more of the story of Dina and Theo, setting up my laptop on the trestle table, I spoke French, I sang at choir and I went to concerts, but I had to do something about the shoulder, back, rib and neck pain. It had not abated at all despite revelation, or despite knowing that it wasn't fatal. The internet self-diagnosis sites informed me the pain would abate but that it would take up to two years.

I was still going to Tristan de Parcevaux and swallowing painkillers to get through each day and, in the evenings, stronger ones to get through the night. Most days it was difficult to think, difficult to write and doing ordinary things like putting the washing-up away was slow work. One day I stubbed my toe on the wet, rolled-up carpet the street-sweepers used on the corners of streets to direct water along the gutters and whimpered. I was 'shamelessly grovelling at the feet of pain' as Montaigne said. My happy disposition was taking a beating.

I decided to go to the American Hospital on the edge of Paris where the doctors all spoke English. I trudged along the streets, lost for a while, but eventually arrived at my appointment where I was diagnosed with 'adhesive capsulitis', or frozen shoulder. I could put up with it and it would go away in time, or I could have a series of cortisone injections to stop the pain and then exercises to restore movement.

I made an appointment for the first injection. Suffering with patience might be a good thing, but I'd reached the end of my small allotment. I couldn't help agreeing with Montaigne that 'without health all pleasure, scholarship and virtue lose their lustre and fade away' and that 'no road leading to health was too rough or expensive'.

A week later I was back out at the hospital where a rheumatologist gave me the first injection. By the next day, the pain had reduced dramatically, not gone altogether, but enough to make the days seem bearable. Under the rheumatologist's direction I booked into a physiotherapy clinic in the sixteenth arrondissement for twice-weekly sessions, to start after my second injection if all went well.

I did feel as if I had failed some test, that I ought to have been able to put up with what, in the scheme of suffering, was minor, but I've long been suspicious of the doctrine that suffering was good for the soul. I'd been afraid to say it out loud, having a superstitious fear of the Fates who like to knock down anyone who defies them, and then I found brave Montaigne saying, 'I disclaim those incidental reformations based on pain.' He suffered a great deal of pain through illness and there was much less relief from pain in his day and yet he still didn't take refuge in it supposedly improving his soul.

Anthony had been in Australia for three weeks for work meetings and arrived back tanned and carrying tales of bright heat and bushfires and days at the beach. While he was still jetlagged, we rugged up in our overcoats and went walking in the Jardin des Plantes, a botanical garden near the Seine in the fifth arrondissement. I put my gloved hand through Anthony's elbow and felt the comfort of his body even though layers of wool separated us. Up on the hill we saw stylish bee-boxes labelled 'L'Hôtel des Abeilles', Bee Hotel, but no bees. It was too cold for gathering nectar. We wandered along a wintry path and on either side hardy marguerites and pansies gave splashes of colour. The pansies reminded me of my mother's garden, their dark red and violet and yellow faces so common and everyday, but if you looked closely, each one individual and beautiful. The branches of bare chestnut trees, twisted and knobbly from being pruned so often into neat cube shapes, reached over our heads in a long avenue. They looked like they were grasping for something, or ready to receive something from the sky with their deformed limbs.

NINE

FEBRUARY

Perhaps the one link possible between two souls was compassion.

Simone de Beauvoir

One chilly day in February I discovered St-Gervais, just behind the Hôtel de Ville in the fourth arrondissement. It was built in the mid-seventeenth century, a French baroque church with Greek columns, a cupola and painted wooden statues. Madame de Sévigné attended St-Gervais – it was only about ten minutes' walk from her house – and commented on the sermons in her letters, but I had only gone in because I was tired from wandering and wanted to sit for a while. At a side altar there was a continual 'Exposition of the Blessed Sacrament', a white host, or flat circle of bread, visible in the centre of an elaborate golden spiked monstrance with people praying in front of it. I sat there, musing, looking at the people kneeling, their hands clasped, their heads bent. What was happening in their minds? What stories were they telling themselves? In my childhood and teenage years I had tried to believe that the white round of bread was Christ and whenever I swallowed it in Holy Communion I tried to believe I was being filled with His spirit. Truthfully, nothing ever happened. Nothing at all.

I often went into churches in Paris. At first it was a tourist impulse not to miss any grand sight: Notre Dame and its rose windows, St-Sulpice and its Delacroix, the extraordinary looming dark splendour of St-Eustache, and then there were the free concerts in churches every Sunday, but there was also childhood comfort.

Every Sunday my parents took my brothers and sisters and me, dressed in our best dresses and shirts and hats, to Mass, first in the tin church up the road with its five pews on either side – we filled up two rows at the back – and then in the solid brick church in town. Mass, the ritual of sitting and kneeling and standing and listening, was tedious, but in the town church, St Patrick's, there was light coming through stained-glass windows, the smell of incense from Benediction and cold smells of concrete, white marble altars, the warm feel of wood under my legs, sweaty in summer, badly sung hymns, babies crying, other people's hats and lacy mantillas, Pauline Frogley in a wheelchair, short Mr Kelly with his tall blonde wife, paintings of soldiers hammering nails into Jesus' hands, prayer books with guardian-angel holy cards tucked in them, the sound of the priest's Irish accent.

Sitting quietly in church looking around was something I knew how to do.

That day in St-Gervais, I sat looking around, feeling critical and tired. There were a few elderly women praying and an anxious-looking man with his hands clasped; what good did they think it would do, talking to themselves in this old building? I kept sitting, resting. The monstrance was polished gold, the altar white marble. Candles flickered on the gold. I could feel the soaring space above and around me, the dim light from the stained-glass windows high above. And then I became aware of a peaceful calm beginning to ease into me. It came first to my breath, slowing it down, and then my ribs expanded, making more room for my heart, and then my body felt warm and my muscles eased. I became still, without thought, centred.

It's a state that arrives sometimes, which many people think of as spiritual. For me, it has never come when it's bidden by prayer or meditation even though I tried for years. In my experience it comes most often in the bush, although, like joy, it arrives when it will. It was the 'peace that passeth understanding' as sacred texts refer to it, deep and warm and calm.

I went back to St-Gervais a few weeks later in the early evening. I didn't want to admit it, but I realise that I must have been trying to find the switch to turn it on again. This time, as I sat on a woven chair in the church gazing at the ornate paintings and stone scrolls, I was startled to hear the sound of chanting. I turned around and saw double rows of robed and hooded monks walking up the centre aisle. For a split second I thought I had fallen back several centuries or was hallucinating, but they were contemporary and real. Their faces were somehow modern – I think it was their shaved chins and the glimpses of ordinary haircuts under their cowls. The rhythmic chanting was powerful, hypnotic, impossible to walk away from, male voices seeming to bind the earth together. Later I found a leaflet in the church, which explained they were an order of city monks founded in the 1970s. They didn't have an abbey but rented apartments because they believed they should not be attached to property and they worked at part-time jobs in offices and shops. But each morning, and at lunchtime, and in the evening, they came together and chanted in St-Gervais. On the leaflet, they had written, 'If you want to know what we believe, come and listen to us sing.'

None of this means that I experienced a renewal of faith in Paris. In fact the opposite happened. In the winter in Paris I finally admitted out loud for the first time that I no longer believed in any kind of God, not the Catholic one I was brought up with, nor the overarching Power, the Brahma, of eastern spirituality. At least not One who could or would intervene in any way. Perhaps Brahma had breathed out the universe and one day would breath it in again, but in the meantime there was just existence and I had to create my own meaning. I was sitting in the lounge-room in the rue Simart on the black couch when I 'confessed' it to Anthony. He grinned and said, 'Me neither.' We had reached the void at the end of clear thinking together, which was some kind of relief.

*

Being brought up Catholic is one of the few experiences I share with most of the French memoirists, all except Rousseau.

Montaigne held to his faith and defended it, but his mind is more that of a sceptic and a freethinker, particularly when he says he has 'a loathing for that distressing and combative arrogance which has complete faith and trust in itself: it is a mortal enemy of finding out the truth'.

Madame de Sévigné is described as 'pious'; she was brought up by an Abbé, her uncle, and often discussed sermons and theological questions in her letters. The loss of both her parents when she was young must have formed in her the idea that the world was fundamentally dangerous, she couldn't afford not to believe in some kind of overarching protection. She was by temperament someone who longed for meaning, but she also seems not to have allowed herself to think outside the intellectual framework she had been given. Today she might be a Buddhist, a rigorous one, or an agnostic, questioning everything with wry humour.

Stendhal and de Beauvoir were avowed non-believers, because faith, they both said, offended their intellects. With Stendhal though, I think it began with emotion. He heard a priest say that his adored mother's death 'came from God'. He was only seven years old and says he 'began to speak ill of GOD'. It's not difficult to see the proud, heartbroken boy raging against the God who had used His power to take all happiness from his life. It is perhaps not a long step from antagonism to disbelief.

In her youth de Beauvoir was a passionate believer, not just because of convention, but because of her desire for expanded experience, and it was for the same reason that she stopped believing: '"I no longer believe in God", I told myself with no great surprise [she was thirteen years old] I was too much of an extremist to be able to live under the eye of God and at the same time say both yes and no to life [...] As soon as I saw the light, I made a clean break.'

I remember the same moment, at the same age – except I didn't make a clean break. I was standing in the dim and dusty Infant de Prague hall, our school assembly hall, where Sister Julian, a short fat nun with a sensitive soul, was trying to teach choir. She was a plain woman and we thirteen-year-olds mocked her because she constantly fiddled with the fob-watch pinned under the folds of her habit, which made it look as if she were stroking her breasts. I had a soft spot for her because she had loaned me Frances Hodgson Burnett's *The Secret Garden.*

I loved the walled garden and the mysterious way it transformed everyone who went in there, but it didn't stop me from joining in the mocking.

It was a winter term and I was wearing an ill-fitting pleated uniform that made me look like a sack tied around the middle. Its hem was lumpy and it was always grubby no matter how many times I rubbed at stains with a washer. It is strange that the banal details of life sear themselves in memory when something life-changing is happening. In one moment, standing there in the hall, the thought appeared, 'There's nothing there. God doesn't exist.' On the outside, to anyone watching, nothing had happened; I was still an awkward pimply girl standing in a country hall, but continents had dissolved beneath me. I had caught a glimpse of the void and leapt back. It terrified me so much that I instantly changed the thought to 'What if God doesn't exist?' and told myself that it was all right, it was just a doubt. Doubts were admissible. I lacked de Beauvoir's courage, which meant it took me many decades to finally face what had happened that day.

Afterwards I went to church with determination. I tried to listen to the priest's words, to meditate on Christ's suffering, to imagine that I was consuming Him in Holy Communion, to feel His loving spirit. It wasn't a spiritual longing or that I had a devoted nature – I had neither – but a fear of nothingness.

When I left school I never went to church again as a believer; faith had disappeared that day in the hall, the loss quickly disavowed but still it had gone, and by the time I had left school, there was no real thought about letting all the practices of religion go. But the inner structures were still there, most of all an urgent requirement for overarching meaning. I know I wouldn't have lasted a moment with Sartre and de

Beauvoir and their friends who, as de Beauvoir says, 'laughed high-minded souls to scorn – in fact, every kind of soulfulness, the inner life [...] fell under their lashing contempt'.

*

I went to the physiotherapy clinic the American Hospital had recommended. The clinic was underground with windows along the top of the wall at ground level giving a view of feet walking past in the outside world. As I walked down the stairs the first day, and every time after, it felt as if I were entering a dungeon with instruments of torture spread out below me. There were benches, ropes, pulleys, chains and various pushing, pulling and walking machines with cogs and wheels. Elderly women and men wearing long underclothes – spencers and tights – slowly pulled on the chains and ropes or bent over benches in a genteel version of an Hieronymus Bosch hell. I had the dizzying sensation of stepping into my own inevitable future where life had slowed down and would one day stop. I wasn't even fifty years old yet. I wanted to turn and run.

'*Bonjour, Madame,*' each of the elderly men and women said.

'*Bonjour, Mesdames et Messieurs,*' I said. We were all in this together.

I stripped down to my tights and long-sleeved t-shirt and then was assigned one of the pulleys with chains and given a piece of stretchy yellow elastic and a chart with a series of exercises. I meekly pulled on the chains, unable to reach my arms more than a few centimetres from my body. My arm ached all over again. An old woman. I pulled on the elastic and tried to stretch my arms behind my back. I eased my neck sideways and back and forth, I rolled my hips from side to side. I thought afterwards that I never wanted to go back.

The dungeon was near the Metro exit at Monceau, which meant I had to change at Gare St Lazare and then at Villiers. St Lazare is a vast station and it was being rebuilt, the renovations requiring a long walk through a temporary corrugated-iron corridor to catch the connecting train. It was above ground so it wasn't warm like the underground corridors. It was, in fact, bitterly cold, colder even than outside in the weather.

Each time as I climbed the flight of steps to the corridor, I could hear the plaintive, singsong of a gypsy woman: '*S'il vous plai-aît, Monsieur. S'il vous plai-aît.*' Please, sir Plea-ease. Over and over, echoing down the tin walls. The sound alone twanged across my nerves. I could feel myself tensing, getting ready to do battle.

And then I rounded the corner and saw her. She was there every time, kneeling on the floor at the other end of the corridor. She wore long skirts and thick stockings and her black hair was pulled back into a bun – she would have looked at home in any of the last few centuries. She had three grimy children with her, one of them a baby in her arms, and they all sat on the concrete in the bitter cold. Her head and shoulders were mostly bowed and if she did look up, her dark eyes were plaintive.

The two older children, a boy and a girl, wore layers of gypsy clothes too, skirts and jumpers, but still they must have been freezing, sitting there on the concrete. They didn't run around or play or even speak. They had no toys or books, they just sat, unnaturally still and quiet. They both had the same thick dark hair as their mother and large dark eyes, although they rarely looked up.

'*S'il vous plai-aît, Mada-ame, S'il vous plai-aît, Monsieur. S'il vous plai-aît.*' Each vowel dragged out, the whining singsong grating on my pain-exposed nerves. She seemed to know, to be targeting me amongst all the hurrying travellers.

I felt hot and cold with discomfort and judgment. And a violent rage. How dare she make her pretty, dull-eyed children sit with her on the concrete in the freezing cold for hours on end? How dare she, more than anything, teach them to kneel before others? It was the tone that wormed into me every time, a tone that pleaded that she was inferior, and we, striding by on our way to work or to physio appointments, were fine lords and ladies who might take pity on her inferiority.

'Just shut the fuck up,' I muttered under my breath.

I looked at her children but I couldn't look at her. They sometimes looked up at me, their large dull eyes and beautiful faces almost Biblical in their sorrow and poverty.

I knew something of the culture and sociology of gypsies: none of the women were allowed to have any sort of education; practically none of the men could get any sort of work – who would give a gypsy a job? And I knew they were hunted from place to place – we don't want them cluttering up the edge of town or the ring-road with their trucks and caravans and clotheslines – but in those moments rushing along the corridor, I didn't care about any of that. I felt no compassion, no indignation at injustice, no rage against the powerful, only rage against her. I just wanted her to take her children home and teach them to stand up straight and look me in the eye.

When I came back from the dungeon two hours later, each time they were still there in the cold corridor.

*

'They have Mercedes-Benz at home, you know.' That's what people tell each other, reassuringly, about the gypsies in Paris.

*

There is a vast amount of inequality, violence – and cruelty – in the history of Paris. It seems close and immediate; real blood was spilled on these cobbles right under my feet. There was the day, Friday 13 October 1307, when the members of the Knights Templar were arrested in their walled retreat in the rue du Temple and tortured, and their leader, Jacques Molay, burned at the stake on a barge in the Seine. And St Bartholomew's Day in 1572 when Catholics massacred Huguenots in a bloodbath in the streets of Paris. And the months of the Terror from September 1793 to July 1794 when tens of thousands of heads were chopped off in the place de la Concorde and all over France. And the Prussian siege in 1870 when Parisians had to eat dogs, cats, rats and the zoo animals in the Jardin des Plantes to stay alive. And the rounding up and loading into cattle trains of Jews in the 1940s. And the day in 1961 when the police killed and threw into the Seine more than 200 Algerians who had been peacefully protesting against the war in Algeria.

It's a 2000-year litany of bloody battles, sieges, starvations, massacres, murders, tortures, beheadings, burnings at the stake, dismemberments – and every other means of causing extreme and detailed suffering. That's not to even mention the casual everyday violence of obscene wealth and vicious poverty; workers poisoned by the fumes in tanneries, babies being left in their tens of thousands on doorsteps, the rich galloping their carriages through the narrow streets, trampling underfoot any man, woman or child who couldn't get away fast enough. Madame de Sévigné describes it as if it were entertaining:

> Yesterday the Archbishop of Rheims was coming back from Saint-Germain in a great haste, like a whirlwind [...] They were passing through Nanterre, *trit trot trit trot*; they met a fellow on horseback [...] the coach and six horses knocked the poor fellow and his horse head over heels and passed over them so clean that the coach was tipped up and overturned. Meanwhile, the man and his horse, instead of amusing themselves by being broken on the wheel and maimed, got up again by some miracle and remounted, one on the other, and fled, while the lackeys and coachman and the Archbishop himself started to shout: 'Stop him! Stop the knave! Give him a good beating!' When telling this story the Archbishop said: 'If I had got hold of that rascal, I would have broken his arms and cut off his ears.'

Her flippancy is hard to interpret. I still can't decide if she was mocking the Archbishop, a supposed representative of Christ-like love and compassion, or is just amused that the man got away.

Montaigne is not ambiguous; in fact, cruelty is the one topic he is adamant about. His revulsion began when he was fifteen and saw an angry mob skin and 'joint' a man like a piece of beef and stuff his orifices with salt. And then came the Wars of Religion, a time of extreme violence that began after a massacre of Huguenots in the north-east in 1562 and spread all over France, reaching a horrific degree of violence in the Perigord where he lived:

> I live in a season when unbelievable examples of this vice of cruelty flourish because of the licence of our civil war; you can find nothing in ancient history more extreme than what we witness every day [...] If I had not seen it I could hardly have made myself believe that you could find souls so monstrous that they would commit murder for the sheer fun of it; would hack at another man's limbs and lop them off and cudgel their brains to invent unusual tortures, not from hatred or gain, but for the pleasant spectacle of the pitiful gestures and twitchings of a man dying in agony.

Unusual in his time, from his own nature and judgment he saw cruelty as the worst vice of all. 'I am so soft I cannot even see anyone lop off the head of a chicken without displeasure, and I cannot bear to hear a hare squealing when my hounds get their teeth into it.' And he makes a ready link between those who would be cruel to animals and cruelty to fellow humans: 'In Rome, once they had broken themselves in by murdering animals they went on to men and to gladiators.'

Even more, and sounding more contemporary than ever, he says: 'There is a respect and duty in man as a genus which links us not merely to the beasts, which have life and feeling, but even to trees and plants. We owe justice to men: and to other creatures who are able to receive them we owe gentleness and kindness. Between them and us there is some sort of intercourse and a degree of mutual obligation.'

As a young child on the farm I could witness violence, or at least its aftermath, without drawing back. Although it wasn't cruelty, which requires the desire to cause pain, farming practices meant the infliction of pain; sheep's throats were cut, chooks' heads were chopped off, cattle were branded with a burning iron, puppies were drowned, lambs and calves were desexed with a sharp knife. My father, who performed all these acts, was in fact a gentle man. It was part of what he had to do as a farmer, so he made sure that axes and knives were razor-sharp so that the act could be done quickly and cleanly. I can see him with the butcher's knife, scraping it this way and that on the whetstone, making sure it was surgically sharp.

I don't think I lacked fellow-feeling for creatures or, if I did, so did my brothers and sisters. We lined up, miniature Madame Defarges – four of us under six years old – watching my father cut the sheep's throat, disembowel it, hang it up on a hook like a large coathanger under the gum tree and skin it. The intestines were given to the dogs, who, in that moment, became unknowable wild animals, snarling as if they had never let us pat and cuddle them. And then one day, I couldn't bear to watch the throat-cutting – the bright blood darkening on the dirt.

It must have been about the same time that I stopped helping out with desexing. It was done with a quick cut of the lambs' testicles, the gonads were drawn out with claws on the other end of the knife, and then the tails were cut off both male and female lambs and tossed into a bucket. It was one of our childhood jobs to catch the lambs in the yard, bring them to the table nailed onto the fence and hold them with both legs forced upwards while my father did the cutting. In memory I can feel the lambs, the woolly back against my chest, my hands grasping the legs tightly. As I grabbed each lamb, I had a quick look to check they were females – the tail-cutting was slightly more bearable than testicle-cutting. And then, by the time I was eleven, I couldn't stand it at all. It was a task my father never insisted on once we said we didn't want to do it.

He was compassionate by temperament, and so was my mother. No creature, man or beast, ought to be hurt if you could help it. For my mother, religion and politics were founded on compassion. She was fiercely sympathetic towards anyone who was ill-treated in any way – Aborigines, refugees – and leapt to the defence of those without power, but it was also a thought-out moral position which she taught all of her children. It makes my rage against the gypsy woman all the more unforgivable.

*

It's probably not so strange that my thoughts were darker in the depths of winter. The cold and grey had seeped into my spirit. Even in the Blue Mountains, wintry for months on end, I hadn't experienced such long and dimly lit cold. I found waking in the dark especially dispiriting and even though it was past time to get out of bed, I often rolled over back into foggy sleep. When I woke again and saw the flat light on the chimney pots across the road, I took refuge in imagining sunlight and warmth in the back yard in the Mountains. Sun on the waratah leaves, on the eucalypts, on my face.

I crept out of bed and started writing later and later each day until, like a proper Parisian, it was 10.30 or 11 am by the time I sat at the trestle desk. I had almost finished what I'd been hoping would be a final draft, but I had thrown so much out that most of what I was writing was new and raw and would have to be rewritten. And there was the added pressure of Kit and Theo arriving the following month. I wanted to have it finished before they came and to let it compost for a few weeks, but the last section still wasn't coming. It was the part after Theo had left the Mountains to live in Melbourne with his father, seven years after his mother's death, and there were years to write about, dozens of visits. It seemed complicated; there were too many comings and goings. I needed to put aside the record, combine some visits, construct the reality of Theo arriving each time, our awkwardness with each other at first, the way he fitted back into our lives.

One afternoon, tired of sitting inside, I persuaded Anthony to come out to the Bois de Boulogne with me. The Bois is a 2000-acre park with lakes and woods and some cultivated gardens and pathways – not quite untamed nature, but large and wild enough for a wander. Sometimes the constructed world is enough to sustain, for months it can be enough, but then I need real air, dirt, trees and creeks. We had been out there a few times to row on the Grand Lac when it was still warm, Anthony doing most of the work, pulling strongly around the islands. This time we rented bikes and rode along the bitumen roads and then off along dirt lanes and paths through the bare oaks and chestnuts. There were muddy tracks, tangled undergrowth, briars, grasses, fallen branches, wild herbs – mint and yarrow. Because it was winter, there weren't many people about, not even the prostitutes who worked from vans along the roads leading into the Bois. The air was cold on our faces but it was exhilarating and I could feel my spirits lift.

We stopped at the Bagatelle, an English garden within the Bois, and had to leave our bikes to walk in. In France, an 'English garden' is one that is a natural messy garden; that is, without the clipped order, the fleurs-de-lys hedges and square trees of a traditional French garden. Its beauty depends on the colour and textures of leaves and flowers, more than on shape.

We came to a rose garden, which wasn't in flower except for the few odd blooms that always seem to come out of season, somehow given the wrong information about the weather and opening out anyway. The garden was in a basin, and we sat down on one of the benches so that we could look down on it from above. Each bed had a low hedge around it delineating the shapes and spaces. I wasn't thinking anything in particular, just looking at the distinct shapes of the gardens and the pattern they made, the way the squares and rectangles and crescents fitted together and how the spaces between them created their own shapes. As I sat there gazing, pieces of writing started to fall into place in my head. It was as if the shapes of the garden had given my brain an idea that I wasn't conscious of and set it to work sorting and shifting and arranging.

Anthony relaxed with his face up to the weak sun, his hands deep in his jacket pockets. We both sat there, an ordinary couple looking at a bare rose garden, neither of us speaking, while the last section of my manuscript came together in my head like bits of an airy jigsaw puzzle.

I don't want to say that writing is always like that, that nature just comes and writes things for me, that I am some sort of vessel, but every now and then, rarely enough, instructions appear that some part of me must be able to read, and I am grateful for that. That's all. I have been back to see the garden in the heat of summer – the scents of red roses and drunken bees stumbling about and every rose colour under the sun, apricot, burgundy, pink-tipped cream, striped, sunset orange – and it's just a pretty garden with intoxicating fragrance filling the air.

Back in the eighteenth arrondissement that night I had a glass of wine with Vicky at Café de la Place. I told her about riding in the woods and about the rose garden and how it had given me what I needed for my writing. She said that if I wanted more nature, why didn't I go to stay at her place at Lacapelle-Biron in the Lot-et-Garonne where she'd raised her two children. I said I might just take her up on that. It was the first time I'd heard the name of the village which has since become part of my life and part of my family's life.

Later I told her about the gypsy woman at Gare St Lazare, about the hunched shoulders, the bowed head, her children, her voice. *S'il vous plai-ai-aît, Madame, S'il vous plai-aît.* Such long plaintive vowels. I needed to confess how enraged the sound of her voice made me.

Vicky smiled in the way people do when you have given yourself away but didn't say anything so I had to keep going.

'She's … she makes herself inferior. In front of her children,' I accused.

'I know. I think I've seen her, the same one,' Vicky said. She was still smiling, but I realised it was because she too was going to confess. 'At the entrance to the Luxembourg Gardens. It's probably the same woman. With her drugged children?'

'That's what I wondered. They didn't play or even stand up; they just sat there. It was her kids sitting there in the cold and her tone of voice that got to me.'

'Yes, the whining sound. And the glazed eyes.'

We were silent for a moment, taking a sip of wine, looking at passers-by on their way back from the evening shopping with bags and children in tow. A perfect little girl in a blue coat carried a baguette over her shoulder like a rifle and her mother smiled down at her.

'You know, it made me feel violent.' I lowered my voice. 'I wanted to punch her.'

Vicky glanced at me, startled.

'So did I. I wanted to … to hit her, hard,' she said. 'Make her stop.'

We looked at each other in shame-faced relief, remembering the leap to violence in our chests. I felt as if I had been unmasked; it was a kind of freedom. And then we talked, back and forth, hardly stopping for breath.

'The gypsies are marginalised. It's not her fault.'

'Often they can't speak much French – they're from Romania. And mostly they have never been to school.'

'And probably no work papers.'

'The women have to support the whole family, or more, and they have learned only to beg.'

'How can the children learn dignity? Who is responsible?'

We both took sips of wine. I could feel the shame spreading in my body, a kind of stain starting in my heart. We were silent a bit longer than was comfortable.

'But why does it make us angry?' I asked finally.

'It's not the begging, it's her manner. There's something about being servile …' Vicky said.

'Servile! That's the word. That's it.' For a moment I was grateful to have an exact name.

We continued, often not looking each other in the eye, dodging around our judgment and the disturbing desire for violence, then tiptoeing towards it, trying to see why servility enraged instead of engendering compassion. If we two reacted like that, two well-behaved women from opposite sides of the world and different backgrounds, then we were, most likely, not the only ones.

'It's why I like defiant children,' I said. 'I get irritated with kids who won't argue back. They make me feel like a tyrant.'

That was getting somewhere near it, the unwelcome sense of being seen to have crushing power. It was a lump in the soul that neither of us wanted to have, and the gypsy woman had made us feel its cartilaginous shape. I thought of the bishop of Nanterre galloping over people in the streets of Paris. *Trit trot, trit trot.*

'*Madame, vous finissez?*' The waiter was picking up my glass. I nodded.

'I'd like another one, please.'

'And the same with animals,' said Vicky. 'It's why I like cats. They are never servile, but dogs can be.'

We both spoke with a mixture of shame and pride. Side-stepping towards it, shuffling back. We kept our voices low. Even though we were speaking in English I didn't want anyone at the next table to overhear us. It was there, whatever it was, in us both and it was not something for the general light of day, but it had marked us. I don't think I got very far with understanding it; it still feels like something of a knot, not large, but dark. Afterwards, when I returned to my reading, I couldn't find anything, even in Montaigne, to help me see it any more clearly.

TEN

MARCH

Our true self is not entirely within.

Jean-Jacques Rousseau

I finished a draft of the manuscript. It's always a relief to finish but this time it felt like perfect timing. It was two weeks before Theo and Kit arrived. Theo's mother had died more than ten years earlier, but I still didn't want to be writing about her – and him – right in front of his eyes.

I was relieved to have the last piece, the closing scene of the story: Theo and I were walking up the street from our house; I was teaching him a song I'd learned at choir: 'We are going/ Heaven knows where we are go-o-ing'. It was rough, there was work to do, but I knew there was a sense of the moment between us that I had wanted to re-create.

Every now and then, the perception of a moment is impressed so sharply in waxy memory that words can be formed in the indents. In the moment of perception I feel the clear imprint calmly, although, in recall, there is urgency, the effort to see each aspect of the moment: Theo's pale face and winning smile as he sings with me, the slope of the hill underfoot, the yellowish light filtering through snow clouds. Then I feel absorbed in the whole as if it is happening again, and in the end, there is relief – and pleasure – when the words are found. It feels as if the moment has not really been remade, but given form for the first time. Proust said that after he had written his first piece when he was a teenager – it was about glimpsing three steeples appearing 'like three birds perched upon the plain, motionless and conspicuous in the sunlight' – he had such a sense of happiness that 'as though I myself were a hen and had just laid an egg, I began to sing at the top of my voice'. I burst out laughing when I first read that, the image of the boy-writer singing like a chook who has laid an egg – oh my, I have just made something new from my own body! I remembered our scraggy chooks and their eggs in dusty nests under the wheat harvester, or on the seat of the old truck or, once or twice, a pullet dropping her first egg in the yard without any care at all. I liked scooping them up when they were warm and clean and fresh, and feeling them nestle, perfect in the palm of my hand.

*

Before Theo and Kit arrived, Anthony and I made a trip to Istanbul so I could have my passport stamped from outside the European Union. Our long-stay visas hadn't arrived in time before we'd left Australia, which meant we couldn't legally stay in Europe more than six months. It was a bit risky – and if we'd been African, very risky – but a trip outside the European Union would re-establish our legal status. It sounds extravagant to dash off to Turkey, but it was easy to book cheap flights with a local airline – one, as it happened, that was later grounded after one of its planes crashed into the Red Sea – and to find a cheap, hot-pink hotel in Istanbul. It was only for four or five days, just enough to leave a bright impression in the still grey days of March.

There was the tiled dome of heaven in the Blue Mosque and frescoed layers of religion in Santa Sophia, the mini-skirts and blue and black hijabs in the street, the rows of carpets with geometric patterns, flowers, birds, vines, and the carpet-sellers offering sweet apple-mint tea. The hawkers in the streets spoke French – '*Madame? Madame?*' and I answered, '*Non, non.*' We took a boat on the Bosporus to a Crusaders' castle and sat on the grass talking about the knights of France and England who had arrived here – was it to destroy Islam or simply for adventure?

At the ancient markets I saw baskets full of dates, nuts, grapes and figs and thought they must have looked the same when the knights strolled past, even when the first Christians before them wandered by wide-eyed. Afterwards we went to the sixteenth-century *hammam* with its crescent moons and stars, and we were steamed and scrubbed and rubbed and washed to pink newborn perfection. The air was cool on our baby-skin but the sky was high and blue and the light falling on stone walls was like the beginning of time.

One afternoon we visited the Topkapi Palace where the sultans of the Ottoman Empire lived and ruled. I traipsed through the rooms of the harem, the Courtyard of the Eunuchs, the Circumcision Room, the gilded bathroom of the Sultan's mother, and the Treasury with its diamonds and emeralds and pearls. In the early morning I woke to the muezzin's call rising and falling like a bird on unseen currents and felt as if I had fallen into a story.

By the time we got back to Paris, Istanbul felt like a kaleidoscope of colour and light, not quite something we had dreamed, but a tear in the fabric that had let another world in. The woman in the *boulangerie* across the road had noticed I hadn't been in for a few days.

'*J'étais en vacances à Istanbul,*' I explained and felt like a local. I was on holiday in Istanbul.

I remembered my childhood longing for difference on the endless days of the farm, to see something new, for something else to happen. Every day there were paddocks, and a dry creek, and a few gum trees and cattle and sheep, and Baron Rock and the shabby farmhouse. The seasons changed and work changed with the seasons, harvesting, shearing, ploughing, hay-making, the same every year. Outside the farm, there was school and church and shopping in town. When we drove in through the hills to town I looked up the valleys and wished I could walk along them, wished my father would take a turn off the road, a detour.

People too were the same. Everyone had a mother who stayed at home and a father who owned a farm and everyone was white. And always the same neighbours; they never moved away and no-one moved in, except once, for a year, a family of share-farmers. Rarely, a stranger arrived at the farm; once a man came selling encyclopaedias, and my brothers and sisters and I were so unused to difference we hid behind the water tanks to watch. The only real difference happened in books.

Here, strangers from all over the world walked past my door, there were detours everywhere I looked; countries with palaces full of fairytale treasure were only an hour or two away. I wondered if having difference so easily available meant that people born here did not have to long helplessly for elsewhere.

But then Rousseau always longed for an imaginary place, 'the castles in Spain' in which he could easily take up residence, and 300 or so years later, Annie Ernaux in a small French town says, 'When a child and teenager, I lived continually in dream and imagination.' Perhaps the longing for another imagined world is a condition that afflicts some people. It's as if reality can never yield quite enough. Perhaps it comes from endless desire, the hungry ghosts of Buddhist mythology who can never be filled. For Ernaux, by an 'inverse movement' as she called it, instead of imaginary life, the reality of her own life became the material of her writing. The same thing has happened to me.

*

In one way I have more in common with Annie Ernaux than any of the other memoirists, even de Beauvoir, because we are alive at the same time. We share the globalised world, the flood of information and communication pouring across us: television, mobile phones, satellites, the internet, Skype, Twitter, the mix of cultures, ideas, peoples. We also have in common an uneducated provincial background – and haven't returned to it except in our writing.

What do I know about Ernaux?

She was born in 1940 in a working-class family in a small town in the Seine-Maritime department of Normandy. Just after the war, her parents moved twenty-five kilometres to Yvetot, a cold town on a windy plain, where they ran a café. She was an only child, her older sister dying of diphtheria two years before she was born. Her father, who had been a farmhand, and mother, who had worked in a factory, strove to give her every advantage, although her mother couldn't help saying, 'You cost us a lot.' She studied at Rouen University, married, had two children, divorced. She lives in Cergy-Pontoise, a satellite town near Paris. Her books, *La Place*, about her father; *Les Années*, 'a sociology of her self'; *Une Femme*, about her mother; and *Retour à Yvetot*, a return to her hometown, explore daily living and the tension between class and writing. Ernaux has spent her writing life reclaiming her past, her father and mother, her class background. She's the only memoirist I've read entirely in French.

*

In *La Place*, Ernaux writes of her father: 'He ferried me from home to school on his bike. From one bank to the other, come rain or shine. His greatest pride, indeed his mission in life: that I should belong to the world that had spurned him. All the while singing "round and round we row".'

I thought of my father who did not even get to high school and who was dedicated to giving his eight children entry to a world that would spurn him. He had a short, stocky, peasant build and a harelip, which made him rather shy and unconfident. He had no pretensions, did not want fame or riches, his family and his faith were all that he required, but he believed the ability to think and write well were important because they could be used to persuade others of the value of living truthful lives under God. We had the smallest farm and the largest family in the district, but by going without comforts – no inside toilet, no toilet paper, no heating except for an open fire in one room, no running hot water – he was able to send us all to the convent high school in town.

One day he and I argued about some idea – I can't remember what it was but it must have been a religious idea as that was the only kind of idea that really mattered to my father – and I used my superior education to demolish him. I was dismissive.

I was in my twenties by then and had been to university. I don't remember what I said; what I remember is the crushed look in his blue eyes as he replied in a hurt voice, 'You don't have to come the Queen of Sheba with me.' Even though I was ashamed, I thought, what an odd, old-fashioned expression to use.

I'm not sure where to meet Annie Ernaux for coffee. Even though she lives outside Paris, she would know it better than I do. In the end I want to show her a place with an Australian atmosphere – and where I can have a good coffee – so I'm back at Café KB, the same place I met Montaigne. There's a *brocante*, a second-hand fair, in the rue des Martyrs and the stall outside the café has old ironwork, kitchen appliances, embroidered tablecloths and lamps piled on tables. Annie Ernaux is waiting for me when I arrive, sitting inside at the window watching the crowd. She is elegant and still beautiful, high cheekbones, blue eyes, thick hair dyed a light copper. She looks refined, sensitive, well-groomed, middle-class, nothing about her appearance gives away her origins.

I sit down and put my copy of *Une Femme* on the table.

'It was the first book I read in French,' I say, forgetting about *Le Petit Prince*. 'I read it first before my mother died and found it …' I stop to search for the right phrase, 'so precise, so true. I like the way you name things without poetic effect, you restore their power to move the reader.'

She listens intently and I can see she likes what I am saying. She says that she wants her words to be understood by the people she comes from.

I tell her I loved her 'washing with bleach' story and recount my 'dirty girl at the water-bubbler' story. She smiles; we understand each other.

I change topic, wanting to discuss de Beauvoir because I know she is an admirer. I say that I like de Beauvoir too but that I liked her better as a young woman, that she became too adamant when she was older. Annie, I think I can call her Annie, defends her, saying that de Beauvoir tried to live to the full extent of her being and that always has to be admired. We talk for a long time. Annie doesn't like the way the rue des Martyrs had become so *bobo* and has pushed out all the workers, but she likes the relaxed atmosphere of Café Kooka Boora and the easygoing baristas. I invite her to come to Australia one day.

*

Kit and Theo arrived in Paris. It was Theo's first overseas trip, except for when he was two months old and his mother took him to her family home in New Zealand for a week or two. Dina's own mother had died before Theo was born, and then within a few years, she was dead herself. She was thirty-seven, Theo was three. It was a long time ago and he wasn't a little boy anymore – he was tall with dark curls and beautiful eyes – but the loss was still, would probably always be, in him. I thought of Stendhal, whose mother died when he was seven: 'It came about that all the joys of childhood ended with my mother.' Years after the Paris trip, on his twenty-fourth birthday, Theo wrote in a letter to his mother, 'I have been sad every day since you died.'

But in Paris he had a reprieve. On the first morning, after he and his father left their bags in our apartment, Anthony and I took Kit and Theo on the Metro down to the Tuileries and stood on the rise above place de la Concorde so that they could see Paris all around them. We looked at the gold-tipped obelisk and in the distance the Eiffel Tower and the Arc de Triomphe then turned and started walking down the Tuileries towards the first pond.

'I love Paris! I'm going to come back and live here!' Theo exclaimed. It was only halfway through his first morning. He looked at me and grinned and I grinned back. We walked around the pond and looked at the wooden boats bobbing on the water as a couple of boys poked at them with sticks. The sun wasn't warm but it was bright enough to make the water glitter. I felt a proprietorial thrill, as if the beauty of Paris somehow had been my skilful doing.

Over the next few days a flurry of sightseeing confirmed my skill. I revealed a golden Joan of Arc on her horse and the faces under the Pont Neuf, the Fontaine des Innocents at Châtelet and the mountains of seafood at the Bastille markets. In the backstreets of Montmartre I revealed the café where we played Scrabble and where the air smelled of hash, and the still wintry vineyard opposite the Lapin Agile, the cabaret frequented by Picasso, Utrillo, Modigliani and friends, the statue of Dalida, and the Roman temple column in St-Pierre, all of it magicked out of the air by me.

*

I wonder why it matters that Theo, or anyone else, should love what I love. There is always a pleasure when others love as I do, always a slight kind of rupture when they don't. I don't think it's that I want to colonise others, make them all horrifyingly like me, but the feeling of being in tune, in harmony with someone else, is one of the deepest pleasures. Most often it is fleeting; once, years ago, I was standing at a pedestrian crossing in Sydney and I caught the eye of a man in a car stopped at the traffic lights – and we suddenly recognised each other as fellow human beings in the world. We both smiled widely. That was more than thirty years ago, but I can still remember exactly where it was – the corner of George and Liverpool streets in the centre of Sydney – and the joy of being one with a stranger. I wonder if that's what Rousseau meant when he wrote, 'Our true self is not entirely within.'

*

Theo went to the Dali museum near the place du Tertre and to the Pompidou Centre and the Musée d'Orsay, spending hours looking at paintings every day. He was only fourteen but he was already creating himself as an artist, filling a notebook with drawings and dressing each day with a kind of romantic flair – a long flowing overcoat, waistcoat, felt hat. A few years later he would be at art school just as his mother had been. Dina had had the same eye for beauty and style and seeing him here in Paris made me wonder how he had inherited her gifts along with her eyes and curls and easy laugh. He wasn't shaped or influenced by her, but he was as much a mirror of her as could be possible.

Some days he hung around the apartment and read or looked up places to see on the internet. He was a long, rangy teenager, but not loud or argumentative, easy to be around. One day I was cleaning the apartment, putting the sheets on to wash and afterwards draping them over the doors to dry, scrubbing the bath, vacuuming around Theo's long legs. He looked up from his book.

'Listen to this,' he said, preparing to read aloud. He'd always done that, read pages out loud and quoted large chunks of films or *The Simpsons* to me.

'No,' I said, 'I'm busy.' I'd always been a bit impatient with whatever hilarious extract from Douglas Adams or Jasper Fforde he wanted to subject me to.

'It won't take long,' he persisted. 'You'll like it.'

'Thanks, but I have to get this done now. We're going out later and I still have to clean the toilet.'

'That's all right,' he said. 'You keep going and I will trot around after you and read to you like a literate puppy.'

I stopped and laughed. 'Okay, you win. You're much too good for me.'

Afterwards we went out to Versailles together. I had been a few times, as anyone who has visitors in Paris must, and was tired of its weary glory, but I had to take Theo. We both read our guide books as the train sped through the south-western suburbs of Paris, occasionally glancing at the bare, cold gardens and state housing towers. There was a brief patch of fields and forest and then we were at Versailles, walking up the hill to the gilded gates of the palace. We trailed around the state rooms with the waves of other sightseers and took photographs in the Hall of Mirrors of infinitely reflecting crowds and cameras. Afterwards we stood on the steps above the Apollo Fountain with its rearing horses and chariots at the beginning of a vista that continued all the way to the horizon. We admired the symmetrical sweep of pools, clipped gardens, lawns, woods; from our feet to the sky an utterly controlled world. Theo remarked that it was 'sort of calming'.

I nodded, wondering if the random chaos of losing a mother when he was so young had made order more necessary. I found it impossible enough years later to comprehend a world without my mother in it; a child without a mother has lost almost all his context, his surroundings almost erased; how does he find a shape against the blankness? Theo draped his arm over my shoulder as we stood there. He often did that, mostly to show how much taller than me he was, and we stared at the panorama in silence.

Later, back in Paris, I asked him if it was okay to use his name in the book I was writing about his mother. The plundering of others' lives can't be hidden. Better to admit it up front. Bees can buzz as shrilly as they like, and sting the unprotected, but without honey they will starve.

'It's okay,' he said. 'I don't care. No-one I know will read it.'

'Thanks,' I said.

I'd been in Paris for nine months, long enough for everyday life to blur into a kaleidoscope of scenes. A few events are anchored in time, but most float, sometimes attaching themselves to weather or another scene. I do know Theo and Kit were there when my choir sang at the launch of a CD – I have a memory of them finding their seats in a row near the front. Anthony came too and Patrick was over from Amsterdam for a short visit.

The CD was a collection of French *chansons* by a friend of Marc's and we were told to ask our family and friends to come to make a good crowd. We arrived at the hall in the twentieth arrondissement and as soon as I saw my choir gathered near the back, I realised I hadn't understood the instructions about what to wear. I thought I'd heard '*toutes couleurs*' so I was wearing a multicoloured patterned top. Everyone else was wearing one plain colour and black trousers. I asked Marie-Louise what we had been told and she said, 'Any colour, but it has to be one colour, not patterned. And black pants.'

I stood on stage and sang, '*La Paysanne*' and '*L'accordéon*', confident at least in the chorus each time. We only had two songs to sing and we had rehearsed the night before but I still needed the song sheets to remember all the words. I could see Anthony, Patrick, Kit and Theo watching me and clapping when we finished. I hadn't quite got it right in my multicoloured top but I was singing in a choir in Paris and my family and friends were witnesses to it.

A few weeks later I was on a stage, of sorts, again, this time doing a reading at Café de la Mairie near St-Sulpice, a church visited for its Delacroix and for the brass meridian line in the floor. The café across from the church was shabby, ordinary-looking, but renowned for its long history of literary events in the upstairs room.

Elaine, whom I'd met a few months earlier and who had owned the Australian Bookshop in Paris, often organised readings for visiting Australian writers. She was one of that fast disappearing breed who devote themselves to literature for love. She even looked like someone from another era, a glamorous 1950s woman in a Max Dupain photograph perhaps, with softly waved hair and soft skin. She offered to arrange a reading at Café de la Mairie for me. Once she had booked it, I worried that I would be speaking to an empty room. I knew practically no-one in Paris; no-one would come.

By the evening of the reading I imagined empty chairs and tables and wanted to call it off. Who can bear to call out '*Regarde*' and no-one turns a head? Not even my mother looks up. As it happened, Elaine had arranged an email-out from the Australian Embassy and a few expats arrived, and my friends came, Vicky, Trish, Camilla and Sylvie – and Anthony, of course. I wondered if the desire to map where

I begin and end in the world is also the desire to understand where others begin and end. The mapping of the self is not really about the past, even though the details are all of the past. As Annie Ernaux remarked, it's not about searching for lost time, but 'to show how we always carry time with us'. When I read her words I could see time past cradled inside each one of us like a nest made of bleached smooth twigs, string, ribbons, wiry grasses. Sometimes all I can do is marvel at its intricacy. Afterwards we went to a café near Mabillon Metro and had more wine and *moules frites*, mussels and chips, and talked about books.

After Kit and Theo left there was a lull. I had looked at everything in Paris, twice, three times. What else was there to look at? And what was the point of endlessly looking? I stayed at home for a while, read through my manuscript, made notes, wrote postcards to my mother, started translating *Une Femme* into English to improve my French grammar. I enjoyed the familiarity of my *quartier*, the greetings from the woman in the *boulangerie*, the nod from the Nigerian man in the sewing shop over the road, but there was still the knowledge that I could not see this place from the inside. I had to keep searching, keep looking. Look at everything.

One afternoon I took the Metro down to Strasbourg–St-Denis to explore the *quartier* around rue St Martin and rue St Denis, two parallel streets which run from near Les Halles all the way up to Gare de l'Est. Both streets had triumphal arches halfway along, marking the old tollgates of Paris where people had streamed through, paying their taxes as they entered the city. The kings and emperors of France, Napoleon's troops too, had entered Paris through the St Denis gate, returning from wars, or from Basilica of St Denis to the north, in extravagant parades of power and domination.

I'd been to the *quartier* only once before with Anthony to try an Indian restaurant in passage Brady one night and thought it had the feel of another country altogether – the smell of curries, the strings of fairy lights decorating the passage, the un-Parisian cries and urgings to go into this or that restaurant. Now, in the late Paris winter, the streets were crowded with market stalls heaped with red, green and yellow peppers, bunches of green bananas, unrecognisable salad leaves, piles of garlic and other roots. The clothes shops had saris and robes in scarlet and royal blue and emerald green, patterned and edged with gold. And, I quickly realised, the streets were streets of men.

There were hundreds of men of Middle Eastern and Indian origin and some Africans. I couldn't see any women at all. My heartbeat sped up, thumped hard enough for me to be conscious of it as I walked. The men were in clusters, walking, standing about, sitting outside cafés, smoking, drinking tea. No women. The men were not threatening in their manner, but my skin prickled. Only men were allowed out here. I was relieved that it was winter and I was well covered from head to toe. I walked quickly, trying not to catch anyone's eyes, keeping my eyes slightly down. Each time I glanced up the crowds of men seemed more dense, more Other. Should I keep going? My heart banged louder.

Then two plump African women in long floral dresses came around the corner of the next street and walked towards me. They were talking to each other and one of them laughed. As they passed a surge of identification and relief washed through me. Without a moment's thought, I turned around and walked back down the street, staying near them, until I reached the Metro.

I thought about it a great deal afterwards, the feelings of alienation and then of identification. There are so many lines around being human – culture, gender, class, status, colour, age – that much of the time it seems almost impossible to recognise one another. For a while on that day, men were no longer fellow humans sharing a street in Paris, but another dangerous species. I kept thinking I should go back there again and walk calmly along the street and see them as human beings, but I never did.

One day I was in the shop in rue Ordener that sold African produce. Ginger wasn't available in the market or supermarket or greengrocer's – and I used it every morning in my breakfast juice – so I always bought it and sometimes honey there. They stocked all sorts of foods that I didn't recognise, cartons and tinned food as well as fresh vegetables and fruits I'd never seen before. There was often a crate of what looked like mown grass right near the checkout. That day, I asked the checkout woman what the grass was – how was it eaten, was it cooked? She was white-skinned but all the others in her shop, all the women doing their evening shopping, were black-skinned. She looked at my white face, held my gaze and said, '*Je ne sais pas. Les Africains la mangent!*' I don't know. The Africans eat it! Her voice, loud enough for everyone in the shop to hear, seared the air with scorn and disdain. I felt dozens of eyes on my pale skin. I looked away from the woman, grabbed my ginger and change and left the shop.

I rarely know what to say when the words should be said aloud in a firm voice. Even in English. The next day at my rendezvous with Sylvie I wanted to tell her about the checkout woman, but whenever I thought of it, the words stuck.

My memoirist companions don't have much to say about people from other countries – except Montaigne. In the 1500s, European exploration of the Americas and Africa and Asia was just beginning and during that time Montaigne had a visitor who had been with the French explorer Villegaignon, when he made the original French settlement in Brazil. Montaigne listened to his first-hand tales of the boundless new territories and peoples who lived differently. Even then, in the sixteenth century, he was doubtful about the morality and value of exploring and seizing of new lands: 'I fear our eyes are bigger than our belly. Our curiosity more than we can stomach.'

He couldn't have known the effects of colonisation then, the exploitation of lands and people, the oppression and destruction of culture, nor the later twentieth-century return of colonised people to the 'motherland', disturbing the towns and suburbs with their dark presence, giving rise to fearful political parties, but he seems to have understood that greedy impulse could only lead one way. He was writing in the 1580s, more than 200 years before Australia was seized by Europeans, who, as educated sons of the Enlightenment, one might think had read and learned from Montaigne.

He says that 'every man calls barbarous anything he is not accustomed to […] indeed we have no other criterion or right-reason than the example and form of the opinions and customs of our own country'.

He launches into a description, no doubt gained from his explorer-visitor, of the country and customs of the people of Brazil: 'They inhabit a land with the most delightful countryside and a temperate climate, so that, from what I have been told by my sources, it is rare to find anyone ill there.' On their way of life and ethics he reports glowingly: 'Their entire system of ethics contains only the same two articles: resoluteness in battle and love for their wives.'

It's a romantic view of the Noble Savage in many ways, but Montaigne uses the comparison to critique his own society. When he commends their punishment of prophets who get it wrong, it seems clear enough that he's talking about the Church: 'Those who come and cheat us with assurances of powers beyond the natural order and then fail to do what they promise, should they not be punished for it?'

In 1562, three indigenous men from Brazil were brought back to France and Montaigne met them in Rouen when they were presented to the king, Charles IX. They were asked, through an interpreter, what they had been most amazed by in France. Their answer as reported by Montaigne:

> They had in their language an idiom which calls all men 'halves' of one another – and they had noticed here [in France] that there were men among us fully bloated with all sorts of comforts while their 'halves' were begging at their doors, emaciated with hunger and poverty: they found it odd that those destitute 'halves' should put up with such injustice and did not take the others by the throats or set fire to their houses.

It stopped me in my tracks.

The idea that we are all 'halves' of each other.

It's a powerful notion with the potential to overturn everything. It's not just a basis for equality, but a radical concept of the self where our skin is not the end of us.

It took the destitute 'halves' in France another 200 years or so before they finally did tire of the injustice and took the bloated Others by the throat and set fire to their houses, but more intriguing is how and when Europeans lost the idea of 'halves'. It was long gone in France by the time Montaigne was writing, but it must have been there in the beginning or communities could not have survived without a powerful reason to look after each other. Somewhere along the way, the idea that part of the self resided in others was lost. More important, the experience, the feeling of not being entirely separate within our own skin, the flow of self into others was lost, except perhaps to babies and some indigenous cultures and to mystics who learned how to melt the dark line between themselves and others.

I wonder at the energy I have used to keep that line distinct, the self behind it all of a piece. Words have something to do with it. Words break the world up into articulated bits, they put a line around the light and dark of being and let us know where we end and others begin.

A list of my halves in Paris: the man in the corner shop, Vicky, Trish, Anthony, Patrick, Matt, Theo, Marie-Louise, Camilla, Sylvie, the doctor at the American hospital, my choir teacher, Jean-Jacques and Ana, Tristan de Parcevaux, my niece, the elderly men and women at the physio clinic, the waiters at Café de la Place, the women in the *boulangerie*, the gypsy woman at Gare St Lazare who drugged her children, the checkout woman in the African shop, all the men in the rue St Denis.

*

As well as going to a concert every week, almost all of them free on Sundays, I visited museums every other week. Towards the end of March, I went to the Musée Guimet on place d'Iéna, which has one of the largest collections of Asian art anywhere in the world. The former colonies of Vietnam, Cambodia and the Lao Republic were a favourite destination for archaeologists, so the museum is a cornucopia of Southeast Asian sculpture.

It was a rainy day and I had to stand in the queue in the drizzle for half an hour. Everyone has the same idea on a rainy Sunday in Paris. Inside it was warm and, despite the crowds, almost immediately I felt calm – the Buddha effect. There were Buddhas sitting, standing, lying, in almost every room: Cambodian, Indian, Chinese, Thai, Burmese. They were mainly marble or other stone, some copper, silver, gold, some were elaborately dressed, most wearing only a draped cloth, some were slender, others were plump, but all of them were extraordinarily serene. I know next to nothing about Buddhist art, but as Stendhal said, 'I don't claim to be describing things in themselves, but only their effect on me.' Looking at their quiet faces made me feel peaceful.

There was one statue in particular that had me circling back to it three or four times. It was from Cambodia, a seated stone Buddha with a broken snake carving behind his head. The identifying label said '*Khmer Angkorien, fin de XII siècle*'. I have the exact details because I bought a postcard of it, which I still have in my study, thumb-tacked onto a corkboard beside my desk along with postcards of Rodin's Cathédrale, two entwined hands, and a Matisse of a cross-legged Arab girl. I look at the photograph of the calm, slightly smiling face, but it doesn't have the same effect as the actual carved stone, the silent presence of it.

It's evident that this statue, and most of the others, must have been ransacked from ancient temples. The label for a large carving of temple gates noted they 'had made their way across the world to Paris', as if they had upped and wriggled across the world on their own. I know that the Khmer Buddha was stolen, or at least obtained, by people who felt they had a greater right to it than the people who had made it and meditated before it, and that it ought to be returned to where it came from, but I was glad it was there in Paris for me to see and feel its imperturbable grace.

ELEVEN

APRIL

To write personal things in an impersonal mode, to try to attain the universal – it's only this way that literature breaks through our separateness.

Annie Ernaux

I longed for spring. I had been waiting for it for too long; I didn't have any way of measuring how long to be patient in a European winter. In the grey light I cultivated the idea that my residual aches and pains would disappear with the warmth, that the sun would somehow dissolve them. Warmth and bright light gained magical or omnipotent properties in my mind and when a few days of warm sunshine appeared in April, I sat out on the balcony on a small stool, lifted my face to the sun, and worshipped. The geraniums in my balcony boxes had new green leaves and buds were forming.

Early spring in Paris makes promises it doesn't deliver. The 'false spring' Hemingway called it, but even in a false spring he said 'there were no problems except where to be happiest'. That's hard to believe, but I like that even Hemingway can be sentimental about Paris. The untruthful glow of nostalgia can blur anyone's eyes.

I took a break from writing, mainly because there were friends coming to stay on and off through April, but I also needed distance from the manuscript. I had picked it up one morning and the rewrite, which had been going so well, suddenly seemed tangled and fragmented. It often happens and it's hard to tell if there's really something radically wrong, or if it's just the mood I'm in. The day before it was clear, today it was confused and should be thrown away. It needed both detachment and deep concentration to sort it out and it was pointless trying to do that with other people around. I've always needed solitude to do that kind of work.

Phil came to visit from Australia and introduced us to the drawings of Sempé, a French cartoonist with a whimsical, tender spirit, like Leunig's, the Australian chronicler of human frailty, and we introduced him to the grotesque faces under the Pont Neuf and the comic-book shops in the rue Dante. Hannah, my eternally travelling niece, came to stay again for a few days with three German friends and they all lay around in the tiny second bedroom talking, sorting out the world until halfway through the day. Peter and Libby arrived too and we walked up to Sacré-Coeur and, instead of music inside his head, Peter heard, by the purest chance, a beautiful young nun singing evening offices. He and Libby had been together since they were teenagers and now, finally, they were in Paris, as shining-eyed as sixteen-year-olds. Since then, Libby has died and Peter sang like an injured angel at her graveside.

I'd found two more conversation partners too – Sabine, a lawyer who loved oriental art, and Bibi, a French-Polish translator, so as well as my Sunday meeting with Sylvie, I was out two evenings and one morning every week. Bibi liked to arrange other outings, so we often went to an exhibition together. Vicky too asked me to go to films with her, and then to a concert, so even though Anthony was away, this time in Norway, I wasn't often alone in the evenings.

Thursday evening choir was still a fixed rendezvous every week. I left my visitors for the evening and took the Metro to Ménilmontant and swung up the hill to the community centre in the rue des Amandiers. As I walked in each time I felt pleasure in being recognised, even though I didn't know any of them, except Marie-Louise, outside rehearsals. When I'd gone to Istanbul in March, I'd had to miss choir and the following week Marie-Louise asked where I had been as she greeted me. Afterwards on the Metro, I realised that now there was a small space in Paris where I was expected to be.

We learned new songs and rehearsed ones we already knew with a particular date in mind; we had a booking, the Fête de la Musique, which is held every year in late June. The Fête happens on just one day, and many of the performances are held in the streets; quartets and choirs and ensembles perform in squares and on street corners so that people can wander all day listening to music wherever they go. Some of the musicians are professional, but there are also amateurs – which of course means 'those who love' – community choirs and solo performers. Our choir was singing in a square on the Canal St-Martin, at 5 pm on 20 June, just before my return flight to Australia, the end of my year. The timing seemed auspicious; I really was going to be singing in the streets of Paris.

One day Sylvie invited me to her apartment for an afternoon tea party to meet some of her friends. I had been told that the French rarely invited anyone outside the family and friends they had known since childhood to their homes, so it felt like an important invitation, a step into an inner circle.

I left early, allowing plenty of time to find Sylvie's place in the sixteenth arrondissement. To Parisians, the sixteenth arrondissement in the west of Paris, bounded by the southward-turning Seine and the Eiffel Tower on one side and the Bois de Boulogne on the other, means wealth and privilege, political and financial power, established families, a district that inhabitants of the working-class east declare they will never go to. Geographically it has no advantages over the east; in fact the south-east, north and north-east have all of the few hills in Paris, traditionally the terrain of the elevated rich, but in Paris, when Baron Haussmann knocked down the poverty-stricken inner city, the poor fled to the edges.

Sylvie's street was on the other side of the *périphérique*, still in the sixteenth, but not in Paris proper delineated by the ring-road, and not in my map-book. I guessed where to get out, but it was the wrong Metro and I had to walk a long way. As I followed the wider, cleaner streets, I saw the brass plates of consulates, discreetly beautiful shops, grand Haussmannian apartment buildings, separate mansions and even large gardens with gold-tipped iron railings. Everyone was dressed quietly, elegantly – no flashes of colour to draw attention – and nearly everyone was white-skinned.

The sun was still weak but for the first time in five months I was outside in the streets without a coat and when I lifted my face I could feel a faint warmth. There were tight green buds on the chestnut trees, the faintest idea of renewal, and some blades of green – probably freesias – poking through in front gardens. I remembered the freesias beside the steps on the farm, one of the few shady, dark places that stayed moist and even mossy in all the heat and dryness, and I remembered how my mother loved their sweet, fresh smell. I could see her placing a cut-glass vase of freesias in the hall – although that was at the house in town, not out on the farm. And then I saw her sitting in her retirement unit; no freesias there and no shady places for them to grow, just sunny pansies in terracotta pots. How strange and strong memory is, with its own structures and its own translucent textures, more fine and enduring than reality.

Sylvie lived in a one-bedroom apartment in an ordinary 1970s block in the avenue Jean-Baptiste Clément. When I arrived her three friends were already there. I can't remember all their names now and I didn't listen carefully in the first place because I was nervous about speaking French all afternoon, but there was one woman, Emanuelle, whom I remember because of her story. Sylvie and her friends were good-looking, thirty-ish, two of them married and one, a sweet-faced woman, had a baby, although not with her that day. Sylvie was single and Emanuelle had an older fiancé she planned to marry soon. She was taller than the others and had short dark hair tossed around her head and her face was full of photographer's angles, but more striking was her rebellious, defiant look. And some kind of pain.

We sat in the lounge-room around a low table piled with pâtisserie delicacies – *charlottes, opéras, tarte aux framboises* – and pots of tea and coffee. They asked me what I was doing in Paris and about Australia and about my family and I started relaxing into the familiar territory of getting to know other women. A few times I asked them to repeat or to speak more slowly but after half an hour or so I found my head shifting into a French mode, as if my brain had realised English was not going to be of any use so it may as well just move to the cache of French it had stored there. After a while the conversation drifted to relationships with men.

'I'm not in love with Jean-Luc. But I don't think it matters,' Emanuelle said. There was a defiant look on her face. For a moment no-one knew what to say. Jean-Luc was her fiancé. Marrying someone you don't love is not what most people will admit to. And then we each started to make our case. Everyone argued that loving the person you were going to marry did matter. We ranged our arguments – how could you get through the difficult times without love, wouldn't children suffer sensing there was no love between their parents, wasn't it a kind of deceit?

'But he knows I don't love him. I have told him. He loves me and accepts it this way. And I don't want to be alone. I don't want to live alone and I want to have children.'

I looked at her, the rebellious tilt of her body, remembering I had heard the same words before. I had a friend in Australia who had once told me that she didn't love the man she was with, but she was in her thirties and didn't want to be alone. She liked and respected him, but wasn't in love with him. I realised I had never known what it was like to be alone.

Perhaps Emanuelle was talking about the difference between loving someone and being in love with them. Perhaps she did love him but not in that heady, drugged, all-absorbing way of being 'in love'. Just as I was trying to work out how to phrase the distinction in French, Sylvie asked it.

'You mean you haven't fallen in love with him or you don't love him?'

'Both,' said Emanuelle.

There was a silence again. Her honesty seemed to break all the rules.

'But what happens if you do fall in love with someone else?

If you are not in love with him, then you could easily fall in love with someone else,' Sylvie responded.

'I have,' she said. 'It was a *coup de foudre* in the place St Sulpice.'

There was the same startled silence. For a few seconds I wasn't sure what she meant and then I realised *coup de foudre*, lightning strike, also meant the shock of love at first sight. Sylvie and the sweet-faced woman argued that there was no such thing, but Emanuelle was adamant. She described it in detail; she was coming into the square walking near Café de la Mairie and he was walking towards her from the direction of the fountain; they looked at each other and they both fell in love in that moment.

'How did you know he fell in love with you? Did you talk to him?' asked the sweet-faced one.

'Of course. Well, he spoke to me first. We sat at the café. I have had an affair with him.'

Another short silence.

'Well, why don't you marry him?'

'He is already married.'

The pain in her face was finally clear. Stendhal said, 'I have never been able to write of what I love, it would seem a blasphemy', but for Emanuelle it was the opposite, she had to get it out in the open. Make it real for all of us. She could not have what she wanted, but at least she had connected it to her friends, to her world.

I understand Stendhal's desire to hide his love, to protect it from a harsh gaze, but to keep things hidden in the end, I think, twists us as we contort ourselves to fit the mask. And yet, oddly for a writer, I'm a secretive person, at least about love. I don't want to reveal that I too have wondered how much and how well I love. I don't want to reveal how much my feelings change; that at times I am passionately in love with Anthony, shining-eyed and melting, at other times I admire and like him, at other times I am hard-hearted and judgmental. Nor do I want to reveal how much my love is self-centred, dependent on my well-being. Nor do I feel inclined to reveal how I cannot bear dependence and instead am drawn to what is withheld. Nor reveal how much my emotions are shaped by physical pleasure, that the intense mind-blowing high of love-making really does create love in me and that I have no idea how there could be ongoing romantic love without quite a lot of sex.

Is this the way it is with other people? The memoirists, or at least the male ones, write only of an all-absorbing romantic love, which, then as now, seems indistinguishable from a volatile mix of sexual passion and fantasy. Stendhal gives a list of eleven women he has loved:

> Virginie (Kubly), Angela (Pietragrua), Adèle (Rebuffel), Mélanie (Guilbert), Mina (de Gresham), Alexandrine (Petit), Angeline, whom I never loved (Bereyter) [why does he include her then?], Angela (Pietragrua) [why twice?], Méthilde (Dembowski), Clementine (Guila) and then adds, 'and lately for a month at most, Mme Azur whose Christian name I've forgotten' [then a new line] and unwisely, yesterday, Amelia Bettini.

Stendhal is just too cool altogether! But he goes on to confess: 'The majority of these charming creatures didn't honour me with their favours, but they have literally occupied my whole life.' Then I remember him as a boy losing his beloved mother and so I'm won over when he says, 'With all of them, and several others, I was always the child; so I had very little success.'

Rousseau had 'extremely violent' feelings of both devotion and sexual passion, sometimes for different women at the same time. He fell in love with many women, starting when he was eleven, and passion and devotion dominated his whole life. Unlike Stendhal, he felt that 'a love known to the person who inspires it becomes more bearable'. During the years he was with his mistress, Thérèse, he confessed – although not to her – to regularly being in love with other women. Madame d'Houdetot, the one he declares was the true love of his life, he 'loved too well to possess'. For him, love was tumult: 'I will not describe the agitation, the tremblings, the palpitations, the convulsive movements, or the faintings of the heart which I continually experienced'. He doubted his feeling for Madame de Warens, with whom he lived for several years, was love because it was accompanied by 'peace of heart, calmness, serenity, security and confidence'.

The obsessive, overpowering intensity of feelings, his devoted limpet-like tenderness, seem, to me, crowding, exclusive. I remember lying with Anthony once in an unpainted wooden house high above a deep valley and, after love-making, we rolled and tumbled together through the dark night above the valley, our still moist bodies and mingled breath indistinct from air and space. Decades later, I can still feel the night air on my skin although we did not leave the loft room where we lay. Surely love has to be spacious, part of everything around it. I barely recognise the claustrophobia he describes as love at all.

Montaigne writes of the 'loving-friendship' of a good marriage, but then spoils it by saying the 'boiling rapture' of intense sexual passion is not a good thing in marriage: 'There is a kind of lewdness in deploying the rapturous strivings of Love's licentiousness within such a relationship, which is sacred and to be revered', and that 'women's reason can be unhinged by arousing them too lasciviously'. Oh Montaigne, how could you! There is nothing wrong with love's licentiousness, or with being, at times, unhinged!

I'm forced to admit Montaigne is not at his best when it comes to women. This is the one topic where he is of his time, seeing women as a necessary and pleasing adjunct to men's lives: 'What more do they want than to be loved and honoured?' and 'reasoning powers, wisdom and the offices of loving-friendship are rather to be found in men: that is why they are in charge of world affairs'. It's also the one area where he is less than ruthlessly open and honest; he becomes theoretical and tells us nothing personal about his thoughts or feelings towards his wife, or any other woman. In his defence, I wonder if women were so highly constructed as fascinating objects by their roles at that time and in that place – and for the next several centuries in Western Europe – that they were near impossible to know as fellow human beings? And then Montaigne does wriggle out of it right at the end of the wonderfully sexy essay 'On Some Lines of Virgil' when he writes, 'I say that male and female are cast in the same mould: save for education and custom, the difference between them is not great.'

But it's not until Simone de Beauvoir that things change much. She still wants to be 'in love' but she didn't think of herself as 'a man's female companion; we would be two comrades'. I wouldn't use the word 'comrade', but I like the idea. I could never be one of those women who subsume themselves in serving a great man – I don't want to look up or down, I want to walk side by side.

In a contradictory fashion, in the same paragraph de Beauvoir says, 'I should be in love the day a man came along whose intelligence, culture and authority could bring me into subjection.' And then again 'from the very start, he would be a model of all I wished to become; he would, therefore, be superior to me'.

I wonder if she was poking fun at her youthful perfectionism, but it does appear to describe how she felt about Sartre. She says she required him to be ahead of her in ability because 'I was grasping rather than generous; if *I* had had to drag someone along behind me, I should have been consumed with impatience.' I admit, with some shame, to understanding that impatience, but I cannot accept being either dominant or dominated in the power battle of love; it has to be equal, or at least constantly shifting.

*

I saw a quote on a poster in the Luxembourg Gardens: *In nature, the bee and the flower desire one another and indulge one another with a true act of love.* I like the phrase, 'indulge one another'; it suggests both equality and pleasure. Bees and honey have long been part of the imagery of love and sex, the penetration of the flower and the sweet liquid on the tongue. Renaissance artists often painted bees with Cupid as a symbol of the delights and dangers of love, the sting of deflowering and the richness of fertilisation and fecundity.

I suppose my conception of love was formed by the sight of my mother, Connie, and father, Don, walking together on the farm in the evening arm-in-arm, talking. And of my mother seated at my father's feet in front of the open fire while he 'rubbed' her head – they never used the word 'massage'. And the pair of them on the old sofa on the back veranda after they moved to the house in town, Dad with his arm over Mum's shoulder, Mum coquettishly holding his finger. There was a feeling of enjoyment of each other's company and of equal exchange of feeling and thought – except my mother was probably the more powerful of the two – which must have sunk into my heart. I didn't observe or think about sexual passion between them, although by the time I was a teenager I had become suspicious of them spending every single Sunday afternoon in their bedroom where we were utterly forbidden to disturb them. And the troubling salty smell their room often had. Then, later on in life, ten years after my father had died, my mother, quiet and not given to exclamation, one day exclaimed: 'Sometimes I *ache* to have Don's arms around me again.' The word 'ache' carried more weight than any word I'd ever heard her use.

*

After Norway, Anthony went to several cities in Germany for work and then Amsterdam to see Patrick. I pictured the two of them walking along the canals, discussing politics as they both liked to do, Anthony with his hands in his overcoat pockets, holding forth, Patrick biding his time. It would be clear to anyone watching they were father and son.

Anthony was gone for nearly two weeks and came back just before Ana and Jean-Jacques were due to arrive. I told him about Emanuelle's confession and about my companions' thoughts on love, especially de Beauvoir's need to gaze upwards.

'She was a Catholic too, wasn't she? Looking up to the Father?' he said.

'Yes, but I don't have that need. I mean, I need to admire you, but that's kind of a sideways gaze.'

'Is that right?' he said wryly. We were lying on the leather couch, a favourite spot where the light flooded in from three directions. Above us on the wall was the small Matisse print, a girl sitting cross-legged against a glorious blue background. Outside, through all three French doors, I could see only sky from where I lay. Anthony leaned over me and opened his laptop on the low table beside the lounge and selected a song to play. For you, he said. It was a romantic love song, 'Come Away With Me'.

'Sometimes you can think about it too much,' he said. 'But, you know, it's mutual. It's a kind of communion. I guess it's what we all want. To join with others – and that's the thing to think about. Why do we want that? And I don't think there's only one person for everyone; that would be mad. It's a matter of opening your heart and mind to the ones who come your way.'

It probably isn't exactly what he said but that was the gist of it. I thought about how both love and precise words are able to *briser les solitudes*, break through separateness. I felt my cheek on Anthony's chest, my stomach along his side, my leg over his legs, the length of two bodies and all the intimate places they touched. I went to reply, and then thought of Stendhal; perhaps it is too risky to let the Fates know what you love.

*

The wait to see Jean-Jacques made us both uncertain. In our minds he was still young and beautiful – and dangerous. He had lived the shadow side for us all those years ago; neither of us was sure how we would relate to a nice middle-aged man who ran his father's driving school. We had laughed by the fire, played at learning French, drunk red wine. It was only a moment ago, on the other side of the world.

And Ana, I remembered a photograph of a pretty brown-eyed young woman. What would we say to each other?

They flew from Lausanne in the evening and booked into their hotel. They had arranged to meet us at our place the next morning.

'I want to see your Paris apartment,' Jean-Jacques said, and I could hear amusement in his voice.

Next morning I waited as Anthony opened the door and then Jean-Jacques stood there smiling, still handsome, but more solid. I saw in his eyes – he could never hide anything – that he too was nervous at meeting us, a middle-aged couple who purported to be the friends of his youth from Australia.

Anthony and Jean-Jacques embraced. Ana and I caught each other's eye and smiled. I think we knew straight away that it was going to be fine.

Jean-Jacques spoke his mixed French and English and Ana spoke careful French for me. How long have you been here? How do you like Paris? We are staying in the Hôtel des Artistes. Where do you want to go? The readjustments of people from each other's past standing in front of each other in different bodies with different faces. Hiding the sadness.

Jean-Jacques wanted to see all the *touristique* sites, he said, as if this were his first time. He had in fact lived in Paris for a year or so after he fled Australia. He had tried to quit heroin before returning home to Lausanne, before his parents saw him, but it hadn't worked. He ended up going into a detox clinic back in Switzerland and then he'd worked there for a couple of years afterwards, helping other people break the addiction.

'This is what we do in Paris, *non*? See the monuments, be a tourist. I want to do everything. You are nice bourgeois in a nice apartment and you can show us Paris.' His eyes were alight with mischief. 'And, Tony, you can give me a joint.'

Anthony did have a joint for him. He had bought some marijuana in Amsterdam on his way back to Paris. He still did have the occasional smoke himself, but I knew he'd bought it this time because he hadn't wanted to be caught without any by Jean-Jacques. We'd argued about it – it was risky and stupid to carry drugs through an airport. It seemed clear enough it was to stake a claim against middle-aged safety.

They had a few puffs – Ana and I didn't bother – and then we walked out into the rue Simart and zigzagged up the backstreets towards Montmartre. We came out behind Sacré-Coeur, near the park in the rue de Bonne where I had watched the little boy call out '*Regarde*' to his mother on our first day. I had been there many times since then; it had become a place to sit and contemplate. It was away from the rush of tourists but still high enough up on the slope to give a feeling of detachment. Jean-Jacques wanted to go to place du Tertre and to have lunch there, so we kept walking.

We wandered around the crowded square packed as always with stalls selling bright paintings of Paris streets and artists offering caricature sketches. Tourists bumped into each other, talked loudly, took photographs. We sat down on the terrace of Mère Catherine: red-checked tablecloths, woven chairs, a ringside view. I felt uncomfortable. I had not so much as stopped in place du Tertre, even though I lived less than ten minutes away, avoiding it or scurrying through if I had to go that way.

'You are not ze tourist?' Jean-Jacques asked, gleefully observing my discomfort.

'Not really.'

'*Pourquoi pas?*' Why not?

'I don't know. I live here.'

'But it is good to be ze tourist. You can enjoy this *très belle ville* like an *innocente*.'

He was right of course, but I wasn't ready to let go my fragile sense of being at home. I turned to Ana and we started talking about our kids. She and Jean-Jacques had two sons and one daughter, the oldest about twelve, I think. Her youngest son, she said, had a developmental disability, which meant he needed and might always need careful attention. She said his need did not oppress her, that it had opened her heart and only made her love more. I knew it was true – in some people there is a largeness of heart, a loving compassion, which only expands more with hardship. I thought how fortunately things turn out sometimes, that Jean-Jacques had found someone who could love so well.

I told Ana that Jean-Jacques had known both our boys in the Mountains; that even when he was an addict he was like a sweet older brother, that he did the same things as our kids, collecting odd things, bones, shells, cicadas, and he liked to play and to dress up in costumes. And like a child, he couldn't hide his feelings. Delight, anger, wonder, pleasure were always right there on his face with no mask.

'He is still like that.' She smiled. 'He's still a little boy.'

Jean-Jacques heard her comment and the sweet-boy smile flashed. '*Un mauvais garçon*,' he said. A naughty boy. He put his arm around Ana's shoulder and I was reminded of my parents.

'He's a good father, very protective,' Ana said. He worked long hours, she said, and she knew she could always depend on him. 'But,' she said, 'he is a child too. He plays games for hours on his computer.'

Afterwards Anthony and I went back to the apartment to do some work. Jean-Jacques begged us to go to the Louvre with them, but neither of us felt like traipsing past endless dark canvases and made excuses. We met up again in the early evening at the Tuileries because Jean-Jacques wanted us all to go on the ferris wheel on place de la Concorde. I hadn't been on a carnival ride since the octopus and the ferris wheel at Wellington showground when I was fourteen or fifteen. Every year the show brought rides and sideshows, Jimmy Sharman's boxing tent and the mysterious half-man–half-woman and the open-mouthed clowns, transforming the dusty paddock into alleys full of strangeness. Seeing it from above in a whirling ride had made it seem all the more fantastical, like a phantom town appearing briefly in our ordinary place.

It was early evening in Paris. The lights came on as we soared up and around, above the rooftops and monuments, high up with the Eiffel Tower and the Arc de Triomphe and all the way to the horizon one minute, and then down with the traffic and cobbles of place de la Concorde the next, and then up with the lights and distance again. The perspective shifted over and over, but slowly enough not to make me feel giddy. The air was cool on my face and the lift and sway of the ferris wheel gondola felt dangerous. Jean-Jacques looked happy.

'*C'est la vie*,' he said.

Jean-Jacques and Ana stayed in Paris four days, which was as long as they felt they could be away from their children. It was probably long enough for all of us; even when hearts reconnect, daily life has to go on. It was time for me to see what had happened in my draft while it had been out from under my anxious gaze. Sometimes things sort themselves out when I'm not working on them. We said goodbye to each other, insisting, as people do, that the next time we meet up must be in Australia.

TWELVE

MAY

Grace and beauty occupy and fulfil me as much or more than weight or profundity.

Michel de Montaigne

Marc gave us the final list of songs we had to learn for the Fête de la Musique. Some we already knew – '*Petit Poucet*', '*La Paysanne*', 'Mercedes Benz' and '*Ai Linda*' and the African song I knew from my choir in Australia, '*Asikatali*' – and some new French songs, '*La Pluie*' and '*Le Jazz et la Java*'. We weren't singing the Bach, no-one else liked it. Except for the choruses, I still found the French songs too much like speech – and with far too many muttering verses. I sang the rousing '*Marchons, Marchons*' of '*La Paysanne*' with gusto and then rushed through the tangle of words in every verse, still hoping only to finish the line at the same time as everyone else.

Marie-Louise helped me with translating words and expressions in the *chanson*. I still have the song sheets with *la recolte*, harvest, and *les sillons*, furrows, and *la charrue*, plough, underlined. They are the words of my childhood, familiar, everyday: the paddocks of ripe wheat on the farm, and the harvester, or 'header' as we called it, and my sister and I squatting in the header box where the yellow grain flowed in, letting it bank and flood around us. I can see the large discs of the plough, and the glistening slices of earth turning over, and the straight furrows behind it and my father saying he loved to look around at the end of the row of ploughing to see how straight the furrows were. I was moved to think of him gaining pleasure from the artistry of his work, straight lines across the paddock.

*

Lilacs bloomed in the gardens behind Montmartre – the sweet, cool smell transported me to my back yard in the Mountains – and the tulips in the Bois de Vincennes spread their so-pretty dresses and the roses in the Bagatelle spilled crimson, orange, pink, white and yellow colours and heady scent into the air. It was reassuringly beautiful – and ordered, almost as if spring had come on the request of the gardeners, each blossom arriving at a predefined time in an already arranged place. Nothing accidental. I wondered if spring was fierce and random in the country, on the farms and in the forests. After so long in the ground, it must burst through with determined abandon, pushing through sticks and leaves and around rocks and through cracks. I started to long for wildness, a place where trees didn't grow in rows and disorderly blackberry bushes straggled in every direction.

Vicky said we should go and enjoy spring at her farmhouse on the edge of Lacapelle-Biron. It was about 600 kilometres south-west of Paris in the Lot-et-Garonne, bordering on the Perigord region famous for foie gras and truffles. After her children had grown and she moved to Paris, the farmhouse was empty for most of the time – she said she wouldn't sell it because she and everyone else in Paris went back to their villages in the summer. It was a necessary return to their *terroir*, their place on the earth, she said. I thought of my father selling our childhood farm while he was in the grip of anxiety and depression and then afterwards, after the electric-shock therapy erased the memory, my mother having to tell him he had sold it. I thought of the Wiradjuri too, who had been displaced from their country nearly 200 years ago. They were still fighting for the right to call their country their own. Not everyone gets the choice to keep his place on the earth.

Vicky didn't want us to pay her any rent. 'Just tidy up the garden for me,' she said. And she even had an old car down there we could use. Her neighbour and friend, Michel, used it most of the time, but he would pick us up from the train in nearby Fumel and drive us to Lacapelle-Biron and then the car would be ours.

'And you can write down there,' she said, 'it's quiet and there's plenty of room.'

We left mid-morning on a Saturday from Montparnasse, a gigantic station under the only high-rise building in Paris. The station was crowded and chaotic but we eventually found the right platform and settled down on the TGV high-speed train. It rocketed to the south-west in less than five hours, but we had to change to a two-carriage local train at Agen so it was early evening by the time we arrived in Fumel and stumbled off with our bags. I had been wondering how we would find Michel, but as soon as I saw him standing on the platform, I recognised him – he was the same shape and size and build as my father, a short, stocky peasant. Vicky had warned me I wouldn't understand his broad south-west accent, but I felt so immediately at home with him that I couldn't help exclaiming, '*Vous me rappelez de mon père. Il était fermier aussi.*' You remind me of my father. He was a farmer also.

He nodded and smiled politely. He was only about ten years older than I was.

Michel drove us through the countryside speaking slow and careful French in answer to our questions. I know I gazed out the window trying to take everything in, but recall only a generalised pretty scene – dense forests, dappled light on the roads, small fields, streams, villages. I do remember my first sight of Lacapelle-Biron as we drove down the hill towards it, a medieval village tucked into the landscape as if it had been there forever. It feels as if my mind took a picture of the village, as if I knew I'd find a connection to this place.

We stopped at a farmhouse just outside the village, set down a short slope from the road.

'Vicky's farm,' Michel said. He gave us the key, said *au revoir* and drove off with his wife, who had been waiting there with her car. We stood there in the midst of the countryside, a French farmhouse to ourselves, a car, and, we found when we went inside, a bottle of wine and a round of cheese.

'*La vie est belle, uh?*' Anthony said. We'd seen a young girl about ten years old exclaim *La vie est belle, uh?* on a news interview one night. It was an item about the summer holidays just after we'd arrived, and we adopted her knowing comment whenever things seemed too good to be true. Life is beautiful, eh?

We woke next morning and looked out the window and saw there was a field with a sprinkling of green, bordered by a stream with a forested hill on the other side. The stream, the Lède, wound its way between the field and forest, and crossed the road a short way up the Gavaudun valley. In the coming weeks we found it turning up here and there, wandering over the countryside, often with a few graceful fishermen standing on its banks. A field, a forest and a stream. I grew up with paddocks and a dry creek that only ever ran with muddy water for a couple of hours after it rained.

'I'm in a book,' I said.

I went downstairs and out to the garden, which ran down to the stream on one side and the field on the other. From here I could see there were distinct new blades pushing through the ploughed earth of the field. Dew glinted on wheat or oats – it was too soon to tell which it was – in the cool morning, like thousands of diamonds shooting red and emerald and blue fire in tiny glittering sparks. And then I was a child walking up the lane through our wheat paddock to catch a ride to school with the teacher – he lived further up the road and gave us a lift in the back of his ute each morning – walking past rows of fresh green wheat blades, each one spangled with dew shooting fire as I walked. And then it was another season and I was a teenager and the wheat had grown as high as my waist and changed colour to a blue-green like water under a summer sky. The wind moved over it and the wheat waved like the sea hundreds of miles away, deep and restless. *Shifting green and blue.* I could dive into it, swim, feel it slide over my body. *Aqua light and shadow.* And then the need to seize the wheat-sea with a net of words, to hold on to it and dive in whenever I wished. *Wind rippling the seed-heads of the sea.*

Eighty years earlier, a couple of hours' drive from Lacapelle-Biron, teenage de Beauvoir felt her soul reach out in the quiet evening dew. Felt the desire to hold beauty. Every summer she visited her aunt and uncle and cousins in the country at Meyrignac, near Limoges.

'Lying in the grass, I gazed up at the moon; it was shining down on an Umbrian landscape [she was reading a life of St

Francis of Assisi] radiant with the first dews of night: I felt breathless with the soft beauty of the moment. I should have liked to snatch it as it fled and fix it forever on paper with immortal words ...'

I wondered if the desire to seize beauty is the first impulse, even before the impulse to attribute it to unseen powers. The old, old longing, against the unstoppable nature of being, to haul the moment out of time, to 'snatch it as it fled and fix it forever on paper'. Simone lay on the grass in the moonlight and felt beauty flood her soul, and then, immediately, came the desire to seize fluid time, to pluck at and fix a moment like a butterfly on a pin.

Rousseau asserted that the only time he had been happy was when he was immersed in nature and that he was never seriously ill when he lived in the country. He said: 'When you see me at the point of death, carry me into the shade of an oak and I promise you I shall recover.' It was his central belief, that nature was inherently good and civilisation destructive: 'Everything is good as it leaves the hand of the Author; everything degenerates in the hands of Man', but it's clear that it wasn't just an idea; he was more content, more at peace, when surrounded by forests and lakes and mountains.

Late in his life he lived for a while on an island in a lake. 'On getting up I never failed, if it was fine, to run out to the terrace and breathe in the fresh and healthy morning air, and to let my eyes skim along the horizon of that beautiful lake whose shores and whose skirt of mountains delighted my gaze.' He couldn't understand how anyone immersed in the natural world could not have faith in God: 'How is it that their souls are not raised in ecstasy a hundred times a day to the Author of the wonders that strike their eyes?'

But it wasn't just a delightful wandering about, floating in beauty. He studied botany and was dedicated to the idea that observing detail revealed wonder: 'Others, when they look at all these treasures of nature, feel only a stupid and monotonous admiration. They see nothing in detail because they do not even know what they ought to look at; and they fail equally to see the whole. Because they have no idea of the chain of relations and combinations, which is so marvellous it overwhelms the observer's mind.'

Simone de Beauvoir, who, I suspect, would have no patience with Rousseau in most situations, might have liked him in the country. When she stayed at Meyrignac:

> The chief of my pleasures was to rise early in the morning and observe the wakening of nature; with a book in my hand, I would steal out of the sleeping house and quietly unlatch the garden gate: it was impossible to sit down on the grass, which would all be white with hoar-frost; I would walk along the drive, beside the meadow planted with specially chosen trees that my grandpa called the landscape garden; I would read a little from time to time, enjoying the feeling of the sharp air softening against my cheeks; the thin crust of rime would be melting on the ground; the purple beech, the blue cedars, and the silvery poplars would be sparkling with the primal freshness of the first morning in Eden: and I was the only one awake to the beauty of the earth and the glory of God …

Like Rousseau's, her romantic love of nature had a strong spiritual meaning: 'Here I could see blades of grass and clouds that were still the same as when He snatched them from primal Chaos, and that still bore His mark. The harder I pressed myself against the earth, the closer I got to Him, and every country walk was an act of adoration.'

There is a quality in her feeling that's even more than a response to beauty. It's the same feeling that came in my childhood when I stood on Baron Rock behind our farm, surrounded by its ancient volcanic rock and twisting gums, and as a young woman in the Blue Mountains immersed in the hot dreaming bush – blue gums, banskia, grevillea – pulsing with imminent revelation. And sometimes even in the cultivated nature of a city. It happened not long ago on a recent return to Paris one afternoon as I walked into the Jardin des Plantes. Just inside the gate was a Wollemi pine, the ancient tree discovered in a lost valley in Australia, and I stopped to pay a brief homage, but didn't feel anything in particular except perhaps a sort of pride. Then I walked through an avenue of chestnuts planted in rows, their branches and leaves clipped into the usual absurd cubes, towards an expanse of rectangular garden beds – and then, without warning, it came. I felt it arrive like waves rolling across the garden beds and up the avenue, a vast and joyful peace, warm and replete. For minutes I was filled with joy and felt I must have been shining. Even when it left it pervaded the whole rest of the afternoon with an afterglow of tranquil happiness. Meaning is given to that glorious feeling, most often awe of the Almighty, but couldn't it be fine, as yet undetectable, waves of energy from trees and plants, from the natural world? It sounds fantastical and I don't have any evidence, but I have felt it and cannot call it God anymore.

*

There were bikes in the back shed at the farmhouse, so after eating toasted baguette with jam at the table in the back garden, we decided to explore. I was here to write, but I needed to locate myself in the landscape first. The immediate area of Vicky's place and two other houses nearby was known as Courrance. It was at the beginning of the Gavaudun valley, which we found later was a picture-book valley: tiny wheat fields, dappled oak and birch forests, the Lède stream wending its way beside the road, delicate sharp-eared deer in the evening, a ruined chateau on a cliff. The village of Lacapelle-Biron was about a kilometre in the other direction so we headed that way first. We pedalled up a slight incline, the soft whirr of the bikes and the cool May morning air and faint scents of grass reminding me of riding to school in the early morning.

As we entered the village we saw a car parked outside a dilapidated stone house, an old black Citroën, looking as if it had driven out of a French war film. Opposite was a shop selling wine and local walnuts and prunes and general goods. Vicky had told us it was run by an elderly woman called Madame Hebiard and that we ought to introduce ourselves to her as '*les amis de Madame Cole*'. Just ahead in the centre of the village was a war memorial, a large slab of rock inscribed with the names of the dead, held up by many stony arms coming out of the soil. Later, when I got to know Madame Hebiard, she told me that during the Second World War, the Germans had rounded up all the men in the village and shot some of them in a field and sent the rest to Dachau and that most of them, including her father, never came back.

A couple of years ago I went to a service at the memorial and saw and listened to the children and grandchildren of the men who disappeared that day, most of them now old themselves. I listened carefully and understood the loss and what was owed in a way that I never had on Anzac Day in my hometown, even though the names of my own great uncles who had died were inscribed on the war memorial there. In my town war had seemed too long ago and too far away.

It was recent history here. Lacapelle-Biron had been in this small fold of the hills since at least the twelfth century, watching wars for centuries. It had been here when the English rampaged back and forth during the Hundred Years War and when the Catholics murdered Huguenots in the name of God in the sixteenth century. It had been here when Montaigne was writing in the tower of his chateau at Bergerac an afternoon's horse and carriage ride away. Its stone houses watched quietly, did not draw attention.

All around the Lot-et-Garonne and the Dordogne, there are many *bastides*, walled towns, built in the twelfth and thirteenth centuries either by the invading English, or to protect against them, with market squares and beautiful arcades on hill-tops, but Lacapelle-Biron is just a huddle of houses and a few shops. It is pretty, as stone villages are, but it is no different from thousands of other French villages. Its main tourist attraction is Chateau de Biron four or five kilometres on the other side, but tourists stop there rather than the village, so Lacapelle-Biron remains quiet. We found two cafés, a *boulangerie*, a *boucherie* and *pharmacie* and a small supermarket and petrol bowsers, all except the cafés with notices stating they would be shut in the middle of the day. It was a small, ordinary village. The few people we saw nodded and said, '*Bonjour Messieurs-dames.*'

Riding to the village became part of the rhythm of our days. I wrote in the mornings and then we took turns to ride to the *boulangerie* to buy a baguette just before lunch. In the afternoons we drove to one of the *bastides* or headed out on foot, following the maze of walking paths through the forests and fields. The footpaths were part of the great network of trails all over France, the *Grande* and the *Petite Randonées*, the *Grande* marked with red and white stripes and the *Petite* with yellow. There was one twelve-kilometre circular path that began directly opposite the farmhouse, or at least we could join it there.

The first time we walked it was late in the evening, during the golden twilight. We had a map but the path was clear enough. It plunged straight up a hill into a small oak wood and then came out on a ridge through a wheat field from where we could see the lie of the land. Across the valley were more wooded hillsides and ahead was Lacapelle-Biron. The path skirted along the edge of the village then veered back into the trees – oaks, chestnuts, birch, locusts. We stopped every now and then to check for the yellow way-markers that appeared on posts, trees, the side of a Telecom box. At one point we came to the ruins of a stone cottage, its roof fallen in, a gnarled oak twisting its roots over the lintel like a tightrope walker over my head. Skinny oaks grew inside the four walls open to the sky. In a short distance, the path came out into a ploughed field, and I suddenly felt the expansion of open fields and a longer perspective.

'Out of the woods,' Anthony said aloud. I suddenly understood what that meant in my body, the physical release of being out of the woods. The language that I had known all my life had lived outside of my skin and I hadn't even noticed.

Ahead on the next hill was the Chateau de Biron, its round towers and chapel and battlements outlined against the sky in the twilight. From the twelfth century it had been the seat of a powerful family, the Gontaut-Birons, but most of it was built in the sixteenth century.

'Fairytale,' I thought. It was impossible to think any other word.

'Fairytale' was in my mind for most of the walk – it was the only context I had for castles and keeps and forests. On the map, Vallon du Loup, the Vale of the Wolf, was marked to the east. I thought about wolves and how quickly I might be able to climb an oak tree. When we crossed the road in front of the chateau we entered another wood, which was dark oak on one side and a delicate tracery of beech on the other. Milky green lichen grew down one side of every tree and I remembered reading that's how people knew which direction they were going in a wood; moss and lichen grow on the north side of trees. In small clearings corn grew or a stone house appeared. White clematis tangled over broken walls along a path worn nearly two metres below fields from a thousand years of walking.

And then we came out at St Avit, a medieval village about a kilometre on the other side of the farmhouse. We peered in the open door of the twelfth-century church and saw swallows and robins swooping inside in the dimness. Outside on its stone roof, plants and grasses grew as if the stones were still back on the hillside 800 years ago. Old roses climbed and fell from stone fences, bees staggered home to hives, a meadow with grasses and poppies wafted sweet smells. Across from the church a cemetery sank into the side of the hill, new and old graves crowding together. The long-ago past dreamed in the air. Our sons would have loved this place, I thought, especially Patrick, who had read medieval fantasy novels right through his teenage years.

From St Avit the path followed an ancient stone wall all the way back to the darkened farmhouse. I felt that my feet had connected not only to the earth, but to all the people who had trodden the path down through the centuries. Farmers like my father, and blacksmiths, beekeepers, women gathering mushrooms, shepherds, lovers holding hands where no-one could see them, children taking bread and cheese to their fathers in the fields, my footsteps on their footsteps, making my faint mark on the earth. I was beginning to know this land close-up at a walking pace, which I've come to believe is the only way to know the land.

*

In one of those unlikely coincidences that pattern life, several years later when Patrick had finished his degree and was working in Paris teaching English, he met a girl at a party whose family came from Lacapelle-Biron. The girl, Céline, thought it quite incredible – and perhaps a chat-up line – that he knew of and had visited her tiny village (fewer than 500 inhabitants) to see his Australian parents at the Englishwoman, Madame Cole's, house. When Céline took him to the village to meet her parents and grandparents, he walked around the streets and pointed out the *boulangerie* and the wifi café and the road to Gavaudun. Céline now lives with Patrick in Australia and when I go back to Lacapelle-Biron these days, I think of her ancestors walking along the paths in the oak forests and along the streams, and wonder at the intricate ways we are bound together.

*

Wild grasses growing on the stony roof of the St Avit chapel; an oak growing out of a lintel – these sights please me. Things that are well ordered reassure for a while – a neat row of trees in a winter park – then I want to rebel. It could be just that I'm not good at order, I've never achieved a 'look' that goes together perfectly, a room where everything is in the same style. Perhaps it's disruption that attracts me, the point between order and chaos where neither dominates. Montaigne aimed for that kind of disorderly order in his writing style, a kind of roughness and disruption: 'I like to imitate the unruly negligence shown by French youth in the way they are seen to wear their clothes …'

I laughed when I read it, thinking of suit jackets worn with t-shirts, and then he went on to say: 'With their mantles bundled over their necks, their capes tossed over one shoulder or with a stocking pulled awry: it manifests a pride contemptuous of the mere externals of dress and indifferent to artifice.'

Montaigne said too: 'Those clever chaps [he meant other writers, not the French youth] […] are always adding glosses […] they never show you anything pure, they bend it and disguise it to fit with their own views.'

Is that what I've done? I have wanted to be honest, but it's easy to add gloss, to make things shine when in life they have an ordinary colour, a plain finish. It's the nature of writing to complete things, to give form, perhaps some bending and disguising can't be helped.

Many centuries later, Annie Ernaux aimed for a style without disguise, for directness and simplicity, although it seems to me for a different reason. For her it was a way of giving allegiance to her country working-class origins, 'to accord the same importance to the words, to the gestures, of the people'.

It makes me curious that an aristocratic man from the sixteenth century and a working-class woman from the twenty-first century had the same desire to disrupt the smooth and stylish surface of language. Was it because they were both from the country, or even just that they were not from Paris and they found its elegant rule overbearing? Like the farmers who come to Paris every now and then: when they are unhappy with the government they shovel cow manure, or sometimes horse manure, onto their trucks and hold their anger and drive up the motorway to Paris and stop in front of the *Assemblée Nationale*, and as they unload the steamy pile in front of the Parliament it breaks the spell of the word-spinners.

I like plain and simple, rough and ready, but I also love fine and precise. I'm not single-minded, I'll be led anywhere. Montaigne said his mind 'bolts like a runaway horse', heads in any and all directions. He leaps from the body's ills to sexual inclinations to dislike of morose temperaments – and back again, quoting Horace here and Cicero there, interrupting his own thought or jumping sideways. 'I leave the choice of my arguments to fortune and take the first she presents to me, they are all the same to me.' It sounds lazy but I want to defend it because I suspect it's what I do as well. He says he gives himself to 'doubt and uncertainty, and to my governing method, ignorance'.

Stendhal said he wanted to use language that the workers at Les Halles, the city market in Paris, used, concrete and direct. He also drew sketches all the way through his memoir – interrupting the flow of words. They are rough and odd, sometimes incomprehensible, messy or spidery corners of his memory, a contrast to his elegant and sharp thinking. And at the end he attached an appendix, which he wrote a couple of years before he died. It's a list of twenty-three articles of privilege he would like to be granted.

Article 3
A hundred times a year he will know for twenty-four hours whatever language he wishes.

Article 7
Four times a year he will be able to turn himself into the animal he wishes and then turn himself back again into a man.

Article 18
Ten times a year, on demand, the privilege-holder will be able to reduce by three-quarters the pain of someone whom he sees …

Article 21
Twenty times a year the privilege-holder will be able to divine the thoughts of all persons around him, at a distance of twenty paces.

It's a peculiar way to end a memoir, and it's scrappy like the drawings, but in this odd list, tacked on the end, the bits and pieces of the boy and the man come to life and someone breathing steps out of the book. Not everything is continuous, part of a whole, makes perfect sense.

I thought of an article of privilege for myself.

Article 1
Twelve times a year the privilege-holder can become anyone who has ever existed for half an hour and then be themselves again without harm or advantage, but keeping the memories, if they so wish, of the other.

Back in Paris after two weeks away, the air was noticeably warmer; summer was coming at last. Bees had returned to the Jardin du Luxembourg and the gardens in Montmartre, collecting nectar for the beekeepers who kept hives in the Gardens and on the roof of the old Palais Garnier opera building and the roof of Temple de l'Étoile near the Arc de Triomphe.

In yet another of those odd patterns in an apparently random world, I've discovered that in Greek mythology a bee settling on the lips signified a truth-teller in scholarship and in poetry. In some African cultures too, honey was put on the lips of newborns so that they would be truth-tellers. In India, the bowstring of the Goddess of love, Kamadeva, is made of honey-bees. And then, in Hebrew, 'honey-bee' has the same root as 'word', both coming from the letters DBR. The letters can be interpreted as 'to pick a direction'. Bees don't so much pick as reveal a direction in the steps of the dance they perform in front of their hives. They show where and how far away the clematis or linden or eucalypt flowers bloom. I thought of words taking me this way and that, perhaps not even revealing a direction for me, but at least uncovering where I have been.

I don't believe anymore in a cosmology where the world is speaking to me, speaking to us all, but I keep wondering about the stinging restlessness that pulled me to Paris in the first place. Was I longing for direction, the ordinary longing of those who have lost their origins? I thought I knew where I'd come from, that I had already 'picked my direction'. The Wiradjuri country of my childhood is my heart and soul and all the sense memories of my body too, which are no small things, but truthfully, my mind has come from elsewhere. The stories that I read, that filled my days, had the weather and geography and animals, snowstorms and wolves and castles, oaks and meadows, of a world that I had not seen. Even language, the English I've always thought of as mine, so deep in my cells, didn't come out of the soil I grew up on, didn't match the landscape or the weather. Here I was finding out what words meant for the first time. I found myself at home on the other side of the world and I found too that I didn't belong. Paradox shifts the lens, brings who I am in and out of focus. There was always, perhaps will always be, a fine split, a self which is never quite whole. And neither does it matter. Nothing on earth is pure and unmixed, even honey, and there will always be flaws and cracks and things that cannot be one. It's the nature of being here in the world and I wonder if I even desire wholeness anymore.

*

It was already late May; we had to leave Paris in mid-June to return to Australia. I remember making lists again, what I had done, what I wanted to do, but when I look in my diary I find most pages just contain a time next to a name, 'Camilla', 'see Trish in Semele', or an instruction, 'Ring Mum', or brief information, 'Felix born today' – my youngest brother and his wife had a baby in the middle of May. I kept tickets for various exhibitions and plays which fill in some of the gaps, and although evidence doesn't really matter because I have not wanted to write a history, I take them out and as mementoes they faithfully give me back to the day and the place and the people.

One Sunday I heard a Congolese choir sing in a church on the other side of Paris. The choir stood in front of the altar, mostly big women in loose dresses, and gave the songs their whole breath and heart and body, and I felt as if I were being shot through with an electric charge. They swayed their hips and arms and stepped back and forth, utterly fluid. At the end they asked people from the audience to join them singing 'Swing Low Sweet Chariot' and some of us stood up and sang. Comin' for to take me away.

Another day I went to hear Trish singing in the chorus in Semele at the Théâtre des Élysées in the rue Montaigne, the glorious sound of endless desire, endless love, filling the theatre. The story of Semele, who desired immortality, and who, of course, was destroyed by her desire, unfolded in a flood of sound and light. There were thunderbolts and gods and hymns – and a huge round bed with satin sheets. I had a balcony seat and felt like one of the gods looking down on the action. Afterwards I had a drink with Trish and a few of the Greek gods and nymphs in the café across the road from the theatre.

Another Sunday I went to a Miró retrospective at the Pompidou Centre and found myself drowning in blue. It looked as if the struggle to find what was essential almost made his art disappear only to be reborn in vast blue canvases. Another day I saw 'Orientalism' at the Institut du Monde Arabe and it was the opposite: souks, bazaars, gold and scarlet robes, sand, azure sky, Matisse's *La petite mulâtresse* (Mulatto Girl), painted Persian carpets, colour and detail on every centimetre of canvas.

I could only try to see every image, hear every note, be attentive to each part of the world. I sang and listened to my voice merging with the rest of the choir, I walked and felt my stride easing the world forward. Montaigne wrote, 'When I dance, I dance. When I sleep, I sleep; and when I am strolling alone through a beautiful orchard, although part of the time my thoughts are occupied by other things, for part of the time I walk.'

I dug in the balcony garden with a kitchen fork and watered my geraniums. I wrote each morning except market mornings when I went with Anthony to the rue Ordener and bought parsley, broccoli and carrots – I knew the best stall and the stall-holder knew me – and still avoided the dark red meat labelled *cheval.* We bought comté cheese in the rue Poteau, after discussing it with the *fromager,* and on the way home we bought tulips from the corner flower shop. I went clothes shopping with Bibi in the Marais and I taped the songs at choir so I could practise them at home for the Fête de la Musique. I rang my mother and talked about my new manuscript as a way of making a spell so that she would stay alive to read it. I met Sylvie every week in Les Éditeurs and, while I was with her, spoke French with a messy ease, my mantle and cape and stockings awry.

THIRTEEN

JUNE

Memory is stronger than reality.

Annie Ernaux

I went to see my first play in French. It was *La Nuit des Rois*, The Night of the Kings, or *Twelfth Night*, so I knew I'd be able to follow the story. Still, even after almost a year in Paris I didn't think I was ready for Shakespeare in French – I was there because Bibi had organised it instead of our usual weekly French conversation, booking the tickets and arranging to meet me outside the theatre.

The actors were a travelling company from the south of France and the theatre was in the fourteenth arrondissement near Montparnasse cemetery. When Bibi and I found our seats there were already musicians playing on one corner of the stage. They were dressed as minstrels in gold and red with vests and trailing sleeves and caps, but somehow looking as if these were the clothes they wore every day rather than being costumes for a Renaissance play. They had an easy-going air; it didn't matter what town or village or even what century they landed up in, they were ready for a jig or a song anytime.

'Don't worry,' whispered Bibi in French. 'I'll explain if you don't understand anything.'

A young woman waddled deliberately onto the stage. Her hips and backside were padded out and she exaggerated her side-to-side motion as if she were a wind-up toy. Everyone laughed as she indicated 'mobile phones off'. It turned out she was the maid, Maria, and as the story unfolded, she nearly stole the show. She only had to appear on stage and the audience laughed.

I don't really remember any of the tangled lovers in the play, what Olivia or Viola or Orsino looked like or wore, only Maria and the other comic characters, Sir Toby Belch, Sir Andrew Aguecheek, and of course Malvolio with his yellow stockings – he had long, very thin legs – was another scene-stealer as he pranced about trying to win Olivia. 'She did commend my yellow stockings of late, she did praise my leg being cross-gartered …' The production was relaxed and the players were noisy and rough and funny as if they had all tumbled off the back of a caravan after travelling muddy roads from the last village. I couldn't follow all the dialogue but the irreverent mood was infectious. The musicians threaded the story together with such energy that I had more fun than I'd ever had watching Shakespeare.

A great while ago the world began
With a hey, ho, the wind and the rain;
But that's all one, our play is done,
And we'll strive to please you every day.

Afterwards Bibi and I found a bar and had a glass of red wine. It was warm so we sat outside and talked about the play and watched passers-by. All the tables were crowded with theatre-goers, laughing and talking as if it were the beginning of the evening.

'The play has made everyone happy,' Bibi remarked. We were both excited to see Maria, slender now, and Sir Toby walk past, laughing and talking with Viola and Olivia. Of course I told Bibi about the day I arrived in Paris nearly a year earlier and about the actor hanging out the window across the courtyard in the rue des Trois Frères. It seemed like an age ago and just yesterday.

*

It was plummeting towards the end. Time had begun to concertina in that way it does, arrival and departure pressed up against each other. I thought of Annie Ernaux, '*je ne suis que du temps qui a passé à travers moi*', I am just time that has passed through me. I am standing in a street and time is streaming through me, imprinting and colouring me like light on transparent film.

I started to think it would be as if the year in Paris had never happened by the time I returned home to my own wintry back yard in the Mountains. Time would close back over it and it would just be a shadowy shape in memory. I had not yet realised that 'memory is stronger than reality', and that even reality, if the present moment can be called that, is mainly made up of memory. It hasn't really been until now, when I have been trying to write of the year with my book companions in Paris, that I've understood most of life is constructed in the mind. Paris was always an imagined place and living there was always going to feel imaginary. And then, writing about the year has, as writing about anything always does, refashioned my experience of it. As Montaigne remarked, 'I have no more made my book than my book has made me'.

I wrote in my diary, 'I don't want to go back to my ordinary life. No! No!', an isolated protest amongst the usual reminder notes. The handwriting was larger than usual and messier, with too many exclamation marks. It was the usual protest against endings, the futile pushing against time that occupies so much human energy.

*

A series of farewells: I visited Simone de Beauvoir's grave in Montparnasse cemetery. She is buried with Sartre, under the same stone inscribed with both their names, a mingling of their bones for eternity, which I think would have pleased the romantic young de Beauvoir if not the older rationalist. The light on the stone was dappled, patterning the faded bunches of flowers – roses and carnations and a small silver bowl of daisies – and the Metro tickets that other people had left, a gesture of solidarity with Sartre's support of the activists who stole Metro tickets to give to workers. It was a warm and gentle summer's day, melancholic weather for a cemetery; graves are better to visit on cold, bleak days when there's not such a strong reminder of how lovely the earth is.

I'd already visited Rousseau's burial place in the Panthéon, a monument in the style of a Greek temple where the Great Men of France are interred. It's an unlikely resting place for a man who only wanted to lie down under an oak. And Stendhal in Montmartre cemetery, his verdigris profile seeming to smile wryly amongst the trees and moss. But not de Sévigné, who died visiting her daughter in Provence. Nor Montaigne, who was buried several times, firstly near his chateau, then at the church of St-Antoine in Bordeaux and, finally, at the University of Bordeaux, although his heart was removed and kept many kilometres away, preserved in the church of St-Michel de Montaigne.

I suspect Montaigne would have been delighted with the fact that there was no certainty or stability in his final resting place and that even his body did not remain whole! He always found it hard to be fixed: 'I do not know whether I have found it harder to fix my mind in one place or my body.' Now he doesn't have to decide, he can be in many places at once.

Some years afterwards, I stood at my mother's grave in the central west. She did stay alive to read the book I wrote in Paris, even though her peripheral vision was so poor she had to use a ruler to keep herself on the line of text, but in the end none of us could keep her alive forever. She died with my younger brother and me on either side of her bed after nearly two weeks of focused breathing, each breath seeming to take all her concentration. On the last day I stared at her wondering who, exactly, it was who was dying, and it came to me that my mother was a constellation of memories, of pre-memory, of feelings, of shared stories. I had stared and puzzled, knowing this shrunken, dying creature was not my mother, and now I saw it; my mother was a vast constellation inside me where she had always lived. She was a construction, a fiction, within me.

Annie Ernaux said that she wanted 'to seize the woman who lived outside of me', when she wrote about her mother, but that seems an impossible task. No-one exists 'outside of me'. I construct every other person and every other person constructs me. Inside my sons, inside Anthony, Vicky, my choir, Tristan de Parcevaux, the Tahitian transvestite on the corner, everyone I pass on the streets, I exist as a fabrication, more or less detailed and probably not looking much like the one I carry of myself.

And places too: the landscape of my childhood, Wiradjuri land, lives in fierce detail inside me; Paris lives in a more impressionist mode. Even with the knowledge of my murderous rage towards a gypsy mother, and the feel of ropes and pulleys in a physiotherapy dungeon, and the smell of urine in alleyways, it is still in soft focus and aglow with warm light. The original imaginary image can never be fully dissolved; it colours everything else after it. Everything, apart from the present moment, this exact instant more fleeting than any clock can measure, is memory.

*

I wish I could convey the almost panicked delight I took in Paris in those last few weeks. The weather had the softness of early summer, the gentle skies that I've come to love as much as the high, wide, endless skies of home. People sat on benches in the parks, men played boules on any available patch of gravelly dirt, children dug in sandpits and sailed boats on the Tuileries ponds. I walked every day, trying to absorb the sight of chestnuts flowering, of houseboats on the Seine and their clotheslines with singlets and t-shirts pegged out, of accordionists endlessly playing 'Those Were The Days' on the Metro, of St Denis carrying his head in the park and *Le Passe-Muraille* walking out of the wall with boys playing soccer in front of him. Trying to absorb it all through my skin. When I was in the apartment I gazed at the window where the younger man still laid out the clothes of the older woman and brought her out each day in her wheelchair, and at the line of people who still queued outside the *boulangerie*, over the footpath and onto the street each day just before noon, and at the light falling on chimney pots across the street which still told me what the weather was like before I got out of bed.

I have some photographs: pink geraniums in white pots along a wall in the Tuileries, the stairwell in the rue Simart looking up five flights, the 'Amélie' shop at the end of the rue des Trois Frères, Colette's grave in Père Lachaise, Anthony rowing on the lake in the Bois de Boulogne, me walking down the stairs in Metro Abbesses, Sylvie smiling at Le Relais Odéon. They were mostly taken in the last couple of weeks.

There were too many goodbyes to say. When I arrived at my rendezvous with Sylvie, I saw she had brought another one of her friends to meet me. She was a soft plump woman with thick pre-Raphaelite hair and friendly, but I had wanted Sylvie to myself for our last meeting.

'You've finished reading Montaigne?' Sylvie asked.

'I don't think I'll ever finish with Montaigne,' I said. I tried to explain that he had become my friend and that it wasn't just in my mind, that it was an emotion. I realised as I tried to find the words that it was love that I felt.

'*Je l'adore*,' I exclaimed and Sylvie and her friend laughed.

We talked as we always did, sitting under the rows of books in Café des Éditeurs. Her friend joined in now and then but mostly she watched us both. I marvelled again that we had met from a note stuck on a wall and we all laughed at the random ways the world can work, the paths that can cross.

Sylvie and I said *au revoir* at the entrance to Metro Odéon near the statue of Danton and as her friend kissed me on both cheeks, she said softly in English, 'Sylvie really loves you, you know.'

I haven't seen Sylvie again since then.

We had a trip out of Paris in the last few weeks too, to the seaside. One Saturday morning Anthony said he felt like walking on a beach.

'Are you trying to get ready for Australia?' I asked.

'Maybe. I just feel like sand and maybe a swim.'

I looked at my fold-out map of France and tried to work out which beach was closest to Paris.

We tossed a change of clothes into a bag and within an hour we were leaving Gare St Lazare on a train to Deauville, a watering-hole for the rich in the nineteenth century. On the other side of the river was Trouville, where the working class had lived. We found the Hôtel des Artistes in Trouville and then we walked on the quay and on the beach and took photos of each other and Anthony took photos of fishing boats. There were rows of brightly painted bathing huts, red and yellow and blue, on the beach, but because there was hardly anyone else about they looked like a stage setting. The tide was a long way out, a shimmer of water lay on the flat sand reflecting a light blue sky. It looked as if I could walk out across the ocean and it would never get deep, as if I could walk all the way to England.

Afterwards we walked around the town and discovered, by reading plaques on the walls, that at different times both Gustave Flaubert and Marguerite Duras lived and wrote here by the sea. *Madame Bovary* and *The Lover.* It was a quiet and pretty town, flowers everywhere, intriguing houses scrambled up the steep streets, the sun shone, there was a market selling local *saucissons* and cheeses and it was summer and the sea-light illuminated everything, but I felt subdued. I knew I couldn't keep pretending I lived in Paris anymore. Dashing away to the seaside for the weekend wasn't going to fool anyone.

*

In one of Montaigne's last essays he writes about his ordinary actions and habits; that he doesn't like fruit except for melons, that he only likes to have sex before he goes to sleep, that he likes drinking wine out of a particular shaped glass and could not drink it out of a cup, that he likes a hard bed with too many blankets, that he feels ill at ease without his head covered, that he can't stand not having a clean napkin at meals, that he doesn't like to stay out in the evening dew, that he has trained his bowels to be regular, that he doesn't dream much.

There was something about this recording of ordinary inclinations that moved me deeply, perhaps more deeply than anything else he wrote. It was as if he was giving me a glimpse of the things I would know about him if I lived with him, the daily ordinary habits that everyone, high or low, allows themselves. It felt like a celebration of being here in the world, of the endless wonderful banalities that occupy so much time. He claimed the unheroic, the unspectacular, the mundane, as part of who he was.

I see now that most of my daily life in Paris was the same as my life in the Mountains and is the same as my life now in Sydney; I dislike drinking tea out of thick-rimmed mugs, I much prefer to have sex in the afternoons (always have), I never go out without wearing kohl and feel undressed if I forget to put earrings on, I cannot bear my feet getting too hot in bed, I always compare my body to other women's in the street, mostly unfavourably but sometimes favourably, I cut avocados neatly and find it disturbing when others dig into them with a spoon, I reverse toilet rolls in public toilets if the paper unrolls from the bottom instead of the top, I am happy to write at a messy desk for months and then take pleasure one day in tidying it up to perfection, I love the feel of early morning streets, the cool air and the unloading of boxes and produce and the early morning smells of bitumen and coffee.

*

Our choir was performing in the late afternoon in the Fête de la Musique. On the last Thursday before the performance Marc reminded us again that we needed to know all the words so that we could sing without looking at our song sheets.

'*Sauf Parti*,' he said with a smile. Except Patti.

When we had sung in the community hall for our families and friends and for the CD launch, the instructions to make sure we knew all the words were always '*Sauf Parti*.' I nodded and smiled back. I didn't mind at all; it didn't matter if I had to hold the words in front of me. I did try to learn them, but even practising every day, only the choruses of '*La Paysanne*' and '*Petit Poucet*' stayed with me. I sang along to our taped rehearsals at home, hoping the neighbours wouldn't mind my repeated attempts at '*La Paysanne*', the rousing chorus of which – even now, if no-one is listening – I can belt out:

En route, allons les gâs!
Jetons nos vieux sabots
Marchons, marchons
En des sillons plus larges et plus beaux.

En route, let's go boys
Throw away our old clogs
Let's walk on, walk on
In wider and more beautiful furrows.

Posters had appeared around the streets and the Fête was listed in the *Pariscope* with performances in every *quartier.* There were soloists – opera, *chanson*, rap – choirs, quartets, chamber orchestras, guitarists, jazz drummers, on every street corner and square. Every performance was allocated a particular place, a square or street corner or hall, and a time, so that audiences could select particular musicians or simply wander around their *quartier* from Mozart to African chanting to the *chanson* of Jacques Brel.

Marc gave us a handwritten sheet with our running order, location and time, and added instructions to meet beforehand for a last-minute rehearsal and voice warm-up. Our allocated spot was on a small square on the Quai de Valmy along one side of Canal St-Martin which runs through eastern Paris, joining the Seine to the Canal d'Ourcq in the north. From Bastille, the canal runs underground for a while and when it emerges it's crossed by high curved footbridges and has locks for the tourist barges that make their slow way up and down. It's mostly in the tenth arrondissement, which also contains the vast Gare du Nord and Gare de l'Est, so it's a crossroads *quartier* for people from all over Europe and Africa. In the years since living in Paris, as I return each year, I've become familiar with the canal and the quays; I ride my *velib*, free city bike, up the canal and back each day for exercise when I'm visiting, but back then I didn't know the area at all.

I caught the Metro to Colonel Fabien, the nearest station according to Marc's instructions: *179 Quai de Valmy (10ème). Metro Colonel Fabien.* Anthony was coming later, and Camilla too, to hear me sing. I kept looking at the paper, checking and rechecking the address. I was rushed and felt hot – I had wanted to leave plenty of time, but a quick meeting with Vicky had turned into a conversation and now I might be late.

I found the quay easily and I could see some people gathering in the distance but realised that must have been another performance as the street numbers were going in the wrong direction. I turned and headed up the other way. As I drew near I started to feel unsure. There didn't seem to be anyone about. There was no square, just the canal on one side and the street and footpath on the other. Not even people shopping. Where was my choir? Where was our audience? Perhaps I'd got the date wrong. I looked at Marc's scrawl headed *Programme du 20 Juin.* That was today. And the time. *Rendezvous à 16h30.* It was already nearly 5 o'clock, I was late. I looked again at the street number on the paper and the number on the wall. *179 Quai de Valmy.* Nothing and nobody here. Had they all arranged to meet somewhere else and hadn't told me? My heart began to thump and although it was only a mild day I was sweating. Even in that moment I knew my feelings were out of proportion to what was happening, but it didn't stop the knotting in my stomach.

I looked down at the paper again, willing it to be different. *179.* Suddenly my brain leapt sideways into a different channel. A French channel. The 7 didn't have a line through it; it was a 1. The street number was 119. It was in the other direction, where I had seen the milling group of people several blocks away in the distance.

I ran about half a kilometre down the quay and arrived at the square just as my choir was arranging itself into sopranos, altos, tenors and basses. They all looked up and exclaimed as I ran up to them, hot, sweaty and breathless. They are pleased to see me, I realised, and felt a rush of delight.

'Patti, you're late. You've missed the rehearsal.' Marc scolded. He had a stand in front of him and was holding his guitar.

'I'm really sorry, I thought the one was a seven.'

He shrugged, puzzled, but let it go. He turned and arranged our song sheets on his stand. There was already a crowd of people waiting. I looked around and saw Anthony and Camilla, who must have arrived before me. How had they got the number right? Anthony raised his eyebrows at my sudden late arrival.

'We thought you had decided not to come,' Marie-Louise whispered. Marc frowned at us. He was ready to start.

He slipped his guitar strap over his shoulder, tapped on the stand, and we began. The first song, '*La Pluie*', 'The Rain', opened with a faint chorus of plinking sounds like rain falling on a roof, the sopranos and tenors and altos alternating, the sound of raindrops rising until it was a clattering storm and then diminishing as the verse began. My breath returned and I could hear each voice and my voice, light and nervous at first. We didn't sound as strong as usual, all of us holding our voices in. We made it through, holding the last note uncertainly, and Marc nodded. He's nervous too, I thought.

The audience applauded, clapping and whooping, and we looked at each other, relieved, smiling. They were our friends and families, there was nothing to worry about. We headed off into '*La Paysanne*' and then the rest of our repertoire with gusto, twelve songs altogether – French, Spanish, English, African. We swayed and clapped. Marc kept one hand on the music, and conducted us with the other. On a few songs, he played along with us on his guitar. My voice rose and fell, disappeared in all the other voices, the notes true and strong, sweet and straggling.

I couldn't stop smiling. I was singing in the streets of Paris. I could feel Marie-Louise's shoulder next to mine. My heart had calmed down after beating too hard from running and now my voice felt strong and round in my throat. I kept my gaze on Marc, letting his eyes hold me, hold us all as one. *Marchons, Marchons.* We all belted out the fighting words. The sun was shining in a milky blue sky, that soft pearly colour that I haven't seen anywhere else, the chestnut trees had new leaves, everyone was smiling. *Ma fren orll drive Porchez.*

*

It was a decade ago, the singing. And everything else that happened that year. I really don't know if I have any better idea of what it all meant. It was a year in Paris. I finished a manuscript, I had coffee with Montaigne and all the other memoirists. I discovered many looking-glasses in other centuries, other minds. I found the imaginary world did not disappear when I stepped into it. I grew in different soil, the red-brown earth of Wiradjuri country, and would always belong to it, but I could see my reflection in mirrors in Paris too.

I have been going back there every year to work since then; I stay no more than a couple of months and I teach memoir classes and write and ride around the streets on the squat grey *velib* bikes, dodging buses and taxis. Several times I have gone back up to the rue Simart and I look up at our apartment on the fifth floor and I'm reassured to see the red geraniums are still growing there.

Every time I return I think, this will be the time that I see Paris for what it really is, just another crowded European city with an overweening pride in its beauty and bloody history.

An elegantly arranged pile of limestone.

A criss-cross of urine-smelling alleys and cold windy boulevards.

A glossy tourist copy of its original self.

And every time, usually on a chilly autumn morning, often rainy, or at least grey, a few days after I arrive, my heart lifts with a piercing joy.

Last time I arrived, just a few months ago, it was mid-September and, in the morning, chilly enough to wear a scarf. I took the train into Paris from the airport and dragged my luggage through Châtelet station and up along the streets of the third arrondissement to the rue des Gravilliers where I'd booked a tiny studio. I was going to spend several weeks trying to finish this book. I knew the street, Trish used to live there, an ordinary working street, and I had often visited her, so it felt familiar.

I saw myself reflected in the window of the *boulangerie* opposite the front door. *This great world of ours is the looking-glass in which we must gaze to come to know ourselves from the right slant.*

The door was open and I could see the *boulanger* sliding baguettes onto wire racks so I went in to buy an almond croissant for breakfast. The first day.

'*Bonjour*,' I said, cheerfully.

'*Bonjour Madame*,' he said with vast indifference. He looked sensitive and life wasn't the way he had wanted it to be.

The studio was up five flights without a lift, again. I felt defeated for a moment, feeling the weight of my bag, but the landlord came downstairs and carried my bag up the narrow sloping flights. He told me that he was a linguist and also wrote novels – there were three of his books on the shelves beside the bed. The room was just big enough for the bookcase, bed and a table at a window looking onto an inner courtyard and, above it, an expanse of sky.

After the landlord-novelist left and I'd unpacked my laptop and manuscript and clothes I went out walking to stay awake. I always walk all the first day, trying to shake off the jetlagged desolation that always visits me. More than 'where in the world am I?', it's 'why in the world am I?' I know joy will come when it wants to, maybe not today, but that's fine, I still have to walk.

I had a few small tasks to do as well, buy a weekly Metro pass, and a *puce*, the word for both a flea and a SIM card, for my mobile phone. I decided to head back to Châtelet first, then to the phone shop in the rue de Rivoli, and then I'd walk along the Seine all the way up to the Port de l'Arsenal near Bastille.

Not far from the rue des Gravilliers a young Iraqi man – a doctor, he said – asked me for directions. People often ask me for directions in Paris, more often than the likely average for any one person could be. Some days it seems that my job is just to wander about helping passers-by find their way. I occasionally know the direction but most often I have to look at my blue map-book, *Paris Pratique*. That particular day, five people asked me which way to go: the Iraqi doctor, an American couple in Châtelet, an elderly French man who must have been from the provinces, a boy on his mobile phone who called out, '*Quel direction est Gare de l'Est?*' as I passed by him in the rue St Martin and then, later in the afternoon in the same street, a young African-French woman with a baby tied on her chest asked for directions to the Beaubourg, Pompidou Centre.

'Just along there,' I said in French, ready to hurry past. 'You'll be there in a second.'

'*Une seconde?*' she repeated, puzzled. I looked at her unfocused eyes and suddenly realised that she was blind. She needed me to be more precise. I hesitated for a moment.

'I could walk with you if you like?' I said.

'Thank you,' she said. 'That would be good.'

'You cannot see at all?'

'I can see colour and general form.'

'Your baby can see?'

'He sees,' she said smiling.

We walked along chatting. Her baby looked sideways at me and I stroked his arm. When the green and blue and red pipes of the Beaubourg appeared, I said '*Voila*' and we parted ways.

I smiled as I walked on, absurdly pleased to have been of use. Sometimes it seems that that is enough anywhere in the world.

ACKNOWLEDGMENTS

I want to acknowledge my book companions:

Simone de Beauvoir, *Memoirs of a Dutiful Daughter*, translated by James Kirkup, HarperPerennial Modern Classics, New York, 2005

Annie Ernaux, *Retour à Yvetot*, Éditions du Mauconduit, Paris, 2013

——*Une Femme*, Gallimard, Paris, 1987

Michel de Montaigne, *The Essays: A Selection*, translated by MA Screech, Penguin Classics, London, 1993

Jean-Jacques Rousseau, *The Confessions*, translated by JM Cohen, Penguin Classics, London, 1953

Madame de Sévigné, *Selected Letters*, translated by Leonard Tancock, Penguin Classics, London, 1982

Stendhal, *The Life of Henry Brulard*, translated by John Sturrock, New York Review of Books, New York, 1995

And:

Colette, *Rainy Moon*, translated by Antonia White, Penguin, London, 1976

Antoine Compagnon, *Un Été Avec Montaigne*, Éditions des Équateurs, Paris, 2013

Sarah Kofman, *Rue Ordener, Rue Labat*, translated by Ann Smock, University of Nebraska Press, Nebraska, 1996

Marcel Pagnol, *My Father's Glory and My Mother's Castle*, translated by Rita Barisse, Farrar, Strauss and Giroux, New York, 1986

Marcel Proust, *In Search of Lost Time*, translated by CK Scott Moncrieff and Terence Kilmartin, Vintage, London, 2002

Voltaire, *Candide*, translated by John Butt, Penguin Classics, London, 1979

I also want to acknowledge lines from 'Stings', in *Ariel* by Sylvia Plath, Faber Paperbacks, London, 1974.

Many thanks are due to my agent, Clare Forster, for encouraging me to write the Paris book; to my publisher, Alexandra Payne, for her faith in it; and to Ian See for his insightful remarks. I also want to thank the wonderful Jo Jarrah for her brilliant editing and Bettina Richter for her endless enthusiasm and determination. And most of all, infinite thanks to Anthony Reeder, my first reader and favourite companion. I hope those dedicated to the facts will forgive the layering of time in this account of my life in Paris.

Bookclub discussion notes are available for this book. Visit uqp.com.au and click on the Bookclub tab to download them.